ED

P **G**

CONCEPTS

STRUCTURED PROGRAMMING CONCEPTS

Keith LaBudde

Professor of Data Processing/Computer Science
Ulster County Community College

McGraw-Hill, Inc.

New York   St. Louis   San Francisco   Auckland   Bogotá
Caracas   Lisbon   London   Madrid   Mexico City   Milan
Montreal   New Delhi   San Juan   Singapore
Sydney   Tokyo   Toronto

This book was set in Optima by Beacon Graphics Corporation.
The editor was Christina Mediate;
the production supervisor was Diane Renda;
the cover was designed by Fern Logan.
Project supervision was done by The Total Book.
Semline was printer and binder.

STRUCTURED PROGRAMMING CONCEPTS

4 5 6 7 8 9 0 SEM SEM 9 0 9 8 7 6 5 4 3

ISBN 0-07-035778-1

 This book is printed on recycled paper containing a minimum of 50% total recycled fiber with 10% postconsumer de-inked fiber.

Library of Congress Cataloging-in-Publication Data

LaBudde, Keith P.
    Structured programming concepts.

    Includes index.
        1. Electronic digital computers—Programming.
2. Structured programming.   3. Business—Data processing.   I. Title.
QA76.6.L3235 1986   005.1'13   86-7458
ISBN 0-07-035778-1

ABOUT
THE AUTHOR

Keith LaBudde is Professor of Data Processing/Computer Science at Ulster County Community College, Stone Ridge, N.Y. He received an M.B.A. from Harvard University and a B.S. in mathematics from the University of Wisconsin. He has taught data processing and computer science at UCCC since 1970. He has also served as a consultant on curriculum development for two-year colleges. Prior to entering academia, he spent 10 years as an operations analyst and consultant in New York.

CONTENTS

PREFACE   xiii

1   The Programming Process   **1**

OBJECTIVES   1
INTRODUCTION   1
EXAMPLE: POSITIVE, NEGATIVE, AND ZERO NUMBERS   2
　　Defining the Problem / Preparing an Algorithm /
　　Preparing a Program Flowchart / Coding the
　　Program / Debugging and Testing /
　　Documenting
EXAMPLE: GROSS PAY   17
　　Problem Definition / Algorithm / Test Input and
　　Output Data / Program Flowchart
SUMMARY   22
KEY TERMS   23
EXERCISES   23

2   Introduction to Structured Programming   **25**

OBJECTIVES   25
INTRODUCTION   25
MODULAR PROGRAMMING   26
　　Implementing the Modular Approach / Problems
　　with the Modular Approach / Examples of
　　Program Modules
TOP-DOWN PROGRAMMING   30
　　Structure Charts / Identifying Modules /
　　Reviewing the Structure Chart / Structure
　　Charts and Flowcharts / Coding the Modules
PROGRAMMING STRUCTURES   34
　　Sequence Structure / Loop Structure / Selection
　　Structure / Structure Charts and Program
　　Structures
STRUCTURED CODING   40
　　Pseudocode / A Structured Program in
　　Pseudocode
ADDITIONAL STRUCTURES   44
　　FOR Loop / PERFORM UNTIL Instruction /
　　REPEAT UNTIL Instruction / CASE Instruction

ix

	SUMMARY	48
	KEY TERMS	48
	EXERCISES	48

3   Conditions that Control Processing   49

OBJECTIVES   49
INTRODUCTION   49
COMPARISONS OF TWO VALUES   49
SORTING THREE NUMBERS   50
COMBINATIONS OF CONDITIONS   52
  Boolean Algebra / Truth Tables / Special
  Boolean Equalities / Boolean Algebra in
  Programming
ORDER OF COMPARISONS   61
INPUT EDITING   62
  Sequence Checking / Restricted-Value
  Tests / Miscellaneous Other Tests / Error
  Routines
DETECTING END OF DATA   64
  Sentinel Value / Counter
SUMMARY   65
KEY TERMS   66
EXERCISES   66

4   Complex Combinations of Conditions   67

OBJECTIVES   67
INTRODUCTION   67
FILE INQUIRY EXAMPLE   67
  Problem Definition / Truth Table / Structure
  Chart / Pseudocode / Program Flowchart /
  Test Input Data / Test Output Data /
  Postscript
DECISION TABLES   77
  Components of a Decision Table / Redundancy
  and Contradiction / Examples of Decision
  Tables / Extended-Entry and Mixed-Entry
  Tables
SUMMARY   84
KEY TERMS   84
EXERCISES   84

5   Control Breaks   87

OBJECTIVES   87
INTRODUCTION   87
GROSS PAY REVISED   87
  Handling the Control Break / Special
  Problems / Structure Chart / Program
  Flowchart / Pseudocode
NASSI-SHNEIDERMAN FLOWCHARTS   93
  Representing the Three Logical Structures /
  Revised Gross Pay Problem
PURCHASE SUMMARY   98
  Problem Definition / Structure
  Chart / Nassi-Shneiderman Flowchart /
  Pseudocode

SUMMARY   105
KEY TERMS   105
EXERCISES   105

6   Multilevel Control Breaks   **107**

OBJECTIVES   107
INTRODUCTION   107
FIELD SALES SUMMARY   107
        Problem Definition / Structure Chart / Program
        Flowchart / Decision Table for Module 200 /
        Pseudocode / Nassi-Shneiderman Flowchart
        of Module 200 / Alternate Handling of
        Output / Accumulating and Printing Totals /
        Group-Printed Field Sales Summary Report
HIPO CHARTS   123
        Preparing a HIPO Chart / Advantages and
        Disadvantages of HIPO
SUMMARY   125
KEY TERMS   126
EXERCISES   126

7   Tables   **128**

OBJECTIVES   128
INTRODUCTION   128
TERMINOLOGY   128
        Single and Paired Tables / Argument and
        Function Tables / Discrete and Segmented
        Argument Tables
ORDER OF TABLE ARGUMENTS   131
        Ascending Order / Descending Order / Neither
        Ascending nor Descending / Postscript
TABLES IN MEMORY   134
        Referencing Table Entries / Getting the Tables
        into Memory / Organizing the Table File /
        Reading the Table File
SEARCHING A DISCRETE TABLE   136
        Sequential Search / Binary Search
SEGMENTED TABLE EXAMPLE   142
        Getting the Table into Memory / Searching the
        Table
USING A TABLE TO ACCUMULATE RESULTS OF PROCESSING   144
TABLES OF VARIABLE SIZE   144
        Discrete / Segmented
DIRECT TABLE ADDRESSING   145
        Determining the Index of the Function / Additional
        Examples of Direct Addressing
MULTIDIMENSIONAL TABLES   147
        Two-Dimensional Tables / Two-Dimensional
        Tables in One Dimension
SUMMARY   153
KEY TERMS   153
EXERCISES   153

8   Multifile Processing: Sequential Access   **155**

OBJECTIVES   155

INTRODUCTION 155

TERMINOLOGY 155

Master and Transaction Files / Sequential and Serial Access / Maintaining, Updating, and Referencing

FILE MEDIA FOR SEQUENTIAL FILES 156

MAGNETIC TAPE 157

Creating a Master File / Updating a Master File / Adding Records to a File / Deleting Records from a File / A Combined Add and Delete Run / Combining Updating and Maintenance / Backup for Tape Files

MAGNETIC DISK 174

Creating a Master File / Updating a Master File / Adding Records / Deleting Records / Combining Updating and Maintenance / Backup for Disk Files

ACTIVITY AND VOLATILITY 182

POSTSCRIPT 183

SUMMARY 183

KEY TERMS 183

EXERCISES 183

9 **Multifile Processing: Direct Access** **185**

OBJECTIVES 185

INTRODUCTION 185

STORING DATA ON DISK 185

INDEXED FILES 187

ISAM Files / VSAM Files / Fully Indexed Files

RANDOM FILES 200

Determining the Location of Records / Random File Processing

SELECTING A FILE ORGANIZATION 202

SUMMARY 203

KEY TERMS 203

EXERCISES 203

APPENDIX—NUMERIC CONSIDERATIONS 204

Objectives 204

Introduction 204

Rounding 204

Determining the Size of a Result 205

Addition / Subtraction / Multiplication / Division

Output Editing 209

Accuracy and Precision 209

Key Terms 210

Exercises 210

GLOSSARY 211

INDEX 218

PREFACE

PURPOSE AND EVOLUTION OF THIS BOOK

This book is intended for use in an introduction to business programming course. This course may be the first data processing course a student takes; it may be taken along with an introductory data processing course; or it may have an introductory course as a prerequisite. No prior knowledge of computers is assumed, so I have included brief discussions of material that students who have taken an introductory course may already have encountered. The extent of overlap with such an introductory course is, however, minimal.

It is the purpose of this text to present certain fundamental programming concepts that are commonly encountered in business uses of a computer. When these topics are taught as part of a language course—as they frequently are, too much time is spent on the concepts, at the expense of an in-depth treatment of the language itself. Moreover, the concepts must usually be taught in more than one course to ensure that the students are able to complete the programming assignments. By covering these concepts in a separate course that will be a prerequisite or corequisite for the language courses, more time is available for the instructors of these latter courses to explore special features of the languages.

When I first started teaching a "programming concepts" course in the early 70s, this type of course was not common and textbooks were few in number. One week before the beginning of the spring semester in 1978, I discovered that the book I had been using was out of print. I was forced to develop a series of handouts to replace the text. This gave me an opportunity to correct deficiencies I had perceived in the text, and after five years of use, these handouts became the basis for a book. The approach taken, however, was unstructured, and therefore not really appropriate for today's programming courses which emphasize the structured approach. When I decided to switch to a structured approach, I found none of the available structured texts really met my needs. I therefore decided to write the book I wanted. This is the result.

CONCEPTS AND TECHNIQUES

This text covers concepts that are generally required in business programming, including the programming process, structured program development, controlling program flow, control breaks, tables, and multifile processing.

A variety of methods for planning and documenting computer programs are presented and illustrated. Included are structure charts, program flowcharts, pseudocode, Nassi-Shneiderman flowcharts, and HIPO charts. In addition, truth tables and decision tables are examined as techniques for dealing with limited aspects of a problem (rather than with the problem as a whole as the other techniques do).

Structure charts, program flowcharts, and pseudocode—the more common techniques used in the development of structured programs—are fundamental to this text. HIPO charts incorporate structure charts and pseudocode, and add information about input and output. Because so many ways have been devised for representing the input and output portions of HIPO charts, I do not cover this technique in great detail. Nassi-Shneiderman flowcharting is relatively new, gaining in popularity, and is, therefore, covered in more depth.

Why present so many techniques? Why not settle on the one or two that are best? For one thing, there is no consensus as to which are best. Each has its advocates, based on the user's prior training and experience. This is true for both data processing instructors and data processing managers.

And tastes in techniques do change. My experience is probably not atypical. I started preparing program flowcharts in 1960, and for a long time I could see no need for any other technique. (Today I am willing to admit that program flowcharts do have some limitations, not the least of which is the difficulty non-data processing people have in understanding them and the effort required to revise them.) Pseudocode at first seemed like a lot of unnecessary work, particularly since my pseudocode ended up being almost like the program itself. I recognize now that my pseudocoding standards were not very well thought out. I feel today that pseudocode may become even more popular because it is easily understood and can be revised readily when a word processor is used in its preparation.

I was very skeptical when I first encountered Nassi-Shneiderman flowcharting, but today it is my preferred way to plan a structured program. I like the way Nassi-Shneiderman flowcharts reveal the structure of program modules; they are relatively compact, easy to read, can be partially prepared with a word processor (though not as easily as pseudocode can), and thus are relatively easy to revise.

We can expect planning and documentation tools to change in the future. New techniques will be developed. Older techniques will become less widely used. Some people will resist the changes. How then to best prepare the students? It is my hope that by exposing the students to a variety of techniques they will be better able to learn and apply any new ones their future employers decide to adopt.

OVERVIEW OF THE TEXT

The first chapter introduces the programming process. The traditional approach to program development is taken, including the development of algorithms and the preparation of program flowcharts. The importance of desk checking is stressed. The approach in this chapter is nonstructured since students seem to find it easier initially to understand this way of handling a problem.

Chapter 2 introduces the fundamental concepts of structured programming. The three basic programming structures (sequence, loop, and selection) are presented, along with some variations. Structure charts, structured program flowcharts, and pseudocode are used to plan and document the structured programs.

In Chapter 3 we examine the use of conditions in loop and selection structures to control the order of processing. Boolean algebra is introduced as a way of dealing with combinations of conditions, and truth tables are used to evaluate compound conditions. The importance of the order in which comparisons are made is examined. Input editing and various methods for detecting the end of a data file are discussed.

Chapter 4 expands the discussion of Chapter 3 by considering complex combinations of conditions that may control processing. Decision tables are introduced as a technique for dealing with the difficulties presented by these combinations.

Chapter 5 begins the discussion of control breaks, a factor in the production of most business reports. Nassi-Shneiderman flowcharting, an increasingly popular technique for the planning of structured programs, is introduced.

The topic of control breaks is examined further in Chapter 6, where multilevel control breaks are dealt with. Group printing and group indication are illustrated. The HIPO chart, another technique for planning and documenting structured programs, is presented.

Chapter 7 deals with tables, the use of which can make the programming task much simpler in many situations. A variety of tables are presented. The advantages and disadvantages of ascending, descending, and unordered argument tables are examined. Ways of placing table data in the computer's memory are considered, as are ways of accessing this data (searching and direct table addressing). Multidimensional tables are examined briefly.

Chapters 8 and 9 consider techniques for processing multiple input files. In the former we deal with the processing associated with sequential master files. This includes creating, updating, and maintaining sequential magnetic tape and magnetic disk files. In Chapter 9 we examine magnetic disk files that have been organized to permit accessing a desired record directly. Indexed files (ISAM, VSAM, and fully indexed) and random files are considered. Again, techniques for creating, updating, and maintaining these files are examined. The chapter ends with a discussion of some of the considerations involved in selecting an organization for a file.

An Appendix has been included that examines numeric considerations that can be troublesome to a programmer. While not strictly relevant to the topic of structured programming, they are very much worth covering if time permits. The student will also find a glossary and an index at the end of the text.

Each chapter starts with a list of objectives the student should be able to meet upon completing the chapter and ends with a chapter summary, a list of key terms for the student to master, and exercises for testing the students' comprehension of the material. The exercises emphasize the application of the techniques presented in the chapter. I believe that the true measure of the comprehension of a new technique is the extent to which it can be applied to a new problem.

FOR THE INSTRUCTOR

We have an extensive set of transparency masters to go with the text. An instructor's manual is provided that contains solutions to the exercises and some suggestions that may help the instructor present the material more effectively.

The amount of time available for a course such as this will vary, so some instructors may have to skim over certain topics and techniques, or even skip some completely. Decision tables and HIPO are likely candidates. The discussion of multidimensional tables in Chapter 7 can also be omitted in a pinch, as can the discussion of Boolean algebra and truth tables. And if time gets really tight, I suppose even Nassi-Shneiderman flowcharts could be omitted.

ACKNOWLEDGMENTS

I thank the following reviewers whose comments and suggestions were so helpful in the final preparation of this book: Professor Neil F. Dunn, Massachusetts Bay Community College; Professor Richard Fleming, North Lake College; Professor Seth Hock, Columbus Institute of Technology; Professor Michael Jeffries, University of Tampa; Professor Norman Liebling, San Jacinto College; Professor Leonard Presby, William Paterson College; Professor Bob Saldarini, Bergen Community College; Professor Tim Sylvester, College of Du Page; and Dr. R. Kenneth Walter, Weber State College.

STRUCTURED PROGRAMMING CONCEPTS

CHAPTER 1

THE PROGRAMMING PROCESS

OBJECTIVES

Upon completing this chapter the student should be able to:

1 List the steps in the programming process.
2 Explain the processing depicted by a program flowchart.
3 Describe good flowcharting practices.
4 Prepare an algorithm, a program flowchart, test input data, and test output data for a simple problem.
5 Define and use the key terms at the end of the chapter.

INTRODUCTION

A *computer program* consists of a group of instructions for a computer that cause it to perform a desired task. The computer program is a means to an end. The end will normally be defined as information that is needed to solve a problem. The *programming process* is, therefore, a problem-solving process, and it consists of the following activities:

1 Defining the problem
2 Preparing an algorithm
3 Preparing a program flowchart
4 Coding the program
5 Debugging and testing
6 Documenting

These activities can be visualized as shown in Figure 1-1. Activities 1 through 5 each include checking procedures that the programmer must

FIGURE 1-1 The programming process.

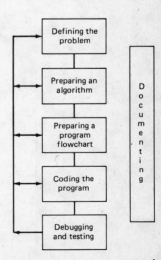

carry out thoroughly before proceeding to the next activity. At any time it may become necessary to return to an earlier activity to deal with unanticipated problems. Activity 6, *documenting* (keeping a written record of what is done), occurs simultaneously with the other five activities.

In the remainder of this chapter we will discuss each of these activities, with particular emphasis on preparing algorithms and flowcharts. Two examples will be used to illustrate the programming process.

EXAMPLE: POSITIVE, NEGATIVE, AND ZERO NUMBERS

Consider a very simple problem in which we are to determine how many positive, negative, and zero numbers there are in a list of numbers.

Defining the Problem

The definition of the problem begins with a statement of the desired *output* (results to be produced by the program). Unless this statement is correct and clear, all succeeding activities will be of doubtful value. The statement should be in writing so that misunderstandings can be minimized. Our statement could be as follows:

Given a list of numbers, find out how many are positive, how many are negative, and how many are zero.

A description of what the output is to look like is another element of the problem definition. Output to be printed can be described using a print chart (Figure 1-2). If output is to be displayed on a CRT (cathode ray tube) terminal, also referred to as a VDT (visual display terminal), it can be documented on a display system layout sheet (Figure 1-3). Output to be placed in a file is described on a record format form (Figure 1-4).

Before proceeding, let us consider how data is organized to facilitate processing. At the highest level we have *files,* which are collections of related records. We can have a file that contains information about students, a file of customer information, or a file with information about products. A *record* is a collection of data that pertains to a particular entity in a file, for example, a student, a customer, or a product. Records are composed of *fields*—also called *items,* such as name, address, age, price, course code. Fields, in turn, are a collection of *characters*: letters, numbers, or special symbols, such as a comma, dollar sign, or decimal point. The record format form shows the arrangement of fields in a record, the size of each field, and the type of characters that can appear in each field.

The *input* (data to be processed) must also be documented as part of the problem definition. If punched cards are to be processed, a multiple-card layout form (Figure 1-5) will be used. Data coming from a file may be described on a record format form. Input coming from a CRT terminal can be shown on the display system layout sheet.

The solutions to some problems involve complex calculations. These must also be described in detail as part of the problem definition.

The definition of the problem will usually be provided to the *programmer* (the person who writes the program) by a *systems analyst* (someone who plans the collection of equipment, programs, people, and procedures that make up a system). For simpler problems, the programmer may prepare the definition. In some smaller computer installations, the functions of analyst and programmer may be combined in a single position.

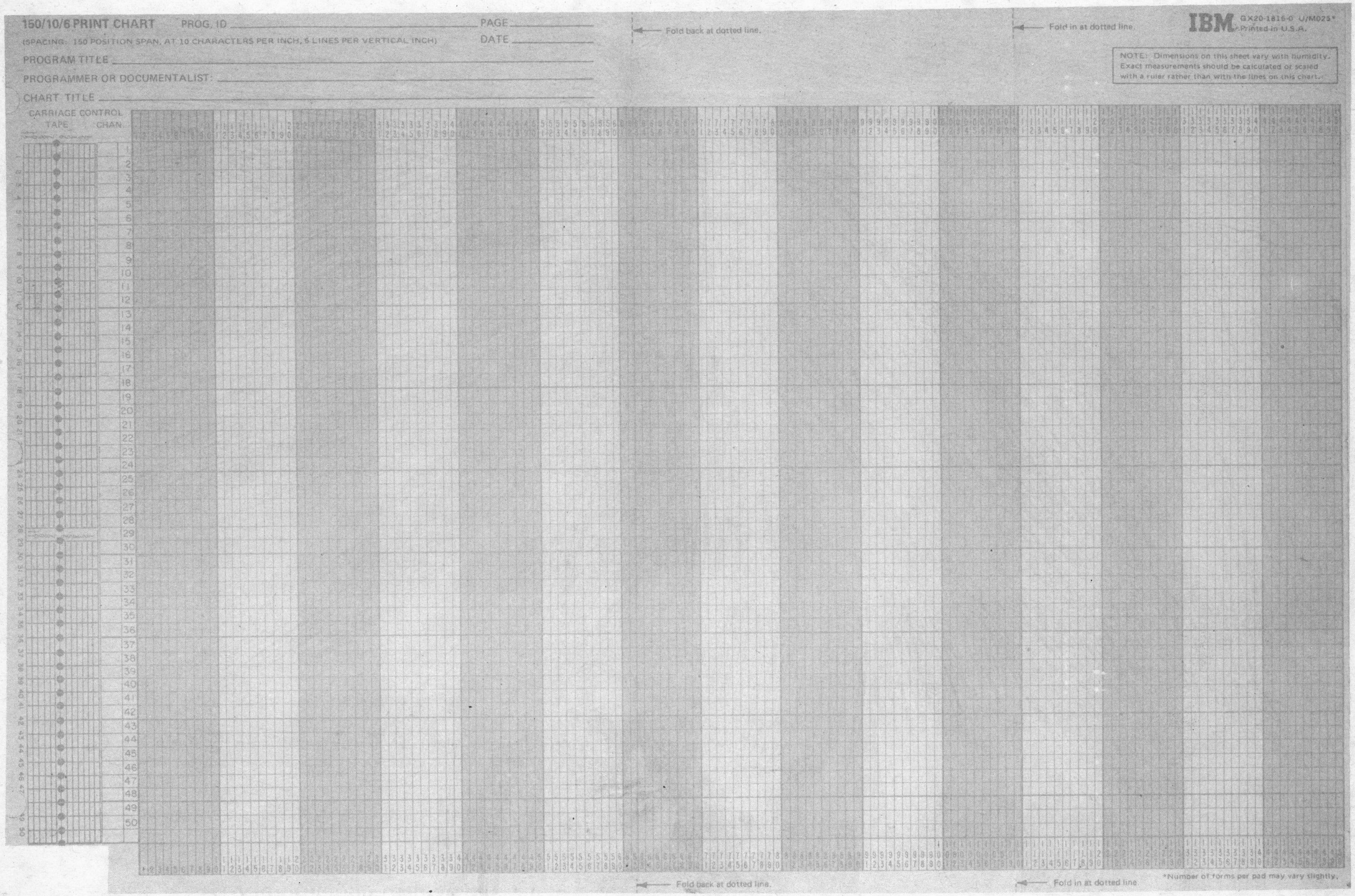

FIGURE 1-2 Print chart.

3270 Information Display System Layout Sheet

IBM

Panel ID

Job No.

Originated by

Subject

Sheet _____ of _____

Date _____

COLUMN

ROW

ATTRIBUTE

ITEM	DISPLAY PRINTER ROW COL	BUFFER ADDRESS DEC HEX	OR-DERS

PROT NO.	HI INT	A/N	SEL PEN DET	NON DISP	MDT ON
UNPR	NORM	NON	NORM	NORM	OFF

DEFAULTS

Example of use:

ITEM	DISPLAY PRINTER ROW COL	BUFFER ADDRESS DEC HEX	OR-DERS	PROT NO.	HI INT		SEL PEN DET	NON DISP	MDT ON OFF
20	03 20		ATT	NUL NON N					
		21	IC	√ N					
		26	ATT	N					
		29	RA	(to <03-42>) with 'x'					
		47	SBA						
		47	NL	-					

Address comments concerning this form to IBM Corporation, SDD, Dept. 520, Neighborhood Road, Kingston, N. Y. 12401

GX27-2951-0 U/M 025*
Printed in U.S.A.
*No. of forms per pad may vary slightly

KEY ASSIGNMENTS

PF1		PF6		PF11	
PF2		PF7		PF12	
PF3		PF8		PA1	
PF4		PF9		PA2	
PF5		PF10		PA3	

FIGURE 1-3 Display system layout sheet.

IBM

RECORD FORMAT

INTERNATIONAL BUSINESS MACHINES CORPORATION

GX20-1702-1 UM/025 †
Printed in U.S.A.

APPLICATION . . . . RECORD NAME . . . . BY . . . . DATE . . . . PAGE . . . . OF . . . .

Field Name

Characteristics*

Position**

**POSITION
Hexadecimal / Decimal
Numbering
from
00 to FF / 0 to 255

HEXADECIMAL

HEX

HEX

HEX

*CHARACTERISTICS

Check the box that corresponds to the characteristics used:

System/360 Characteristic Codes

General Characteristics

A - alphabetic or blank
X - alphanumeric
9 - numeric
V - assumed decimal point

Examples of Signed Fields:
X9999   999X
X9999V99   9999V9X

A - address value, full word
B - binary
C - character, 8-bit code
D - floating-point, double word
E - floating-point, full word
F - fixed-point, full word
H - fixed-point, halfword
P - packed decimal
S - address, base displacement
> - address, external symbol
X - hexadecimal, 4-bit code
Y - address value, halfword
Z - zoned decimal

SORTING FIELDS (Major to Minor)

1		7
2		8
3		9
4		10
5		11
6		12

WHERE USED

Input From	Output To

REMARKS

File Description
Recording Mode
Records per Block
Record Size
Label Records are
File Identification
File Serial Number
Retention Cycle
Organization Type

fold to here

Date	Revisions By

† The number of forms per pad may vary slightly.

FIGURE 1-4 Record format form.

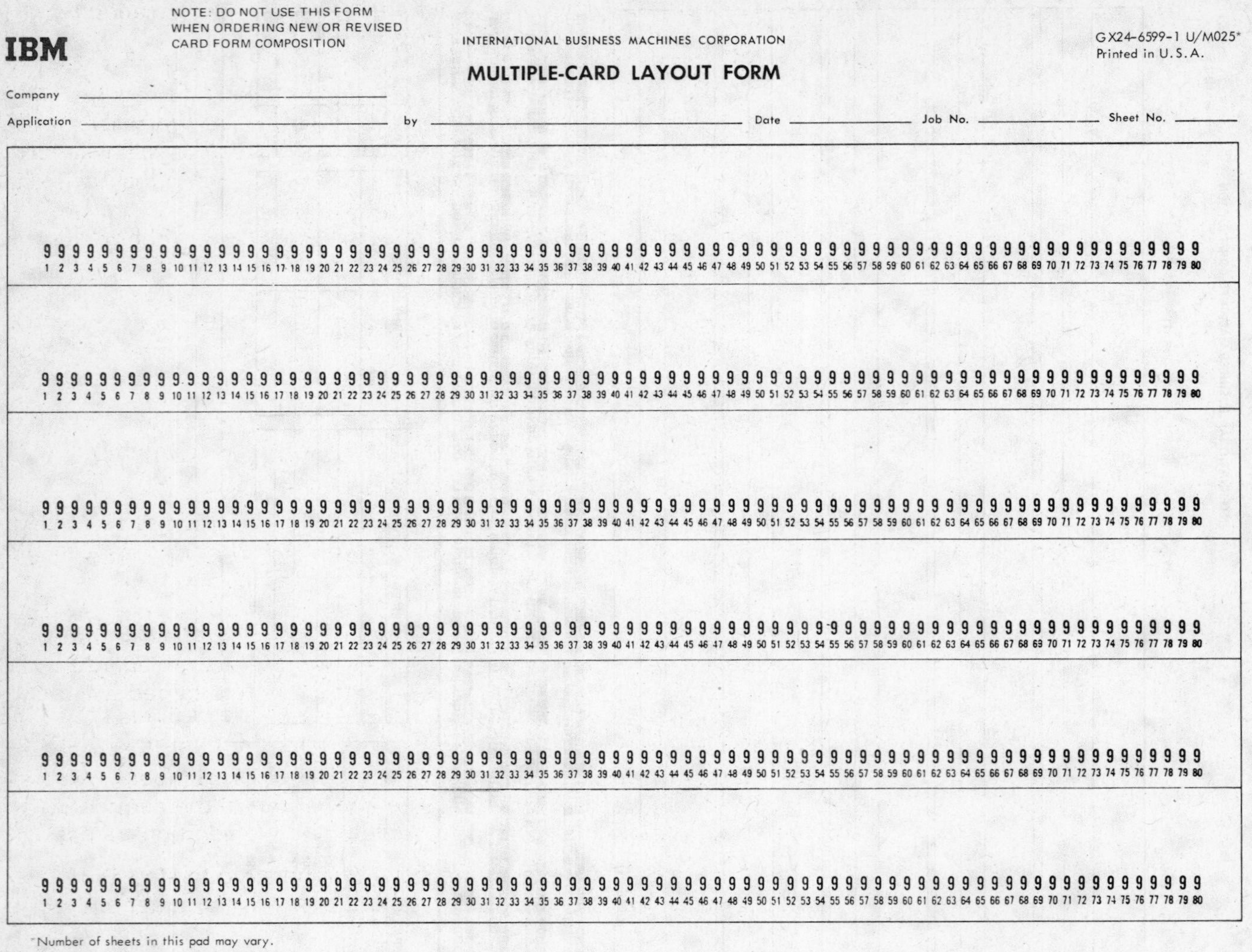

*Number of sheets in this pad may vary.

FIGURE 1-5 Multiple-card layout form.

Preparing an Algorithm

Once the problem has been defined, we can prepare an *algorithm* (a description of the sequence of steps required to solve a problem). In defining an algorithm that will work on a computer, we must consider the computer's limited capabilities:

• A computer can perform arithmetic operations (usually limited to addition, subtraction, multiplication, and division).

• It can compare two things and, on the basis of the result of the comparison, choose among alternative courses of action.

• It can move data about in its *memory* (a part of the computer in which data and instructions can be stored).

• The computer can also *input* (*read in*) data and *output* (*write out*) results.

Despite these limitations, we can use the computer to solve very complex problems. The trick is to figure out the exact sequence of steps to be fol-

6

lowed such that the computer will provide us with the information we desire. This sequence of steps is the algorithm.

An Initial Algorithm   Much of what we human beings do requires little conscious thought because we use our past experiences. This makes it difficult at first for us to define a sequence of very simple steps that will make this machine we call the computer do what we want. It is not that the steps themselves are difficult or complex, but rather that we must provide the machine with much more detailed instructions than we would have to give to a human being in order to get the job done. If we wanted a student in this course to tell us how many of our list of numbers were positive, how many negative, and how many zero, the original statement of the problem would probably be sufficient instruction. If we want a computer to do the job, we will have to prepare an algorithm such as the following:

1. If the number is positive, add one to the positive counter.
2. If the number is negative, add one to the negative counter.
3. If the number is zero, add one to the zero counter.

(A *counter* is a device for keeping track of the number of times something occurs.) These steps will be *executed* (performed) one at a time in the order given.

Refining the Algorithm   This takes care of one number, but we are supposed to process a list of numbers. Let us assume that the computer will get its list of numbers one at a time. Once we have determined whether a number is positive, negative, or zero, and have *incremented* (added one to) the appropriate counter, we must go back and get another number, process this number, and so on, until we run out of numbers. We also must make some provision for getting the answer out of the computer. We will therefore refine our algorithm to incorporate two additional steps:

1. Read a number; if there are no more numbers, go to step 5.
2. If the number is positive, add one to the positive counter and go to step 1.
3. If the number is negative, add one to the negative counter and go to step 1.
4. If the number is zero, add one to the zero counter and go to step 1.
5. Print counters.

Steps 1, 2, 3, and 4 illustrate how we can alter the normal sequential execution of our algorithm; the *go-to* instruction causes a *branch* (also called a transfer of control) to a step that is not next in sequence.

This version of the algorithm is better, but there are still a few improvements that can be made. For one thing, if we reach step 4, we will know that the number in question is zero. If it is not zero, that is, if it is either positive or negative, we will increment a counter at step 2 or 3 and go back to step 1; therefore, step 4 can simply be:

4. Add one to the zero counter and go to step 1.

There also is a problem with the incrementing of the counters. Each time we find a positive number, we add one to the positive counter, but we do not know what the counter was equal to initially. Our algorithm assumes that the counters are all set to zero when we start out, but we cannot safely make that assumption. We may in fact be attempting to add one to some number other than zero (in which case our results will be wrong), or to something that is not even a valid number (in which case the computer will stop with what is known as an *execution-time error,* an error that occurs while a program is being executed). Murphy's law seems to have been written with computers in mind:

Anything that can go wrong will.

When we write programs, we must try to anticipate all the problems that may arise and find ways to avoid them; therefore, we will include a step that will *initialize* the counters (set their initial values) to zero. A final refinement for our algorithm is the inclusion of a step to indicate that the job is done. This results in the algorithm shown in Figure 1-6.

The process we have gone through here in developing our algorithm is fairly typical. We started out with an algorithm that contained the main processing steps required, but we had to go through a series of refinements to make the process more efficient and to include some steps that we had failed to consider in our initial solution. Unless a problem is very simple, even an experienced programmer will have difficulty defining an initial solution that is completely correct.

Desk-Checking the Algorithm How do we know that this algorithm produces correct results? Before proceeding to the next activity, the preparation of a program flowchart, we can check our algorithm by making up a list of numbers and seeing what happens when we attempt to process this list with our algorithm. This is referred to as *desk-checking* the algorithm. Table 1-1 shows the steps in the order they will be executed, and what will happen to our counters, if we process the following list of numbers:

$$16, 3, -7, 0, 4, -6, -2, 8$$

The final results in Table 1-1 indicate that our data consists of four positive numbers, three negative numbers, and one zero. This checks with the test data, so we have verified that our algorithm does produce the correct results. The algorithm that we have created and tested becomes an important part of our documentation.

Preparing a Program Flowchart

When we are completely satisfied that our algorithm is correct, we are ready to prepare a *program flowchart,* a symbolic representation of our algorithm. The preparation of the program flowchart consists of translating the algorithm into a form in which the steps are shown by a set of outlines which has been adopted as a standard by the American National Standards Institute (ANSI). The program flowcharting outlines we will need are

FIGURE 1-6 Numbers algorithm.

1. Set positive, negative, and zero counters to 0.
2. Read a card; if there are no more numbers, go to step 6.
3. If the number is positive, add one to the positive counter and go to step 2.
4. If the number is negative, add one to the negative counter and go to step 2.
5. Add one to the zero counter and go to step 2.
6. Print counters.
7. Stop.

TABLE 1-1   DESK-CHECKING NUMBERS ALGORITHM

		Counters		
Step	**Number**	**Positive**	**Negative**	**Zero**
1	None	0	0	0
2	16	0	0	0
3	16	1	0	0
2	3	1	0	0
3	3	2	0	0
2	−7	2	0	0
3	−7	2	0	0
4	−7	2	1	0
2	0	2	1	0
3	0	2	1	0
4	0	2	1	0
5	0	2	1	1
2	4	2	1	1
3	4	3	1	1
2	−6	3	1	1
3	−6	3	1	1
4	−6	3	2	1
2	−2	3	2	1
3	−2	3	2	1
4	−2	3	3	1
2	8	3	3	1
3	8	4	3	1
2	None	4	3	1
6	None	4	3	1
7	None	4	3	1

shown in Figure 1-7. The processing to be done at each step is written inside the appropriate outline. There are flowcharting templates available that contain these outlines; one should always be used to produce a legible flowchart.

The algorithm was stated in everyday English — more or less — but now we will be planning a solution that takes into account the capabilities of the computer. For example, how will a computer know if a number is positive? As humans, we look for the presence of a plus (+) sign — or the absence of a minus (−) sign — in front of a nonzero number. But to get the computer to determine if a number is positive, we are forced to use its limited capabilities. Its ability to compare two things helps us here, for what, after all, is a positive number? It is a number that is greater than zero. Similarly, a negative number is one that is less than zero. So if we compare a number to zero, we can find out if it is positive, negative, or zero.

A Flowchart for Our Problem   Figure 1-8 is a program flowchart derived from the algorithm of Figure 1-6. (The numbers at the upper left of the outlines are not used in standard flowcharts, but are included here to identify parts of the flowchart in the discussion that follows.)

This flowchart, like all program flowcharts, starts with the terminal outline (1). The word inside this outline need not be START, but it should be appropriate (for example, BEGIN).

A flowline takes us from the terminal outline to the process outline (2) in which the three counters, here called POSCTR, NEGCTR, and ZEROCTR, are initialized to a value of zero. POSCTR, NEGCTR, and ZEROCTR are

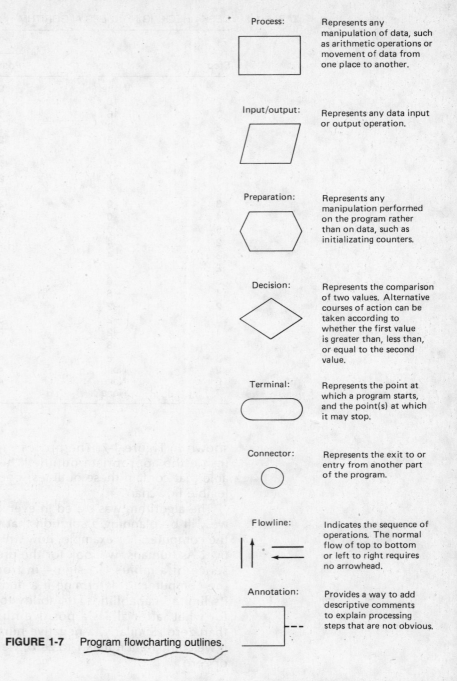

Process: Represents any manipulation of data, such as arithmetic operations or movement of data from one place to another.

Input/output: Represents any data input or output operation.

Preparation: Represents any manipulation performed on the program rather than on data, such as initializating counters.

Decision: Represents the comparison of two values. Alternative courses of action can be taken according to whether the first value is greater than, less than, or equal to the second value.

Terminal: Represents the point at which a program starts, and the point(s) at which it may stop.

Connector: Represents the exit to or entry from another part of the program.

Flowline: Indicates the sequence of operations. The normal flow of top to bottom or left to right requires no arrowhead.

Annotation: Provides a way to add descriptive comments to explain processing steps that are not obvious.

FIGURE 1-7   Program flowcharting outlines.

symbolic ways of referring to the locations in the computer's memory in which we will accumulate our counts. The use of POSCTR, NEGCTR, and ZEROCTR to represent the counters is the programmer's choice, although each programming language imposes some limits on the names that may be used. The names used in the flowchart should be the same as the names that will be used in the program. They should also be chosen to help the reader recall what is being represented; that is, they should be mnemonics.

Note the arrow (←) in "POSCTR ← 0." The arrow indicates that we are replacing the value currently in the memory locations used for POSCTR by

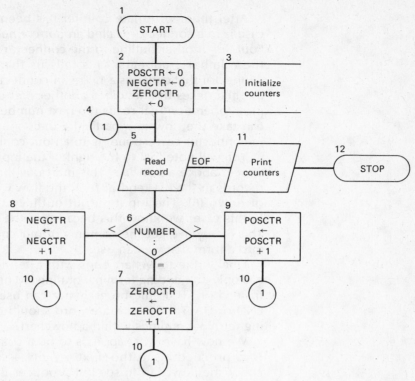

FIGURE 1-8 Numbers program flowchart.

the value zero. The annotation outline (3) explains what is being done in the process outline (2).

A flowline now takes us to the input outline (5). Although this outline is used for both input and output, we know that here it is being used for input because of the word "Read" inside the outline. This represents the reading of a record that contains a number to be analyzed. You may have observed that we have skipped over the connector outline (4). We will be coming back to it shortly.

After the input operation — assuming that there was a record to read — a flowline takes us to the decision outline (6). Here the number read from the record (identified by the name NUMBER) is compared to zero, just as in steps 3, 4, and 5 of the algorithm. This comparison took three steps in our algorithm, but we can show it in a single outline. We are able with one comparison to determine if NUMBER is greater than ($>$), less than ($<$), or equal to ($=$) zero. Each exit from the decision outline is labeled with the appropriate symbol: $>$, $<$, or $=$. If NUMBER $=$ zero, the flow will be to the process outline (7), where ZEROCTR will be incremented by adding one to it. This is indicated on the flowchart as:

$$ZEROCTR \leftarrow ZEROCTR + 1$$

That is, take the contents of ZEROCTR, add one to it, and place the result back at ZEROCTR. Similarly, if NUMBER $<$ zero, the flow is to (8), where NEGCTR is incremented; if NUMBER $>$ zero, the flow is to (9), where POSCTR is incremented.

After the appropriate counter has been incremented, the flow in each case is to a connector (called an *out-connector* because the flowline comes "out" of another outline to the connector). Inside the out-connectors (10) the number 1 appears. This tells us that the flow is to move to an in-connector that contains a 1. The in-connector (4) is a connector with a flowline that takes the flow *in* to another part of the flowchart, in this case the input operation that reads the next number. More than one out-connector can take the flow to a particular in-connector, but there can be only one in-connector corresponding to an out-connector.

You will note that to the right of the input outline (5) the characters EOF appear above a flowline. This indicates that when there are no more data records in the file (end-*of*-*f*ile), the flow will move to the right (11) instead of down (6). The input/output outline (11) is used for output purposes in this case; we know this because of the word "Print" inside the outline. This is how we get the contents of our counters out of the computer and into a form that we can use.

Finally, the flowchart ends with a terminal outline (12). This flowchart has only one ending terminal outline, so our program will always end here. Instead of STOP, the programmer can use any appropriate word, such as END or HALT, but the same word should be used consistently for all ending terminal outlines within a flowchart.

We now have what appears to be a completed flowchart. However, before proceeding to the next activity—coding the program—we must check the flowchart to see if it produces the correct results. In going from the algorithm to the flowchart we altered the way in which we were doing things (for example, there is only one comparison: of NUMBER to zero), so it is possible that the flowchart we have created from our algorithm may not yield the correct results. It is possible that we may have made a *logic error* (an error in our reasoning, as reflected in the flowchart). Just as we tested the algorithm, we should now test the flowchart of Figure 1-8 with the same set of data. This exercise will be left to the student.

The completed flowchart now becomes an important part of our documentation.

Some Flowcharting Guidelines   The following are some guidelines that will prove helpful in preparing a program flowchart; this is not an exhaustive list of all the do's and don't's of flowcharting, but it does cover the most important considerations:

1 A flowchart should be read the way a printed page is read: from top to bottom and from left to right. Any bottom-to-top or right-to-left flow should be clearly identified by an arrow on the flowline unless the flowline is an exit from a decision outline.

2 Every program flowchart starts with a single terminal outline (usually in the upper left corner) and ends with one or more terminal outlines.

3 The descriptive names that identify data items being used and the operations being performed should be used consistently.

4 The words used inside the outlines should be chosen so that they will have meaning for anyone reading the flowchart.

5 The contents of a decision outline should consist of the two items being compared (either two descriptive names or a name and a constant), separated by a colon, as shown in Figure 1-8.

6 Each exit from a decision outline should be labeled with the appropriate condition: $<$, $>$, $=$, $\leq$ (less than or equal), $\geq$ (greater than or equal), or $\neq$ (not equal).

7 Try to leave white space in the flowchart by using connectors instead of flowlines that wander all over the flowchart.

8 Be consistent in the level of detail shown; for example, if descriptive names are used in calculations, they should also be used when moving data.

9 There should be only one flowline into an outline. Any merging flows should be brought together on a flowline.

10 With only two exceptions, there should be only one flowline out of an outline. The obvious exception is the decision outline. The other one is the input outline, where the EOF condition may be represented by a labeled flowline that exits from the right of the outline.

11 Use the process outline for operations performed on data (for example, initializing a total field to zeros) and use the preparation outline for operations performed on the program itself. These latter operations will be encountered in subsequent chapters.

12 Entering and exiting flowlines should be positioned in the center of an outline.

13 Use annotations to explain anything that may not be obvious. Remember, the purpose of the flowchart is to document the processing steps; therefore, the processing represented by the flowchart should be easily understood by anyone likely to read it.

The above guidelines apply to standard program flowcharts. In the next chapter, we will encounter modifications to guidelines 5, 6, and 10, to accommodate structured programming techniques.

Coding the Program

When we are satisfied that the logic of the flowchart is correct, we can go on to the next activity: coding the program. The use of the word "coding" deserves some comment. The coding that is done in spy stories consists of taking important information and rewriting it in a form that can be understood only by somebody who knows the secret of the rewriting process and can thus decode the message. "Coding" has entirely different implications for us. We are going to write instructions for the computer in a form that is relatively easy for somebody else to understand. A special *translation program* will be used by the computer to convert the *source program* that we write into an *object program*. The object program will be in a *binary* form (composed of 1s and 0s), which the computer can use but which we humans have difficulty understanding. *Coding,* then, refers to the writing of instructions for the computer. There are a variety of languages that have been designed to make it relatively easy to give instructions to the computer. The exact form that these instructions take will be determined by the computer language that is used. For each language, there are coding forms on which the programmer can write the instructions.

Programming Languages   *High-level languages* are the most widely used type because they are relatively easy to learn, the resulting programs are generally easy to understand and modify, and programs written for one computer can usually be used on another computer with only minor modifications. In this text we will refer to the following high-level languages:

BASIC (*Beginner's All-purpose Symbolic Instruction Code*): an easy-to-learn and easy-to-use language that was originally developed for students to use in solving algebraic problems but has been modified to handle business data processing also. BASIC is widely used on personal computers.

COBOL (*CO*mmon *B*usiness *O*riented *L*anguage): designed for business data-processing requirements, COBOL was originally used on large computers but is now available even on some personal computers.

FORTRAN (*FOR*mula *TRAN*slator): designed for mathematical problem solving, FORTRAN has been modified over the years, most recently to include structured programming capabilities. It is available on most computers.

Pascal: a general-purpose programming language designed with the needs of structured programming in mind. Pascal is available on most computers.

RPG II (*R*eport *P*rogram *G*enerator): a powerful, relatively easy-to-learn language for business applications. RPG II is widely used on smaller business computers but is also available on large computers and some personal computers.

ANSI standards exist for BASIC, COBOL, FORTRAN, and Pascal. These are all procedure-oriented languages; a programmer using one of these languages must define the step-by-step procedure to be followed. A compiler is used to translate each source program instruction into one or more object program instructions. (There are also BASIC interpreters, which will be discussed below.) RPG II is an example of a problem-oriented language,

FIGURE 1-9 Numbers program flowchart with two-way branches.

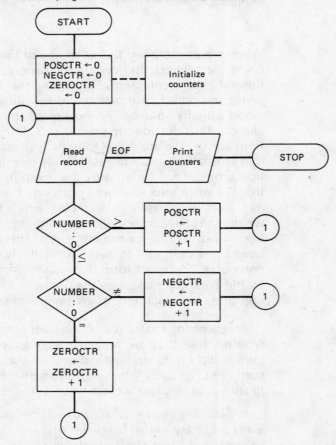

one in which the programmer describes the problem but does not define all the steps that must be followed; a generator program uses the problem descriptions in the source program to generate an object program.

An assembler language is a low-level language. Assembler language source programs are translated into object programs by an assembler program which produces one object program instruction for each source program instruction. There are many assembler languages; each type of computer has its own unique version. Assembler languages are relatively difficult to learn and understand, and programs written for one type of computer usually cannot be used on another computer without extensive revisions. It is not surprising, then, that assembler language programming is not widely used for business data processing.

Coding from the Flowchart A programmer writes a computer program by expressing in a programming language the processing steps shown in a program flowchart. The flowchart in Figure 1-8 can be used with any of the languages described above. However, because of the way the testing of NUMBER is shown in the flowchart, it is better suited to languages such as RPG II, assembler, or FORTRAN, which allow for three-way branches (three exits from a decision outline, labeled "<," "=," and ">").

If we intended to use COBOL, BASIC, or Pascal, we would probably draw the flowchart as shown in Figure 1-9, using two-way branches (two exits from a decision outline, labeled "<" and "≥," or ">" and "≤," or "=" and "≠"). Because our concern in this text is with structured programming techniques which use two-way branches and because two-way branches can be used in any programming language, we will restrict ourselves to the use of this type of branching in future flowcharts. Examples of two-way branches are shown in Figure 1-10.

Desk-Checking the Flowchart Before proceeding to the next step in the programming process, the programmer must *desk-check* the code for *syntax errors* (violations of the rules of the particular programming lan-

FIGURE 1-10 Two-way branch examples.

guage being used) and compare the program to the flowchart to be sure that the program contains no logic errors.

Debugging and Testing

When a program has been coded, carefully examined for syntax errors, and checked against the flowchart for logic errors, the programmer can convert the code to a machine-readable form (a form that can be read by the computer). With today's computers, that usually means entering the program through the keyboard of a CRT terminal, a task that the programmer is likely to perform. An experienced programmer may actually be able to code a portion of the program at the terminal rather than first writing it on a coding form. When the program is in a machine-readable form, it is submitted as input, along with data specially prepared to check the logic of the program, to a translation program (for example, a compiler, generator, assembler, or interpreter).

Using a Compiler, Generator, or Assembler   If a compiler, generator, or assembler is used, the entire program is processed as a unit. The translation program checks for syntax errors the programmer may have missed and produces both a *listing* (printed copy) of the program and diagnostic messages that tell the programmer what syntax errors were detected and where they are in the program. If syntax errors *are* detected, assembler programs and some compilers and generators will go no further. However, some compilers and generators are capable of making assumptions about what code is appropriate when certain kinds of syntax errors are detected. Translation programs with this capability may thus be able to produce an object program which can be executed. Since the compiler or generator will probably make some incorrect assumptions, the resulting program output is unlikely to be what the programmer had in mind, but even a little output may prove useful in starting the process of removing logic errors.

If the translation program is incapable of producing an object program, the programmer has only the listing and diagnostic messages to work with in correcting the syntax errors. If there is any program output to work with, the programmer must review it to identify the logic errors that have resulted in incorrect output. When the syntax and logic errors have been corrected (to the best of the programmer's abilities), the program is resubmitted to the translation program and the process of correcting the syntax and logic errors is repeated. When all syntax errors have been eliminated, the program can be *run* (executed) to produce output.

Beginning programmers have a tendency to think that when a program produces output, the job is completed. The program output must be carefully examined to ensure that it is correct. If it is not, the sources of the problems (the logic errors) must be identified and corrected. The process of detecting and correcting errors (*bugs*) in a program continues until the desired output is obtained. This process is referred to as *debugging* and *testing* a program.

Using an Interpreter   If an interpreter is used, the syntax of each instruction is checked as it is entered. Instructions that contain syntax errors are corrected and reentered; instructions without errors are executed immediately. The resulting output must be examined to identify logic errors in the program. The logic errors must then be corrected and the program rerun (interpreted and executed again). This process continues until all bugs have been removed from the program. No object program is produced. Each time the program is run, it must be interpreted again.

Documenting

Although the preparation of documentation has been left until last in our discussion of the programming process, documentation actually begins with the definition of the problem. We must keep a written record of everything we do in creating a program. In the process described above, we have prepared the following documents:

• A definition of the problem, consisting of a written problem statement; descriptions of output and input, including some or all of the following: print chart, multiple-card layout form, record layout form, and display system layout sheet; and descriptions of any complex processing
• An algorithm
• A program flowchart
• A source program, as recorded in the program listing produced by the translation program
• A record of the test input data and the resulting output

All of these serve as documentation for our program.

The importance of these documents can not be overemphasized. Any program that is going to be used regularly is almost certain to be changed at some time. The requirements may change, or an error in the program that was not detected with the test data may be discovered. In any event, when the time comes to change a program, even the programmer who wrote it is likely to have difficulty remembering the details of the program unless it has been well documented. And if the original programmer is no longer available, it may be virtually impossible to modify the program unless very careful and detailed documentation exists. Without adequate documentation, it may be necessary to rewrite completely a program that must be changed.

EXAMPLE: GROSS PAY

It is time to review the programming process, and there is no better way to do this than by working through another problem.

Problem Definition

Given a file of employee records, we are to produce a report of the employees' gross earnings (earnings before taxes and other deductions are subtracted). Each input record contains the employee number, the hours worked, and the hourly pay rate. To simplify the problem, we assume that employees are being paid just straight time — no overtime or holiday pay; therefore, an employee's gross pay will merely be the product of the hours worked and the pay rate.

There will be a line in the report, called a *detail line,* for each employee. Each detail line contains information about a single entity, in this case, an employee. This detail line will contain the employee's number and gross pay. There also will be a line printed at the end, when all employee records have been processed, that will contain the sum of all employees' gross pay.

This is referred to as a *total line* because it contains a summary total derived from the records of more than one employee.

Since we are not planning to code a program in a specific language, we need not be concerned with the exact form of the input and output; therefore, our task is limited to preparing the following:

- An algorithm
- Test input and output data
- A program flowchart

Algorithm

On the basis of our prior experience with the Numbers problem, we can make a first pass at our algorithm. As we write it, we will probably have to leave a few steps incomplete.

Developing the Algorithm   Referring to Figure 1-6, we see that the first step in that algorithm was an initialization step. Most algorithms will require such a step at the very beginning. Next will come an unknown number of steps for processing each employee record, and, finally, the processing required when there is no more data. We can therefore break the algorithm down into three identifiable components at this time

- Initialization
- Processing of data
- End-of-file processing

It is more than likely that we will not know when we begin to write the algorithm precisely what will require initialization, but this step can be completed as we develop the remaining steps. The most difficult of the three components to visualize is usually the second one, the processing of data. In this case, the processing for each employee record will include reading a record, computing the gross pay, adding the gross pay to the final total, and printing a detail line for the employee. When there are no more employee records to process, all we have to do is to print out the total that we have accumulated of all employees' earnings and terminate processing.

We can therefore devise a preliminary version of an algorithm that looks like the one in Figure 1-11. Step 1 will be completed when we discover what needs to be initialized. We know that we have to read a record and that eventually we will run out of data and have to branch to some step down the line; however, at the beginning, we are not sure just what step that will be, so step 2 is also left incomplete.

We compute an employee's gross pay in step 3. To finish our processing of an employee, we must add each employee's gross pay to the final total

FIGURE 1-11   Gross Pay algorithm, first pass.

1. Initialize ?.
2. Read a card; at EOF go to step ?.
3. Multiply hours by rate to get gross pay.
4. Add gross pay to total.
5. Print employee detail line.
6. Go to step 2.
7. Print total line.
8. Halt.

and print out a line in our report for the employee, as in steps 4 and 5. In the Numbers problem, we had to accumulate counts of each type of number. Here we are accumulating a total of an amount that we are calculating, but the process is quite similar. Any field that is being used to accumulate a total, whether it is a counter or a sum of some other amounts, must be initialized; therefore, we will have to initialize the final total field to zeros in step 1.

The detail line that we are to print is to contain the employee number and the gross pay. We can assume that step 3 will place the gross pay in the output record, but how does the employee number get there? Once again, it depends on the programming language being used. BASIC, FOR-TRAN, Pascal, and RPG II allow the programmer to specify in the output instruction the name by which a field was identified in the input. Assembler and COBOL, however, require that the programmer write instructions to move the contents of an input data field to an output record. To make sure that our solution is complete, let us assume that we need another step to move the employee number into an output record. Once we have performed this step, we can print the detail line and go back to step 2 to get the next record.

When we have completed processing all the employee records, we will print out the total of all employees' earnings and then halt. Step 2, therefore, must specify that at EOF we will go to the step that prints the total line.

Alternative Algorithms We can now complete our algorithm, as shown in Figure 1-12. It should be noted that there is some flexibility in ordering some of these steps. Steps 1 and 2 must be in the order given. We want to initialize the final total only once, so it must be outside of the *loop* (a group of processing steps that is used repeatedly) starting at step 2 that is used to process the employee records. Reading the employee record must be the first step in the loop because we can do nothing else until we have data to work with. However, we can move the employee number from the input area to the output area at any time between the reading of the record and the printing of the detail line. Calculation of the final total must follow the calculation of the employee's gross pay, but it need not follow it directly. It could occur after step 5 or 6 of Figure 1-12. Figure 1-13 contains an acceptable alternative to the algorithm of Figure 1-12.

Test Input and Output Data

We should not assume that either of these algorithms is correct. Rather, we should desk-check them with some data. We must prepare input test data

FIGURE 1-12	FIGURE 1-13
Gross Pay algorithm completed.	Gross Pay algorithm, alternative version.
1. Initialize final total.	1. Initialize final total.
2. Read a card; at EOF go to step 8.	2. Read a card; at EOF go to step 8.
3. Multiply hours by rate to get gross pay.	3. Move employee number to output record.
4. Add gross pay to total.	4. Multiply hours by rate to get gross pay.
5. Move employee number to output record.	5. Print employee detail line.
6. Print employee detail line.	6. Add gross pay to total.
7. Go to step 2.	7. Go to step 2.
8. Print total line.	8. Print total line.
9. Halt.	9. Halt.

for our algorithm, as in Table 1-2. If our algorithm is correct, we should get the output shown in the table. (The first column contains the employee number; the second, the employee's gross pay and the total for all employees.) Will we? Table 1-3 steps through the algorithm of Figure 1-12.

TABLE 1-2   GROSS PAY INPUT AND OUTPUT DATA

Input data		
Employee number	Hours	Rate
1234	40	6.00
3748	35	8.00
6240	40	7.50
Output data		
1234		240.00
3748		280.00
6240		300.00
		820.00

TABLE 1-3   TESTING ALGORITHM OF FIGURE 1-12

	Input records			Output records		
				Detail		
Step	Employee number	Hours	Rate	Employee number	Gross pay	Total pay
1	?	?	?	?	?	0
2	1234	40	6.00	?	?	0
3	1234	40	6.00	?	240.00	0
4	1234	40	6.00	?	240.00	240.00
5	1234	40	6.00	1234	240.00	240.00
6	1234	40	6.00	1234	240.00	240.00
7	1234	40	6.00	1234	240.00	240.00
2	3748	35	8.00	1234	240.00	240.00
3	3748	35	8.00	1234	280.00	240.00
4	3748	35	8.00	1234	280.00	520.00
5	3748	35	8.00	3748	280.00	520.00
6	3748	35	8.00	3748	280.00	520.00
7	3748	35	8.00	3748	280.00	520.00
2	6240	40	7.50	3748	280.00	520.00
3	6240	40	7.50	3748	300.00	520.00
4	6240	40	7.50	3748	300.00	820.00
5	6240	40	7.50	6240	300.00	820.00
6	6240	40	7.50	6240	300.00	820.00
7	6240	40	7.50	6240	300.00	820.00
2	None			6240	300.00	820.00
8	None			6240	300.00	820.00
9	None			6240	300.00	820.00

Output is produced by steps 6 and 8, as indicated by the boxes in the table. This is the same output shown in Table 1-2, so the algorithm in Figure 1-12 is correct. Similarly, Table 1-4 shows that the alternative algorithm, Figure 1-13, also produces the correct output.

Program Flowchart

Since there are several algorithms that will work for our Gross Pay example, there also are several acceptable flowcharts. The one shown in Figure 1-14 is for the initial algorithm of Figure 1-12. [Note the use of an asterisk (∗) to represent multiplication. This is the symbol normally used in both flowcharts and programs. Division is represented by a slash (/).] How would this flowchart have to be modified to represent the logic of the algorithm in Figure 1-13?

Before proceeding to coding the program, we must desk-check our Figure 1-14 flowchart. We should process our test input data through the flowchart to see if we get the correct output. When we are satisfied that we have a flowchart that will yield the desired results, we can include it in our documentation.

TABLE 1-4   TESTING ALGORITHM OF FIGURE 1-13

| | Input records | | | Output records | | |
| | | | | Detail | | |
Step	Employee number	Hours	Rate	Employee number	Gross pay	Total pay
1	?	?	?	?	?	0
2	1234	40	6.00	?	?	0
3	1234	40	6.00	1234	?	0
4	1234	40	6.00	1234	240.00	0
5	1234	40	6.00	1234	240.00	0
6	1234	40	6.00	1234	240.00	240.00
7	1234	40	6.00	1234	240.00	240.00
2	3748	35	8.00	1234	240.00	240.00
3	3748	35	8.00	3748	240.00	240.00
4	3748	35	8.00	3748	280.00	240.00
5	3748	35	8.00	3748	280.00	240.00
6	3748	35	8.00	3748	280.00	520.00
7	3748	35	8.00	3748	280.00	520.00
2	6240	40	7.50	3748	280.00	520.00
3	6240	40	7.50	6240	280.00	520.00
4	6240	40	7.50	6240	300.00	520.00
5	6240	40	7.50	6240	300.00	520.00
6	6240	40	7.50	6240	300.00	820.00
7	6240	40	7.50	6240	300.00	820.00
2		None		6240	300.00	820.00
8		None		6240	300.00	820.00
9		None		6240	300.00	820.00

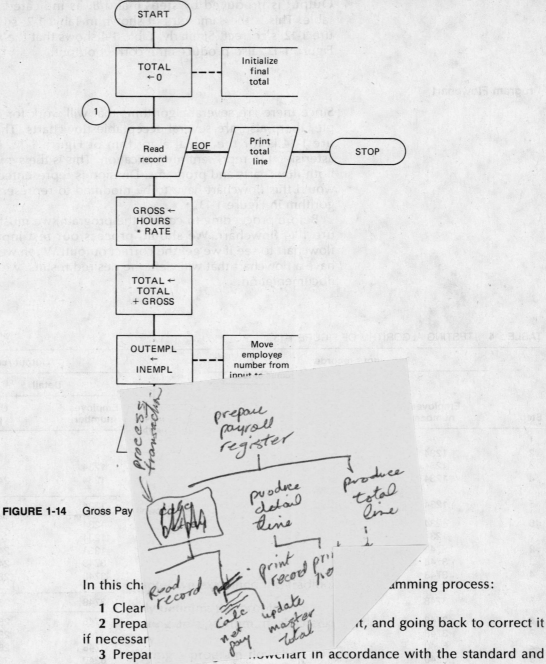

FIGURE 1-14 Gross Pay

SUMMARY

In this cha[...] [...]mming process:

1 Clear [...]

2 Prepa[...] [...]t, and going back to correct it if necessar[...]

3 Prepai[...] [...]wchart in accordance with the standard and desk-checking the flowchart

4 Coding the program from the flowchart and desk-checking the coding

5 Debugging and testing the program

6 Documenting the program, a process that should be going on at all stages in the development of a program

In the next chapter we will see how the second and third steps are changed by the structured programming approach.

KEY TERMS

algorithm
binary
branch
bug
character
coding
computer program
counter
debugging
desk checking
detail line
documenting
EOF
execute
execution-time error
field
file
high-level language
increment

initialize
input
item
listing
logic error
loop
memory
object program
output
program flowchart
programming process
record
run
source program
syntax error
testing
total line
translation program

EXERCISES

1 A payroll register is to be produced. The input consists of employee number, employee's gross pay, income tax, union dues, and other deductions.

The printed payroll register is to contain a detail line for each employee and a final total line as follows:

Detail Line: Employee number, gross pay, income tax, union dues, other deductions, and net pay (gross pay − income tax − union dues − other deductions)

Total Line: Total net pay for all employees

Documentation for this problem is to consist of the following: algorithm, program flowchart, test input data, and test output data.

2 An inventory report is to be produced. The input consists of item number, opening inventory amount, amount purchased, and amount sold.

The printed inventory report is to contain a detail line for each item and a final total line as follows:

Detail Line: Item number, opening inventory amount, amount purchased, amount sold, and ending inventory amount (opening inventory + purchases − sales)

Total Line: Total opening inventory, total amount purchased, total amount sold, and total ending inventory

The total opening inventory is the total of the opening inventory amount for all items. The other totals are computed in a similar fashion.

Documentation for this problem is to consist of the following: algorithm, program flowchart, test input data, and test output data.

3 A savings account balance report is to be produced. The input consists of account number, balance forward, deposits (sum of all deposits), withdrawals (sum of all withdrawals), and interest earned.

The printed account balance report is to contain a detail line for each account and a final total line as follows:

Detail Line: Account number, balance forward, deposits, withdrawals, interest earned, and ending balance (balance forward + deposits − withdrawals + interest)

Total Line: Total balances forward, total deposits, total withdrawals, total interest earned, and total ending balances.

The total balances forward is the total of the balance forward amount for all accounts. The other totals are computed in a similar fashion.

Documentation for this problem is to consist of the following: algorithm, program flowchart, test input data, and test output data.

CHAPTER 2

INTRODUCTION TO STRUCTURED PROGRAMMING

OBJECTIVES

Upon completing this chapter the student should be able to:

1 Prepare a structure chart.
2 Discuss the essential features of a structured program and why they are considered essential.
3 Prepare a structured program flowchart.
4 Write a structured program in pseudocode.
5 Define and use the key terms at the end of the chapter.

INTRODUCTION

In the early days of programming—the 1950s and 1960s, when computers were slower, of limited capability, and more expensive—there was a premium placed on writing programs that required as little storage as possible and could be executed in the minimum amount of time. One result of this emphasis was that programmers often spent a great deal of time devising clever techniques and algorithms to save computer time and memory. Some of these early programmers were truly ingenious, and their programs could properly be considered works of art. Sometimes, however, because of amazing ingenuity, inadequate documentation, or both, the programming logic used by these programmers was extremely difficult to understand.

Today, as hardware costs continue to fall and programmer salaries continue to rise, the writing of programs consumes an increasing portion of data-processing costs. In addition, as much as 80 percent of programming effort is spent on maintenance programming, that is, modifying existing programs to correct errors or to meet changing needs. When the logic of a program is not easily understood, maintaining the program is at best very difficult. In some cases, it is virtually impossible. If the original programmer is no longer available, somebody else must become familiarized with the program logic before any changes can be made. If the program logic is obscure, it may be cheaper to completely rewrite the program than to try to modify it. If the program logic is convoluted enough, and enough time has passed, even the original programmer may not remember why something was done in a particular way.

A program that is difficult to maintain can greatly increase data-processing costs, so it is not surprising that data-processing managers are less interested in clever code and more interested in an organized, systematic approach to programming. Today we see a major emphasis on writing programs with straightforward, easily understood logic, programs that can be written and maintained with a minimum expenditure of time and effort.

The term *structured programming* refers to a collection of techniques that have evolved from the pioneering work of Edsger Dijkstra. These techniques are meant to increase programmer productivity by reducing the time required to write, test, debug, and maintain programs. Structured programming emphasizes the truly creative part of the programming process — the careful and systematic planning of programs. Coding (that is, translating the plan into instructions for the computer) is largely a clerical task once the syntax rules of a language have been mastered. In this chapter we will discuss how structured programming has evolved from modular programming. We will examine the fundamental structures used in structured programming, and we will begin to use structured flowcharts, structure charts, and pseudocode as tools for planning programs.

MODULAR PROGRAMMING

One of the early attempts at improving programmer productivity through better planning was the use of *modular programming*. In modular programming, the program is broken down into *modules* (pieces), each of which performs a single, limited function and is written and debugged separately from other modules. Because the purpose and size of each module are limited, the likelihood of errors is reduced.

Each program contains a main program module, which ultimately controls everything that happens; it transfers control to submodules so that they may perform their functions, but each submodule returns control to the main module when it has completed its task. If the task assigned to a submodule is too complex, it must itself be broken down into other modules, which it controls. This process of successively subdividing modules continues until each module has only a limited task to perform. This task can be input, output, manipulating data, controlling other modules, or some combination of these. A module may temporarily transfer control (*branch*) to another module, but each module must eventually return control to the module from which it originally received control.

Modules are independent in the sense that no module can have direct access to any other module except its calling module and its own submodules. However, the results produced by one module can be used by any other module when it is given control.

Because the modules are independent, different programmers can work simultaneously on different parts of the same program. This reduces the time that elapses between beginning and completing a program. In addition, a module can be radically changed without affecting other modules as long as its original function remains unchanged.

Implementing the Modular Approach

Modular programming is implemented by using *subroutines,* a group of instructions that performs a limited processing task, such as printing a portion of a report, reading an input record, or calculating a square root. Subroutines can be discussed from a variety of perspectives, but we will restrict ourselves here to considering external and internal subroutines. Since internal subroutines are more frequently used in business data processing, we will discuss them first. We will then briefly look at external subroutines.

Internal Subroutines   An *internal subroutine* is part of the program that uses it. The task performed by the subroutine may be one that is required at more than one place in the program, but the code appears in the program only once. The program transfers control to the subroutine when the task needs to be performed. When the task is completed, control is returned to the instruction following the one that transferred control to the subroutine.

The instructions that transfer control to the subroutine and back again are commonly identified as *call* and *return* instructions, respectively. A subroutine returns control to the instruction following the call instruction when it has completed its task. This is possible because at the time a subroutine is called, the location of the instruction to which control is to be returned is stored in a *register,* a special-purpose memory device in the computer. This location is the position in memory of the instruction following the call instruction. When it is time to return to the calling program, the location to which to return is retrieved from the register. Figure 2-1 illustrates how a subroutine can be called from more than one place in a program.

The calling of an internal subroutine is represented in a program flowchart by a horizontally striped process outline, as in Figure 2-2. The name of the internal subroutine is written in the striped area.

The flowchart of the internal subroutine will be part of the flowchart of the program that calls it. Like a program flowchart, the subroutine flowchart begins and ends with a terminal outline. Inside the beginning terminal outline appears the name of the subroutine, and inside the ending terminal outline is placed the word RETURN. Figure 2-3 illustrates the flowcharting of an internal subroutine that performs a series of calculations.

One disadvantage of subroutines is that using them results in generally slower execution speed for the program as a whole, but the high speed of today's computers has reduced the significance of this disadvantage. Another drawback is that some languages impose strict constraints on how data is passed to and from a subroutine and problems may arise if these

FIGURE 2-1   Transfer to and from a subroutine.

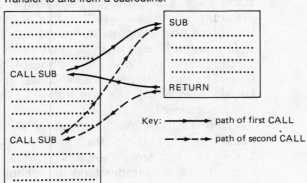

FIGURE 2-2   Calling internal subroutines.

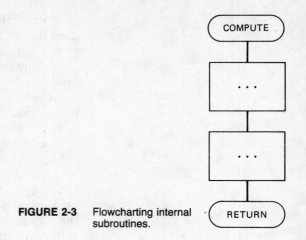

FIGURE 2-3   Flowcharting internal subroutines.

constraints are not closely observed. On balance, however, the disadvantages of using modular programming are far outweighed by the benefits: reductions in the time required to write, test, debug, and maintain programs, resulting in substantial cost savings.

External Subroutines   *External subroutines* are used for tasks that more than one program is likely to want performed: for example, calculating a square root. The term "external" is used because the instructions for doing the processing will not be part of the program using the routine. The external subroutine is treated almost like a separate program. Its instructions are translated like any other program, and the resulting object code is stored in a library where it is available to any program requesting it. As a result, the work of designing, writing, and debugging needs to be done only once.

To use an external subroutine, the programmer needs to know where to find it, what its name is, how to send data to it, and how the answer will come back. Once these technicalities are dealt with, however, the programmer can make use of the code to perform a task, with confidence that the subroutine will provide correct results.

The use of an external subroutine is represented in a program flowchart by the predefined process outline of Figure 2-4. The processing represented by the outline is not explained in the flowchart in which it appears. Usually a flowchart or a description of the processing is available in some other document.

External subroutines are frequently used for complex processing that is needed by many users, such as mathematical or statistical routines or the sorting of files. Any programmer can access and use external subroutines without having to understand the techniques involved.

FIGURE 2-4   Calling external subroutines.

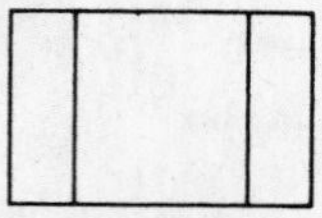

Problems with the Modular Approach

The modular programming approach initially met with some resistance from programmers because it restricted their activities. When portions of a program are allocated to different programmers, no one programmer can be said to "own" the program; instead, it belongs to a team. Team programmers, for example, no longer have free rein to make up names to refer to data, for all programmers must use the same names for certain items of data. For each file, standard field names are established that must be used in programs that process the file. Even when the programmer is free to create a name, there are frequently naming conventions that must be followed.

A more significant difficulty with the modular approach lay in determining exactly what constitutes a module. Early modular programming efforts often produced programs that consisted of one very large module and several small ones. Definitions of the functions to be performed by modules simply were not as limited as they should have been. To counteract this problem, arbitrary limits were set on the number of instructions that a module could consist of. (For example, an often-used rule of thumb was that a module should consist of no more than 50 statements, about the number that fit on one page of a program listing.) These arbitrary rules helped programmers to identify a module with a function that was too broadly defined, but at the same time use of the rules in some cases delayed the development of good programming practices. Instead of designing modules to do a particular job, programmers defined them in terms of an arbitrary number of instructions.

A further early difficulty with the modular approach lay in the emphasis placed on the planning phase of programming, an emphasis that is sometimes unsettling to both programmers and managers. Clearly, planning is essential if the functions of the modules are to be properly defined. Programmers and managers frequently work under severe time pressures, however, and there is a natural tendency to want to get on with the coding. The time spent in planning the program produces no actual code, so it may appear that progress is not being made. In the long run, however, the time invested in careful planning pays off in lower programming costs.

If the modules are assigned to different programmers, someone has to coordinate the project to ensure that each module performs its assigned function and that proper field names are used. With some languages (notably COBOL), if programmers must make up a name for the results of the processing done by a particular module, they have to make sure that the same name has not been used by another programmer for a different purpose. Modular programming thus requires a substantial amount of coordination and standardization.

We humans tend to resist change, so the early resistance to modular programming was not surprising. Today, however, the obvious advantages of the modular approach have made it an integral part of all structured programming efforts.

Examples of Program Modules

The Numbers and Gross Pay examples in Chapter 1 have three major functions:

1 Reading the data
2 Processing it
3 Printing the results

The third function for the Gross Pay problem can be subdivided into

3a Printing detail output
3b Printing final output

We will return to these two examples as we examine some of the tools used in planning structured programs.

In addition to the modules noted above, each program also needs a main program module. Execution begins and ends in this module. In between, the main module transfers control to the other modules at the appropriate times.

TOP-DOWN PROGRAMMING

The top-down approach has evolved as a useful technique in planning a modular program. In *top-down programming* we first define the main program module, which initiates program execution, calls other modules to perform specific functions, and then terminates execution. If the function to be performed by a module called by the main program module is sufficiently complex, this submodule must in turn be broken down into subordinate modules that will handle pieces of the larger function.

Structure Charts

The *structure chart* is a commonly used planning tool in top-down programming. [This tool is sometimes referred to as a *hierarchy,* or *hierarchical, chart* or a *visual table of contents (VTOC)*.] There is no standard for structure charts, and the technique discussed below, which seems to be a workable, logical way to use the tool, is a blending of ideas from a variety of sources.

Rectangles are used to represent modules, as shown in Figure 2-5. Each module is assigned a number, with zero reserved for the main program module. This module represents the entire program, and is referred to as a level-0 module. Below it are shown level-1 modules that are called by—and are therefore directly under the control of—the main program module.

There may be up to three level-1 modules. The first module defined at (*main*) level-1 is the one that will be executed repeatedly, for example, a module that processes input data records. A second module handles the processing that is required before the data itself can be processed (for example, loading a table, as discussed in Chapter 7). Processing that is done after the last data record has been processed (for example, printing a final total) is placed in a third level-1 module. The modules are ordered from left to right in the order in which they normally are executed, as shown in Fig-

FIGURE 2-5   Level-0 and level-1 modules.

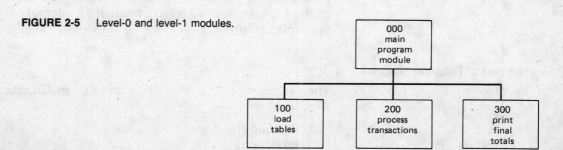

ure 2-5. Level-2 modules are added for any level-1 modules that have an involved task to perform. Some of these level-2 modules may in turn have to be broken down into submodules, and some of these may also have to be subdivided. The subdivision of modules ends when each module has a clearly defined, single function to perform. In general, a module should be small enough to be easily coded and tested.

A properly subdivided module will have at least two modules at the next lower level. If a module has only one subordinate module, it should therefore be reexamined. (An exception to this rule is discussed in the next section.) Excessive subdivision of a module, on the other hand, is more difficult to identify. This condition may not make itself apparent until the calling module is flowcharted and the complexity of its logic revealed. In that situation, the way in which the module is subdivided should be reconsidered. Figure 2-6 shows a completed structure chart for a program that updates an inventory file.

Identifying Modules

A module name is a short description of what the module does. The identification of a module also includes a number. There is a great diversity of opinion about how to number modules. The system described here has the advantages of being both simple and flexible.

The numbers for modules that show the processing that takes place before the data records are processed have the number 1 in the first position. In Figure 2-6, module "100 load product table" has two subordinate modules, one to read the table records, and another to store the table

FIGURE 2-6   Structure chart for a program to update an inventory file.

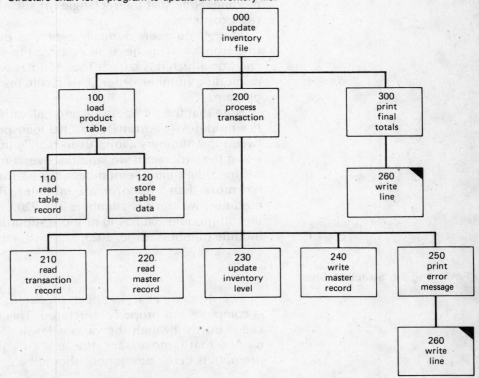

data. The numbers of these modules also contain the number 1 in the first position.

Module "200 process transaction" has five subordinate functions:

- Reading transaction record
- Reading master record
- Updating inventory level
- Writing master record
- Printing error message

(Transaction records contain data about a business activity, such as a sale or a receipt of merchandise; files of transaction records are retained for a relatively short period of time. A master file is retained indefinitely; its records contain information that must be used regularly, such as the amount of an item that is in inventory.) The numbers of all modules subordinate to module 200 contain the number 2 in the first position. Modules 210 through 250 are level-2 modules, as are modules 110 and 120, but because of space limitations, they are drawn at what appears to be a lower level. An alternative way of dealing with the space-limitation problem is to use more than one page for the structure chart. We can put on one page the level-0 and level-1 modules and then have a separate page for each level-1 module and its subordinate modules.

The modules for the processing that takes place when there are no more data records have the number 3 in the first position, unless modules that were previously defined are also used here. In that case, the earlier module number is used. For example, module "300 print final totals" has a single subordinate module ("260 write line"), which is the same module called by "250 print error message." This is an example of the exception referred to in the previous section. A module may have a single subordinate module if that single module is subordinate to at least one other module. Note that the rectangle for such a module is shaded in the upper right corner.

Module numbers normally appear as part of the module names used in the program. This helps in relating the source program to the structure chart on which it is based. The modules will usually appear in the program in module number order. This facilitates locating modules in the source progam.

Note that the numbers 110 and 120, rather than 101 and 102, are used for the modules subordinate to "100 load product table." Leaving gaps between the numbers allows us to readily insert a module between two others in the program if we later discover a need to do so.

Three-digit module numbers can be used as long as no level-1 module has more than 9 subordinate modules. If module 200 has 9 subordinate modules, we can use numbers 210, 220, . . . , 290 for the subordinate modules. If module 200 has 10 or more subordinate modules, we use four-digit module numbers: 2010, 2020, . . . , 2100, etc.

Reviewing the Structure Chart

After a structure chart has been prepared, it must be reviewed to be sure it is complete and properly structured. This review starts at the top and proceeds down through the various levels. To determine if everything is included that is necessary, the *user* (the person or group for whom the program is being developed) should be consulted. The user is most familiar with the problem and can offer valuable comments about the complete-ness of the structure charts.

Whether the chart is properly structured is for the most part a question of whether each module is assigned a single, limited function. If any module has not been subdivided properly, the structure chart must be revised.

Structure Charts and Flowcharts

The process of developing the structure chart begins with defining the main program module. If a module contains any obvious subordinate functions, they are broken out and placed at the next lower level, under the module to which they are subordinate. A module usually has either zero, or two or more subordinate modules; it will have a single subordinate module only if the subordinate module performs a function that is required elsewhere in the program.

This top-down design of the program focuses attention first on the overall structure of the program and leaves the details of the particular individual functions until after the structure chart has been prepared. This contrasts with program flowcharting, in which we immediately plan the detailed processing steps, developing a sequence of these steps as a solution to the problem. Typically, a program flowchart must be revised frequently, for example, when one or more required processing steps have been omitted, or the steps have been listed in the wrong order. Because in developing a structure chart the processing details are left until the end, structure charts require far less revision.

The structure chart is a tool for planning the structure of a program. It shows the functions to be performed and the relationship between modules, but it usually provides too little information to serve as a basis for coding a program. It does not show the exact processing steps, nor does it show under what conditions and in which order the modules will be used. For these reasons, the use of structure charts does not preclude the use of program flowcharts. In fact, after a structure chart has been prepared, flowcharts of the individual modules may be prepared as an aid in writing the code. The logic of some modules will be so simple that it will be possible to write the code without the use of flowcharts. For others modules, flowcharts may be required as part of the documentation of the program.

Structure charts are easier than flowcharts for the user to understand. For this reason, they are an effective tool for communicating the design of a program to the user and for obtaining suggestions for corrections and improvements. Later in this chapter we will examine an alternative to program flowcharts that both shows the processing details and is easily understood by a user.

Figure 2-7 contains a structure chart for the Numbers problem of Chapter 1. This contrasts with the program flowchart of Figure 1-8. Since there was no processing required before the first data record was read, there are only two level-1 modules.

Coding the Modules

In top-down programming, the level-0 module is coded first. It is tested using *dummy modules* for the level-1 modules. These dummy modules can be called by the level-0 module; they give the appearance of performing the desired function without actually doing so. They do, however, permit

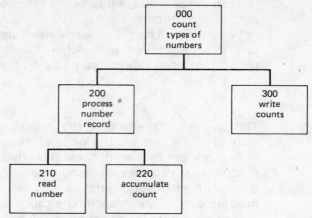

FIGURE 2-7 Structure chart for Numbers problem.

the testing of the level-0 module. When the level-0 module checks out with the dummy level-1 modules, attention can be turned to coding the actual level-1 modules.

When an actual level-1 module is coded, it will use dummy modules for its subordinate functions while its logic is being tested. When the level-1 module (along with its dummy modules) yields correct results, it replaces the corresponding dummy level-1 module in a test of the level-0 module. If the level-0 module (which had previously performed properly) now fails, the problem can be traced to the new level-1 module. This incorporation of new modules into the program one at a time greatly facilitates identifying and correcting the source of problems.

Once a level-1 module checks out (both by itself and with the level-0 module), attention can be directed to developing and testing modules to replace its dummy modules. In this way, the program is literally coded from the top of the structure chart down to the lowest-level modules. When the last dummy module is finally replaced and produces satisfactory results as part of the entire program, a usable program exists.

Since a structure chart gives no indication of the size of its modules, it is possible that during the coding of a module we may discover that it is too large. Then the structure chart will have to be revised to make the function of each module more manageable. This will require the recoding of those modules whose functions have changed.

PROGRAMMING STRUCTURES

One of the early objectives in designing structured programs was to eliminate the confusion resulting from the use of branch, or go-to, instructions. It is sometimes difficult to follow the flow of a program through a series of branches. In addition, because branch instructions enable the programmer to transfer control to any instruction in a program, when a problem does occur, it may be hard to determine what processing led up to the problem. For example, a problem occurring in a portion of a program that can be reached by any of three different branch instructions may be the result of an error in the code preceding any of the three branches. Knowing which of the three branch instructions was executed immediately prior to the occurrence of the problem would be a big help in identifying the problem.

If the portion of the program where the problem appears is in an internal subroutine accessed by means of a call instruction, the register containing the return address can be checked to determine what processing immediately preceded the call of the subroutine.

There is no universal agreement that a program must be completely free of branch instructions. There are some who feel that a limited use of branch instructions under special circumstances (for example, within a module) is acceptable. However, there are a significant number of advocates of structured programming who take the position that branch instructions should not be used at all. The solutions that we will develop will use no go-to instructions; that is, they will be part of what is sometimes called *GOTOless programming.*

Three logic patterns, or structures, have been identified which are sufficient for any structured program: the sequence structure, the loop structure, and the selection structure. None of the three requires the use of branch instructions.

Sequence Structure

In the *sequence structure,* instructions are executed in the order in which they are encountered. Figure 2-8*a* shows a generalized sequence structure, and Figure 2-8*b* shows a specific sequence structure from the program flowchart of Figure 1-14. Note that the only way to enter a sequence structure is at the top, and the only way to exit from it is at the bottom.

The rectangle in the generalized sequence structure can represent any unconditional operation:

- An *I/O* (input or output) operation
- An arithmetic operation
- An operation involving moving data about in the computer's memory

One outline not allowed in a sequence structure is the decision outline.

FIGURE 2-8   Sequence structure.
(*a*) Generalized; (*b*) from Gross Pay problem.

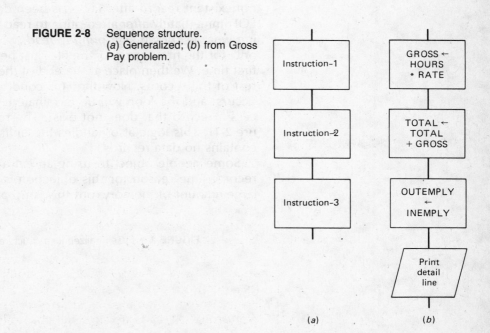

(*a*)   (*b*)

The processing steps in a sequence structure can be combined and represented by one rectangle with a single entry point and a single exit point. If the processing steps constitute the task of a module, when we combine them into a single rectangle we are in effect using that rectangle to represent the entire module. This is the reverse of the process that we go through in top-down programming, where we take a rectangle representing a module and break it down into discrete processing steps. Each module can thus be viewed as a structure with a single entrance and a single exit.

Loop Structure

The *loop* (or iteration) *structure* provides for the repetition of one or more instructions for as long as a given situation, referred to as a *condition,* exists. When a condition exists, it is true (T); when it does not exist, it is false (F). The loop is executed as long as the condition is true.

Figure 2-9 illustrates the loop structure. As with the sequence structure, there is a single entrance and a single exit from the loop structure. Neither of the examples in Chapter 1 contains an obvious example of the loop structure, although both of them contain loops that read and process records. If we modify the flowchart of Figure 1-14 slightly, however, we get the example of the loop structure shown in Figure 2-10. The condition that controls the loop is "not EOF." As long as end-of-file is not encountered, the loop—including the reading of a record—will be executed. The test for EOF cannot be part of the input operation; it must be at the beginning of the loop. We no longer show an EOF exit from the input outline. The use of connectors to return the flow to the beginning of the loop is not a branch. The connectors are used to avoid having a flowline that clutters up the flowchart.

There is a problem with the flowchart in Figure 2-10 when we do reach EOF because there is no exit from the loop until just prior to reading another record. Unless we change the flowchart, we will attempt to process a nonexistent record after EOF has been detected. We really should test for EOF immediately *after* attempting to read a record. This can be done by using what is known as a *priming read,* which is an initial read that is used only for the first record in the file, just before the condition is checked the first time. We then place at the end of the loop the input operation for the rest of the records. Now the EOF condition will be detected as soon as it occurs, and the loop will be terminated. No attempt will be made to process a record that does not exist. The revised flowchart is shown in Figure 2-11. This logic also handles the unlikely situation of an input file that contains no data records.

Some people object to using an extra input operation just for a single record. One reason for this objection is that input instructions require a large amount of memory, but this is no problem if a single copy of the in-

FIGURE 2-9 Generalized loop structure.

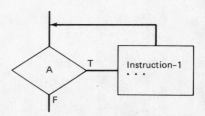

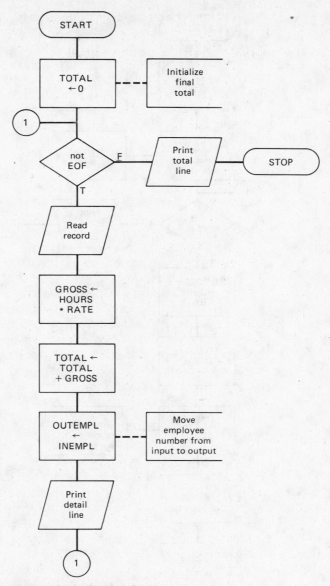

FIGURE 2-10   Modified Gross Pay flowchart.

put instructions is placed in a module that can be called. This requires a modification of the structure chart to include the priming read as part of what is done before the first data record is processed. This is illustrated by Figure 2-12, a structure chart for the Gross Pay problem of Chapter 1. The number assigned to the module that reads a data record starts with the number 2 rather than 1 because all but the first read will be controlled by module 200. Module "240 write line" is used for the printing of both the detail line and the total line, a technique that is characteristic of structured COBOL programming. In other languages, the output would probably be handled differently.

An instruction in the loop will be executed only if the not-EOF condition is true. Since no branch instructions are allowed, there is no way to get into the loop without first satisfying this condition.

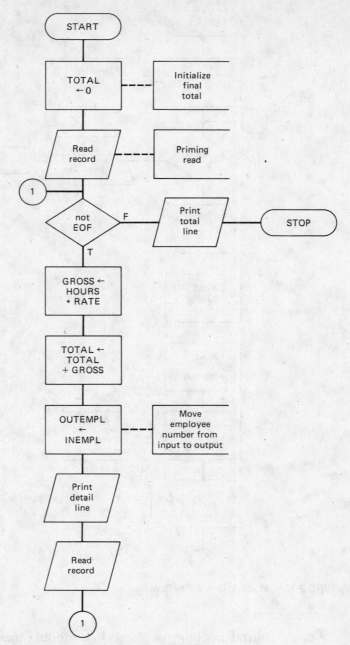

FIGURE 2-11 Gross Pay flowchart with priming read.

The activities that make up a loop structure can be represented by a single rectangle. This rectangle can then be combined with other rectangles in a sequence structure into a single rectangle representing a module.

Selection Structure

The third structure, called the *selection structure,* is illustrated in Figure 2-13a. Note that flowcharting guidelines numbers 5 and 6 must be modified to accommodate the selection structure. Exits from the decision outline are

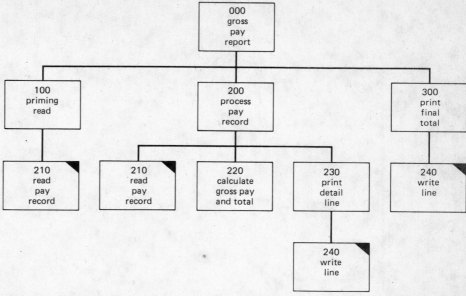

FIGURE 2-12   Gross Pay structure chart.

labeled "T" and "F" instead of with the relationships "<," ">," "=," etc. The relationship becomes part of the condition inside the outline rather than a label for an exit. A condition is tested, and one of two alternative courses of action is selected depending on whether the condition is true or false.

Note that like the sequence and loop structures, there is a single entry point and a single exit point from the selection structure. Because of the single exit point, whatever structure follows the selection structure will be executed, regardless of the status of the condition. A selection structure derived from the Numbers flowchart of Figure 1-9 is shown in Figure 2-13*b*.

In some situations, there may be no action taken if the condition is false. This situation is flowcharted as shown in Figure 2-13*c*.

Like the activities represented by a loop structure, selection-structure activities can be combined and represented by a single rectangle, as part of a sequence structure.

Structure Charts and Program Structures

We can use sequence, loop, and selection structures to flowchart the program represented by a structure chart. The processing to be performed by any module can be represented as a sequence of these three structures. Since both loop and selection structures can be represented by a single rectangle, an entire program module can be represented by a sequence structure. And since a sequence structure can also be represented by a single rectangle, we can represent any module by a single rectangle. Thus, we have what appears on the structure chart: a rectangle representing an entire module.

If we start at the lowest level in a structure chart and work our way up to the next higher level, we can combine all modules subordinate to a calling module into a single rectangle which represents the function performed by the calling module and its subordinate modules. This process can continue

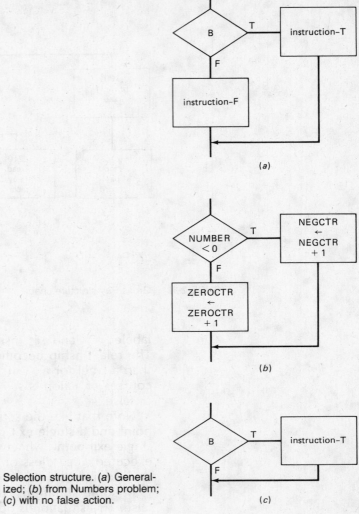

FIGURE 2-13   Selection structure. (a) Generalized; (b) from Numbers problem; (c) with no false action.

until the level-1 modules are combined into the level-0 module that represents the entire program.

Remember: A significant feature of the three structures is that each has a single entry point and a single exit point. One can neither enter (branch into) the middle of a structure nor exit (branch out from) the middle of a structure.

STRUCTURED CODING

How the sequence, loop, and selection structures are coded depends on the programming language used. Of course, not all programming languages provide these structures, but COBOL, FORTRAN 77, Pascal, and some versions of BASIC permit the writing of any program using these structures (or variations thereof) without recourse to branch instructions. In the other versions of BASIC and in assembler and RPG, the programmer must improvise these structures, and branch instructions must be used. (RPG III, available on the IBM System/38, does include these structures.)

Nevertheless, programmers using assembler, RPG II, and those versions of BASIC not providing these structures can still benefit from the application of the principles of modular and top-down programming.

Pseudocode

To illustrate structured coding, we will use a *pseudocode* (literally, a fake code), a recognized alternative to flowcharting for planning structured programs. Pseudocode is an extension of, and a replacement for, the algorithm developed in Chapter 1. Normally either pseudocode *or* flowcharts are used to show the details of the processing taking place in program modules; however, we will use both techniques.

There are no generally accepted standards for pseudocode. We will work with a form that has a minimum number of rules and is essentially *language-independent* (not oriented to any particular programming language). Since pseudocode instructions are written in English, they can be easily understood and reviewed by users. The only syntax rules to be concerned with involve the loop and selection structures. In our pseudocode instructions, the only capitalized words are those associated with these same structures: DO WHILE, END DO, IF, THEN, ELSE, and END IF.

Sequence Structure   The pseudocode for the sequence structure in Figure 2-8 is shown in Figure 2-14. We simply express in English what it is we want to do, in the order in which we want to do it.

Loop Structure   The loop structure is illustrated by the *DO WHILE* instruction:

```
DO WHILE (condition-A)
    instruction-1
    instruction-2
    . . .
END DO
```

[The ellipses (. . .) indicate where other instructions may appear.] As long as condition-A is true, all instructions between DO WHILE and END DO will be executed. Obviously, at some point one of the instructions in the loop must do something to make condition-A false, or we will have an endless loop. It is important to note the indention of all instructions within the loop. Indenting these instructions three or four spaces makes the structure of the program more obvious. Also observe that END is aligned left with DO WHILE.

It might be argued that there is, in effect, a branch back to the beginning of the loop, but a programmer can implement the DO WHILE instruction without writing a single branch instruction.

FIGURE 2-14   Sequence structure pseudocode.

```
multiply hours by rate to get gross pay
add gross pay to total gross pay
move input employee number to output employee number
print detail line
```

Selection Structure The selection structure is illustrated by the *IF-THEN-ELSE* instruction:

```
IF condition-B THEN
    instruction-T
ELSE
    instruction-F
END IF
```

This structure allows for a choice between two alternative courses of action. If condition-B is true, instruction-T is executed; if condition-B is false, instruction-F is executed. (Instruction-T and instruction-F may each actually represent a number of instructions.) Again, indention is used to make clear the structure of the program. The ELSE and END instructions are both placed directly below the IF. Note that this structure provides for choosing between two alternatives without using any branch instructions.

As noted earlier, it is possible that no action may be taken if the condition is false. Then the IF-THEN-ELSE is written as follows:

```
IF condition-B THEN
    instruction-T
ELSE
    (null)
END IF
```

In this case we have a *null ELSE:* that is, if condition-B is false, nothing is done. This fact is explicitly indicated by writing "(null)" indented under ELSE; this arrangement means that there can be no question about a missing alternative.

A Structured Program in Pseudocode

The use of pseudocode is illustrated in Figure 2-15, which is based on the structure chart of Figure 2-7, with a priming read added. Modules are ordered by number. Indention within the DO WHILE and IF-THEN-ELSE structures is consistent.

Note that the instruction executed when NUMBER is not positive (the ELSE instruction) is another IF-THEN-ELSE instruction. An IF-THEN-ELSE within another IF-THEN-ELSE is referred to as a *nested* IF instruction. The nested IF may also be part of a THEN (true) alternative. The entire nested IF is indented, and each IF has its ELSE and END IF. We can also have nested DO WHILE instructions; that is, a DO WHILE may be one of the instructions encountered within a loop. Similarly, a DO WHILE can be one of the instructions in an IF-THEN-ELSE, and an IF-THEN-ELSE can be used in a DO WHILE loop.

The initialization of the counters takes place in the main program module. A case can be made for making this part of the 100 module, since it is done before processing any transactions. However, the pseudocode is supposed to be language-independent. Putting the initialization in the 100 module presumes that instructions must be executed to set the counters to zero. This is the case with Pascal and BASIC, but not with COBOL, FORTRAN, RPG II, and assembler. Therefore, we will put the initialization at the start of the 000 module, where it can easily be handled either way.

```
000-count-types-of-numbers
set positive, negative, and zero counters
    to zero
call 100-priming-read
call 200-process-number-record
call 300-write-counts
stop

100-priming-read
call 210-read-number
return

200-process-number-record
DO WHILE not EOF
    call 220-accumulate-counts
    call 210-read-number
END DO
return

210-read-number
read number record
return

220-accumulate-counts
IF number > 0 THEN
    add 1 to positive counter
ELSE
    IF number < 0 THEN
        add 1 to negative counter
    ELSE
        add 1 to zero counter
    END IF
END IF
return

300-write-counts
print contents of positive, negative, and
    zero counters
return
```

FIGURE 2-15   Numbers problem pseudocode.

Some authorities advocate using in the pseudocode the field names that will appear in the actual program, but since this also introduces an element of language dependence, we will not follow this practice. It is true that if a programmer knows what language a program will eventually be written in, using actual field names in the pseudocode will improve the quality of the documentation for that program. However, the programmer should be aware that using field names may result in a pseudocode that looks just like a program in an actual language. If that happens, pseudocode is no longer beneficial; it is just a duplication of effort.

A limitation of pseudocode becomes apparent when we compare the pseudocode of Figure 2-15 with the structured flowchart in Figure 2-16: pseudocode does not reveal what is happening as well as a flowchart does. On the other hand, it is generally easier to write a program from pseudocode than from a flowchart, and pseudocode is more easily understood by the user.

Note that in Figure 2-16 only the module number is placed in the striped area of an outline representing a call; because of space limitations, the rest of the module name is written in the lower part of the outline. Similarly, we are also restricted to showing just the module number in the terminal outline representing the start of a module.

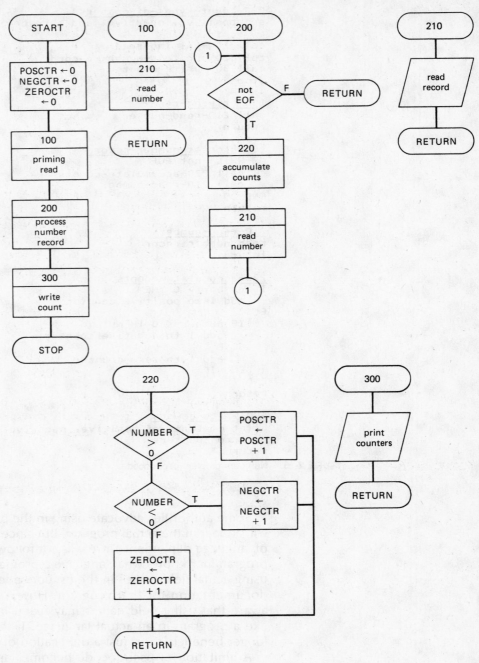

FIGURE 2-16 Structured Numbers flowchart.

ADDITIONAL STRUCTURES

Some programming languages provide other structures, particularly for looping. These structures are presented here simply to provide a more complete picture of the possibilities for structured programming in the various languages. Only the three structures already presented will be used in this text. Observe how indention is used to make the instructions easier to read.

FOR Loop

BASIC, FORTRAN 77, Pascal, and COBOL provide FOR loops that are controlled by a counter. (The COBOL equivalent of a FOR loop is the PERFORM statement with the VARYING option.) The format of the FOR instruction differs considerably from language to language; however, we will visualize this type of instruction as follows:

FOR i = j to k by l
    instruction-1
    ...
END FOR

Counter i is assigned an initial value of j; as long as the value of i is not greater than the value of k, the instructions between the FOR and the END FOR will be executed. After all instructions in the loop have been executed, the value of i is increased by the value of l, and i is again compared with k. The flowchart of a FOR loop is shown in Figure 2-17. This is equivalent to the following sequence using a DO WHILE:

set i to j
DO WHILE i ≤ k
    instruction-1
    ...
    add l to i
END DO

The preparation outline is used to show the initializing and incrementing of counter i. This outline is used instead of a process outline because i is not a data field; it is a field used to control the execution of the program.

PERFORM UNTIL Instruction

COBOL has a PERFORM UNTIL instruction instead of a DO WHILE instruction:

PERFORM subroutine UNTIL condition-C

FIGURE 2-17   FOR loop.

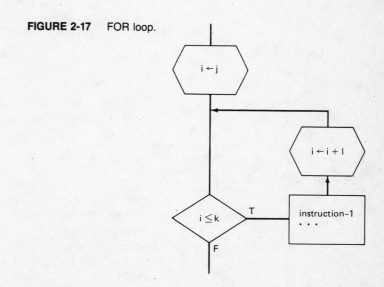

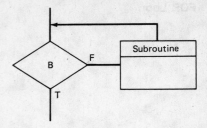

FIGURE 2-18 PERFORM UNTIL loop.

Figure 2-18 shows that as long as the condition is *false,* the loop will be executed. This resembles the DO WHILE loop; the only difference is a reversal of the labels on the exits from the decision outline.

REPEAT UNTIL Instruction

Pascal has a REPEAT UNTIL instruction, but it is quite different from COBOL's PERFORM UNTIL:

> REPEAT
>   instruction-1
>   . . .
> UNTIL (condition-P)

In this case, the instructions in the loop are executed before the condition is tested, as shown in Figure 2-19. This means that the instructions will always be executed at least once, even if the condition is true to begin with.

CASE Instruction

Pascal also provides for multiway branches for those situations in which the contents of a field determine which of several alternative instructions will be executed. The instruction that does this is the CASE instruction:

> CASE field-v OF
>   v1: instruction-1
>   v2: instruction-2
>   . . .
>   vn: instruction-n

FIGURE 2-19 REPEAT UNTIL loop.

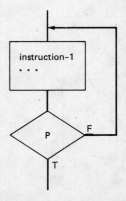

If field-v = vi, instruction-i (where i is between 1 and n) is executed. (Instruction-i may actually consist of several instructions.)

The CASE instruction can be represented in a flowchart as a series of selection structures, as shown in Figure 2-20a. The corresponding instructions would appear as follows:

```
IF field-v = v1 THEN
    instruction-1
ELSE
    IF field-v = v2 THEN
        instruction-2
    ELSE
        . . .
            instruction-n
        END IF
    . . .
    END IF
END IF
```

FIGURE 2-20 CASE statement. (a) Nested IFs; (b) alternative.

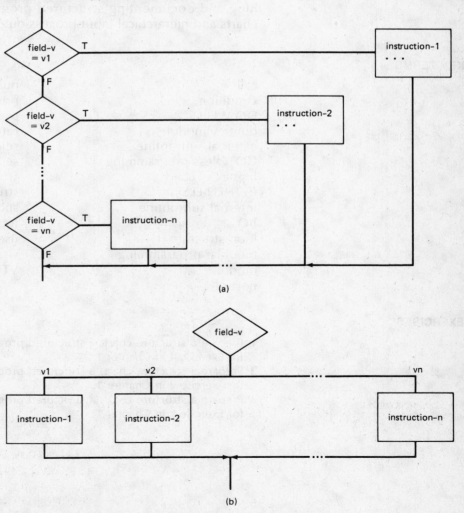

The CASE instruction can be represented more simply in a flowchart, as shown in Figure 2-20*b*.

SUMMARY

The major purpose of structured programming is to produce on a timely basis programs that provide correct results and are easy to understand and modify. This chapter has by no means been an exhaustive examination of structured programming. We saw how modular programming has been extended, via the top-down design of programs, into a structured programming approach. We also saw that a good structured program is modular and does not contain branch instructions (that is, is GOTOless). The use of a structure chart for the top-down planning of a program was introduced. Some of the flowcharting practices learned in Chapter 1 had to be modified to accommodate the structured approach. Pseudocode was presented as a substitute for the algorithm and as a possible alternative to the program flowchart.

We saw that three basic programming structures (sequence, loop, and selection) are sufficient for the development of a program, and we learned how to represent them in program flowcharts and in pseudocode.

In subsequent chapters we will look at two other techniques for planning and documenting structured programs: Nassi-Shneiderman flowcharts and hierarchical input-process-output (HIPO)charts.

KEY TERMS

call	null ELSE
condition	priming read
DO WHILE	pseudocode
dummy module	return
external subroutine	selection structure
GOTOless programming	sequence structure
hierarchy chart	structure chart
IF-THEN-ELSE	structured programming
internal subroutine	subroutine
I/O	top-down programming
loop structure	user
modular programming	visual table of contents
module	VTOC
nested	

EXERCISES

1 Prepare a structure chart, a structured program flowchart, and the pseudocode for Exercise 1 in Chapter 1.
2 Prepare a structure chart, a structured program flowchart, and the pseudocode for Exercise 2 in Chapter 1.
3 Prepare a structure chart, a structured program flowchart, and the pseudocode for Exercise 3 in Chapter 1.

CHAPTER 3

CONDITIONS THAT CONTROL PROCESSING

OBJECTIVES

Upon completing this chapter the student should be able to:

1 Prepare truth tables for combinations of conditions.
2 Prepare flowcharts and pseudocode for problems involving combinations of conditions.
3 Determine the optimum order in which to make decisions.
4 Incorporate appropriate input editing routines into a program.
5 Utilize a sentinel value or counter to signal the end of input data.
6 Define and use the key terms at the end of the chapter.

INTRODUCTION

One of the reasons the computer has proved so useful in problem solving is that it is able to choose among alternative courses of action on the basis of conditions that arise during the processing of data. In this chapter we shall examine more closely the use of conditions in handling a variety of situations that the programmer must contend with when writing computer programs.

COMPARISON OF TWO VALUES

The comparison of two values is represented in a program flowchart by the decision outline. In structured programming, the condition in an IF-THEN-ELSE instruction usually consists of a comparison of two values; the condition in a DO WHILE instruction may also be such a comparison.

In the IF-THEN-ELSE we select one of two alternative courses of action based on the result of the comparison. If we compare the contents of two fields, we can choose from among the alternatives in any one of the six ways shown in Figure 3-1. (The symbol ≠ means "not equal to"; sometimes <> is used. Similarly, we sometimes see ≮, meaning "not less than" instead of ≥, and ≯, meaning "not greater than," instead of ≤. Throughout this text we will use the symbols ≠, ≥, and ≤.)

FIGURE 3-1 Possible IF-THEN-ELSE alternatives.

Possibility	Alternative-1	Alternative-2
(1)	field-1 ≥ field-2	field-1 < field-2
(2)	field-1 ≮ field-2	field-1 ≥ field-2
(3)	field-1 ≤ field-2	field-1 > field-2
(4)	field-1 > field-2	field-1 ≤ field-2
(5)	field-1 ≠ field-2	field-1 = field-2
(6)	field-1 = field-2	field-1 ≠ field-2

On closer examination we can see that possibilities (1) and (2) are really interchangeable, since we can write the IF-THEN-ELSE for (1) in the two ways shown in Figure 3-2. Either version of the instruction produces the desired results. In a similar way, (3) and (4) are interchangeable, as are (5) and (6).

SORTING THREE NUMBERS

Given that we have numbers stored at three locations in the computer's memory (identified as A, B, and C), how can we get the largest of the three numbers at A, the next largest at B, and the smallest at C? This is a problem that every programming student has probably been presented with, for it introduces some key programming concepts.

Let us start with a simpler problem. Given numbers at two locations (X and Y), how do we get the larger at X and the smaller at Y? We must start by comparing the contents of locations X and Y. If the contents of location X is greater than the contents of location Y (hereafter abbreviated as X > Y), there is nothing more to be done. If X < Y, we must exchange the contents of the two locations. But what if X = Y? We could exchange the contents, but we would not accomplish anything noticeable; therefore, we will treat the equals condition in the same way we treat the greater-than condition: we will do nothing. Figure 3-3 shows the flowchart for handling this two-number problem.

How do we represent the logic for this problem in pseudocode?

```
IF X < Y THEN
        exchange X and Y
ELSE
        (null)
END IF
```

This is what we want to do, but let us provide the computer with a little more information about what "exchange" means. How about the following?

```
IF X < Y THEN
        move Y to X
        move X to Y
ELSE
        (null)
END IF
```

FIGURE 3-2   IF-THEN-ELSE alternatives for possibility (1).

```
IF field-1 ≥ field-2 THEN
    alternative-1
ELSE
    alternative-2
END IF

        (a) Version #1


IF field-1 < field-2 THEN
    alternative-2
ELSE
    alternative-1
END IF

        (b) Version #2
```

FIGURE 3-3   Sorting two numbers.

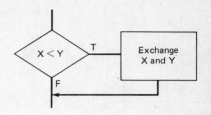

This seems like a rather obvious way to exchange the contents of locations X and Y, but Table 3-1 shows us the effect on the contents of locations X and Y when the instruction is executed. We have not accomplished what we set out to do.

Things start to go wrong when we move Y to X because we destroy the number that is at location X. Before we move Y to X, we must save the contents of X somewhere so it will be available later to move to Y. The way in which we do this is to introduce a third location, where we can temporarily save the contents of X:

```
IF X < Y THEN
        move X to TEMP
        move Y to X
        move TEMP to Y
ELSE
        (null)
END IF
```

Now the desired results are obtained, as shown in Table 3-2.

Since the problem of sorting three numbers can be broken down into a series of problems involving two numbers, we are ready to proceed. By comparing A and B we are able to get the larger of the two at A; then comparing A and C enables us to get the larger of these two (and thus the largest of the three) at A. Having done this, comparing B and C allows us to find the smallest number and store it at C, with the middle number at B. A flowchart of the comparison and exchanging logic is shown in Figure 3-4.

TABLE 3-1   TRYING TO EXCHANGE CONTENTS OF MEMORY

	X	Y
Initial contents	24	27
Move Y to X	27	27
Move X to Y	27	27

TABLE 3-2   EXCHANGING CONTENTS OF MEMORY

	X	Y	TEMP
Initial contents	24	27	?
Move X to TEMP	24	27	24
Move Y to X	27	27	24
Move TEMP to Y	27	24	24

FIGURE 3-4   Sorting three numbers.

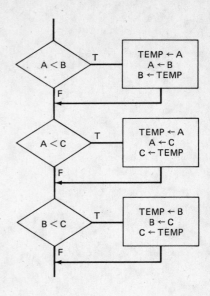

When the contents of any pair of locations are the same, no exchange is made.

Figure 3-5 shows us the corresponding pseudocode. As we would expect from looking at the flowchart, we see the same sequence of code three times, with just the field names changed.

COMBINATIONS OF CONDITIONS

We are often confronted with situations in which we must test more than one condition before we can select the correct course of action. Consider, for example, a request for a list of the names of employees who are both male and are 65 years of age or older. Figure 3-6 is a structure chart for this problem. Since there is no end-of-file processing, there are only two level-1 modules.

Figure 3-7 is a flowchart for this problem. It is assumed here that the field in the input record in which a person's sex is recorded will contain a letter 'M' or 'F' to designate male or female. Unless the employee is a male

FIGURE 3-5   Pseudocode for sorting three numbers.

```
IF A < B THEN
    move A to TEMP
    move B to A
    move TEMP to B
ELSE
    (null)
END IF
IF A < C THEN
    move A to TEMP
    move C to A
    move TEMP to C
ELSE
    (null)
END IF
IF B < C THEN
    move B to TEMP
    move C to B
    move TEMP to C
ELSE
    (null)
END IF
```

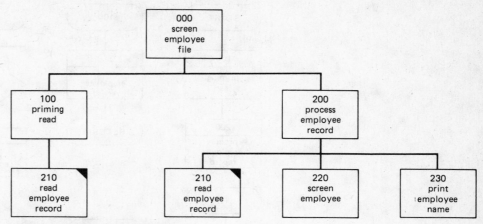

FIGURE 3-6   Screen Employee File structure chart.

(sex = 'M') *and* 65 or older (age ≥ 65), that employee's record is ignored and the next record is read. (The use of single quotes around the letter indicates that we are going to compare the contents of the sex field to the letter 'M' and not to the contents of a field named M. The letter in quotes is referred to as a *literal,* since we are using the letter — quite literally — as a letter in our comparison, not as a field name.) Only if both conditions are satisfied will the name be printed. The corresponding pseudocode is contained in Figure 3-8.

If we had wanted a list of employees who were male *or* at least 65 years old, only module 220 would have to be changed. Figure 3-9 shows the revised module. Notice that in this case, the employee must satisfy only one of the conditions to be included in the list. Only if the employee fails to meet both conditions will the record be ignored. The pseudocode for revised module 220 is shown in Figure 3-10.

Boolean Algebra

When we deal with combinations of conditions, it is sometimes convenient to use *Boolean algebra* (also known as Boolean logic). Instead of working with numbers, and symbols that represent numeric values, Boolean algebra deals with symbols that have values of "true" or "false." (When the value associated with a symbol may vary, the symbol is referred to as a *variable*.)

Instead of the operations of addition, subtraction, multiplication, and division, Boolean algebra uses AND, OR, and NOT operations. The condition for being included in the list produced by the logic of module 220 in Figure 3-7 can be stated as the following Boolean expression:

$$(sex = 'M') \text{ AND } (age \geq 65)$$

Just as Boolean variables have values of true or false, so do Boolean expressions. It is convenient when working with Boolean expressions to use a shorthand notation in which a single letter represents a condition. If we let A represent "sex = 'M'" and B represent "age ≥ 65," then the above Boolean expression becomes

$$A \text{ AND } B$$

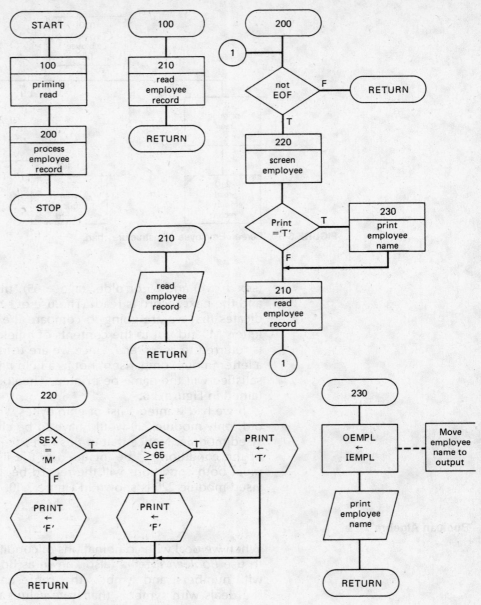

FIGURE 3-7 Screen Employee File flowchart.

We say that this expression is true if condition A and condition B are both true.

Similarly, the Boolean expression that represents the logic of module 220 in Figure 3-9 is

A OR B

This expression is true if *either* A or B is true and also if *both* A and B are true.

The NOT operation is used to change the value of a Boolean expression from true to false, or from false to true. The rules for the AND, OR, and

```
000-screen-employee-file
call 100-priming-read
call 200-process-employee-record
stop

100-priming-read
call 210-read-employee-record
return

200-process-employee-record
DO WHILE not EOF
    call 220-screen-employee
    IF print = 'T' THEN
        call 230-print-employee-name
    ELSE
        (null)
    END IF
    call 210-read-employee-record
END DO
return

210-read-employee-record
read employee record
return

220-screen-employee
IF sex = 'M' THEN
    IF age ≥ 65 THEN
        move 'T' to print
    ELSE
        move 'F' to print
    END IF
ELSE
    move 'F' to print
END IF
return

230-print-employee-name
move employee name to output record
write output record
return
```

FIGURE 3-8 Screen Employee File pseudocode.

FIGURE 3-9 The Boolean expression (sex = 'M') or (age ≥ 65).

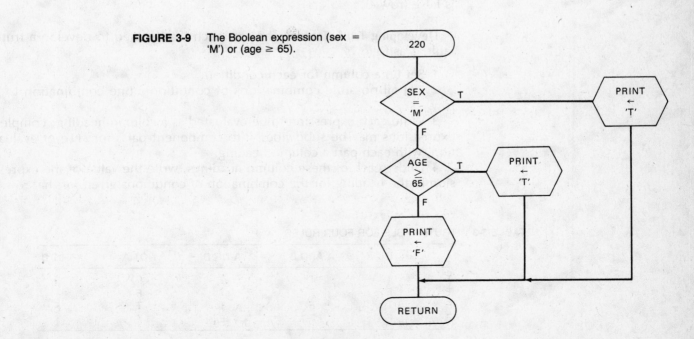

FIGURE 3-10 Revised module 220 pseudocode

```
220-screen-employee
IF sex = 'M' THEN
   move 'T' to print
ELSE
   IF age ≥ 65 THEN
      move 'T' to print
   ELSE
      move 'F' to print
   END IF
END IF
return
```

NOT operations can be summarized as follows:

- The expression A AND B is true if A is true and B is true.
- The expression A OR B is true if A is true or B is true, or both are true.
- If A is true, then NOT A is false.
- If A is false, then NOT A is true.

Truth Tables

The *truth table* is commonly used to represent the possible values of combinations of conditions. The four rules given above are illustrated by Table 3-3. The four rows of the table represent the four possible combinations of the values of two conditions, A and B. These combinations are shown in the first two columns. The letters "T" and "F" stand for "true" and "false," the two possible values of a condition. If A is true, B could be true or false; if A is false, B again could be true or false. The three other columns show the value of the expression in the column heading, given the combination of values in the first two columns. Each row applies to one combination of values for the two conditions.

If we look at the column headed "A AND B" we see from the first row that this expression is true if A is true and B is true, but it is false if A is true and B is false (row 2), or A is false and B is true (row 3), or A is false and B is false (row 4).

Developing Truth Tables The approach that is used to develop a truth table is as follows:

1 Set up a column for each condition.

2 List all possible combinations of conditions, one combination to a row.

3 Write each expression to be evaluated as a column heading; complex expressions may be subdivided into component parts for ease of evaluation, with each part a column heading.

4 Under each of these column headings, write the value of the expression in the heading for the combination of conditions given for that row.

TABLE 3-3 TRUTH TABLE FOR FOUR RULES

A	B	A AND B	A OR B	NOT A	NOT B
T	T	T	T	F	F
T	F	F	T	F	T
F	T	F	T	T	F
F	F	F	F	T	T

In the above table there are two conditions (A and B), each with two possible values (T and F), and thus there are four ways of combining the values of these two conditions. In general, if there are n conditions, the number of possible combinations of the values of the conditions—and thus the number of rows in the truth table—will equal 2^n. If there are three conditions (A, B, and C) there will be eight (2^3 or $2 \times 2 \times 2$) ways in which their values can be combined, and eight rows in the truth table. The first three columns of the truth table in Table 3-4 show these eight combinations. The remaining columns give the values of the expressions in the column heading for the combinations of conditions given in the first three columns. For example, row 6, column 4, gives the value of "A AND B OR C" as false when A and C are false and B is true.

Evaluating Boolean Expressions   A Boolean expression without any parentheses is evaluated in the following order:

1 All NOTs are evaluated first.
2 All ANDs, are evaluated next.
3 Finally, all ORs are evaluated.

Thus the expressions in Table 3-4 are evaluated as shown in Figure 3-11. In the expression "A AND B OR C," A AND B is evaluated first; the resulting value is then ORed with C to get a value for the entire expression. In the expression "A AND NOT B OR C," NOT B is evaluated first; this value is ANDed with A and the result is ORed with C. Similarly, in the expression

TABLE 3-4   TRUTH TABLE WITH THREE CONDITIONS

A	B	C	A AND B OR C	A AND NOT B OR C	A OR B AND NOT C
T	T	T	T	T	T
T	T	F	T	F	T
T	F	T	T	T	T
F	T	T	T	T	F
T	F	F	F	T	T
F	T	F	F	F	T
F	F	T	T	T	F
F	F	F	F	F	F

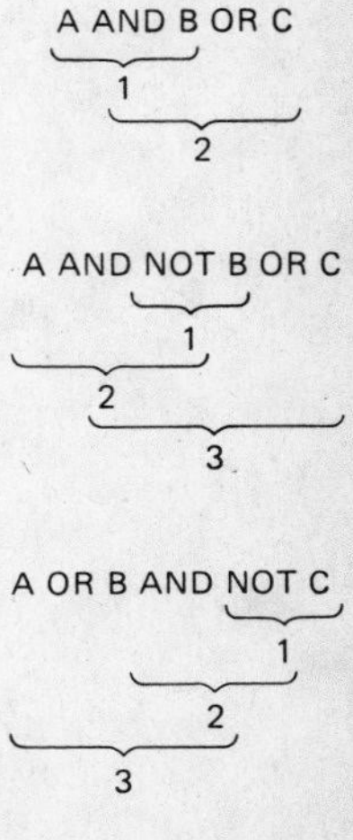

FIGURE 3-11   Evaluating Boolean expressions.

A AND B OR C

A AND NOT B OR C

A OR B AND NOT C

"A OR B AND NOT C," NOT C is evaluated first and then ANDed with B; the result is ORed with A to yield a value for the expression.

When parentheses are used in a Boolean expression, the portion of the expression inside the parentheses is evaluated first, starting with the innermost set of parentheses. The normal order of NOT, AND, and OR is used within the parentheses. Table 3-5 illustrates how the placement of parentheses affects the value of an expression. To evaluate the expression "A OR (B AND C)," the "(B AND C)" is evaluated first, as shown in column 4. The value of "B AND C" is then ORed with A to produce column 5. Similarly, in evaluating "(A OR B) AND C," the expression "(A OR B)" is evaluated first, as shown in column 6, and then ANDed with C to produce column 7.

The expressions in columns 4, 5, and 6 of Table 3-4 are equivalent to the following expressions with parentheses:

(A AND B) OR C
(A AND NOT B) OR C
A OR (B AND NOT C)

While parentheses were not required in Table 3-4, their use does help to clarify the meaning of the Boolean expressions. Parentheses should be used whenever there may be any possible confusion over what is intended. They can also be used to alter the normal order of evaluation. Table 3-6 shows what happens when parentheses are inserted into the expressions in columns 5 and 6 of Table 3-4. In the expression "A AND NOT(B OR C)," the order of operations is: first OR, then NOT, and finally AND. For the expression "(A OR B) AND NOT C" the order also is OR, NOT, AND. You should be able to verify the contents of these truth tables.

TABLE 3-5 THE EFFECT OF PARENTHESES

A	B	C	B AND C	A OR (B AND C)	A OR B	(A OR B) AND C
T	T	T	T	T	T	T
T	T	F	F	T	T	F
T	F	T	F	T	T	T
F	T	T	T	T	T	T
T	F	F	F	T	T	F
F	T	F	F	F	T	F
F	F	T	F	F	F	F
F	F	F	F	F	F	F

TABLE 3-6 MORE EXAMPLES WITH PARENTHESES

A	B	C	A AND NOT (B OR C)	(A OR B) AND NOT C
T	T	T	F	F
T	T	F	F	T
T	F	T	F	F
F	T	T	F	F
T	F	F	T	T
F	T	F	F	T
F	F	T	F	F
F	F	F	F	F

Special Boolean Properties

In the algebra with which we are familiar we work with equalities; in Boolean algebra we deal with equivalencies. Two Boolean expressions are *equivalent* if they have the same values for all combinations of conditions. Truth tables can be used to prove the equivalence of Boolean expressions.

There are situations in which a knowledge of some Boolean properties will enable a programmer to write code more efficiently. For example, consider the distributive property

$$A \text{ AND } (B \text{ OR } C) = (A \text{ AND } B) \text{ OR } (A \text{ AND } C)$$

The left side, with one AND and one OR, requires less work to evaluate than the right side, which contains two ANDs and one OR. Verify that Table 3-7 does indeed demonstrate that they are equivalent. Note that columns 5 and 8 are exactly the same.

In the following example the left side has one AND and one OR, while the right side has an additional OR:

$$A \text{ OR } (B \text{ AND } C) = (A \text{ OR } B) \text{ AND } (A \text{ OR } C)$$

This illustrates another distributive property of Boolean expressions. Table 3-8 demonstrates the equivalence of these two expressions.

Two equivalencies are not immediately obvious, and these have given programmers some very real problems. Table 3-9 proves the first of these:

$$NOT \ (A \text{ AND } B) = NOT \ A \text{ OR } NOT \ B$$

TABLE 3-7   A AND (B OR C) = (A AND B) OR (A AND C)

A	B	C	B OR C	A AND (B OR C)	A AND B	A AND C	(A AND B) OR (A AND C)
T	T	T	T	T	T	T	T
T	T	F	T	T	T	F	T
T	F	T	T	T	F	T	T
F	T	T	T	F	F	F	F
T	F	F	F	F	F	F	F
F	T	F	T	F	F	F	F
F	F	T	T	F	F	F	F
F	F	F	F	F	F	F	F

TABLE 3-8   A OR (B AND C) = (A OR B) AND (A OR C)

A	B	C	B AND C	A OR (B AND C)	A OR B	A OR C	(A OR B) AND (A OR C)
T	T	T	T	T	T	T	T
T	T	F	F	T	T	T	T
T	F	T	F	T	T	T	T
F	T	T	T	T	T	T	T
T	F	F	F	T	T	T	T
F	T	F	F	F	T	F	F
F	F	T	F	F	F	T	F
F	F	F	F	F	F	F	F

TABLE 3-9 NOT (A AND B) = NOT A OR NOT B

A	B	A AND B	NOT (A AND B)	NOT A	NOT B	NOT A OR NOT B
T	T	T	F	F	F	F
T	F	F	T	F	T	T
F	T	F	T	T	F	T
F	F	F	T	T	T	T

The other is quite similar and is proved in Table 3-10:

$$NOT\ (A\ OR\ B) = NOT\ A\ AND\ NOT\ B$$

In spite of what the truth tables reveal, neither of these equivalencies is immediately obvious. That they are equivalent may become more apparent if we think of A and B as representing the following conditions:

A   Have nickel
B   Have dime

Boolean Algebra in Programming

Almost all programming languages incorporate Boolean algebra in some way. In BASIC, COBOL, FORTRAN, and Pascal it is used in IF-THEN-ELSE instructions. The exact form of the instruction varies with the language, as is revealed by the following examples of the IF-THEN portion of the instruction from these four languages:

```
BASIC    IF (S$ = 'M') AND (A >= 65) THEN
COBOL    IF (SEX = 'M') AND (AGE IS NOT LESS THAN 65)
FORTRAN  IF ((SEX .EQ. 'M') .AND. (AGE .GE. 65)) THEN
Pascal   IF (SEX = 'M') AND (AGE >= 65) THEN
```

When more than one condition is combined in this fashion, we have a *compound condition*. (A single condition will be referred to as a *simple condition*.) Conditions are evaluated following the order of NOT, AND, and OR, with expressions in parentheses evaluated first. If there is more than one operation of a particular type (for example, more than one AND), the expressions are evaluated from left to right.

RPG uses Boolean algebra extensively. Conditions are represented by *indicators*, which are said to be "on" or "off," rather than "true" or "false." Indicators can be combined by means of NOTs, ANDs, and ORs in a variety of ways to control calculations and output. RPG also uses Boolean logic in identifying input records.

TABLE 3-10 NOT (A OR B) = NOT A AND NOT B

A	B	A OR B	NOT (A OR B)	NOT A	NOT B	NOT A AND NOT B
T	T	T	F	F	F	F
T	F	T	F	F	T	F
F	T	T	F	T	F	F
F	F	F	T	T	T	T

We can use Boolean expressions to simplify our pseudocode by eliminating some of the nesting of IF-THEN-ELSE instructions. Module 220 of Figure 3-8 can be written as

```
IF (sex = 'M') AND (age ≥ 65) THEN
        move 'T' to print
ELSE
        move 'F' to print
END IF
```

Similarly, module 220 of Figure 3-10 becomes

```
IF (sex = 'M') OR (age ≥ 65) THEN
        move 'T' to print
ELSE
        move 'F' to print
END IF
```

Clearly, the compounding of conditions can result in pseudocode that is easier to understand. Care should be taken, however, particularly when a number of conditions are compounded, to make sure that the compounding does not result in an expression that is so complex that the relationships between conditions are obscured. Another problem with compounding, the fact that it results in a less efficient program, will be discussed in the next chapter.

ORDER OF COMPARISONS

As we have seen, even though two ways of writing a Boolean expression may produce the same results, one of the ways may require fewer operations and thus be more efficient. Similarly, two program flowcharts may produce the same correct output, but if the program produced from one of them requires fewer processing steps it may be more efficient.

Figure 3-7 is a good illustration of this fact. Let us assume that the file being processed contains records for 1000 employees, with the following characteristics:

Characteristic	Number	Percent
Males	550	55
Females	450	45
Age < 65	950	95
Age ≥ 65	50	5

Let us also assume that the proportion of males among employees who are younger than 65 is the same as the proportion among employees who are 65 or older. If we follow the logic of Figure 3-7, we will make the first decision (sex = 'M') 1000 times, once for each employee, and the second decision (age ≥ 65) 550 times, once for each male, for a total of 1550 decisions.

If we change the order of the decisions and consider age first, we will still make the first decision (now: age ≥ 65) 1000 times, but the second decision (sex = 'M') will have to be made only 50 times, once for each person 65 or older. The total number of decisions made in this case is only

1050, whereas the sequence given in Figure 3-7 requires 1550 decisions. The number of decisions made has been reduced by almost a third. Therefore, Figure 3-7 should be changed to check age first and then sex.

Under what conditions would the sequence of decisions of Figure 3-7 be the correct one? It would be correct only if the number of males among the employees was less than or equal to the number of employees who were 65 or older. Since all 1000 employees are subjected to the first decision, the key consideration here is: How many of these 1000 can we eliminate from further consideration by this first decision? In general, when you have a series of conditions in an AND relationship, the condition that should be checked first is the one that the largest number of records will fail to meet.

The picture is a bit different when the decisions are ORed, as in Figure 3-9. In this case, since once an empolyee meets one of the criteria, that employee can be included in the list and no further testing is required, we want to use our first decision to select the largest number who meet one of the conditions. Therefore, we will consider first the employee's sex, since 550 are male and should be included in the list. This leaves 450 to be tested for age, for a total of 1450 decisions. If we considered age first, we would pick up only 50 for our list and would have to test 950 again for sex, thereby making 1950 decisions. Thus the flowchart in Figure 3-9 is a good solution given the age and sex assumptions we have made.

A programmer does not always have readily available the information needed to determine the best order of comparisions, but it is worth some effort to try to gather it, particularly if a program is to be used frequently with large volumes of data.

INPUT EDITING

A programmer designing a program that will process data being entered into the computer for the first time must be aware of the necessity for editing the data. *Input editing* includes a variety of checks that are made in an attempt to prevent erroneous data from getting into computer files and reports. Once bad data gets into the computer, correcting it and getting the correct information out to users who have been misinformed can be a formidable task.

A detailed examination of the different types of input editing that can be performed is a proper subject for a systems design course. We will concern ourselves here with some of the more widely used techniques:

- Sequence checking
- Restricted-value test
- Miscellaneous other tests

Sequence Checking

Most *batch processing* (processing in which data is accumulated over a period of time and then processed as a group, or batch) is designed to handle data that has been sorted on a key field (or fields). Since it is possible that the sorting step might inadvertently be overlooked or done improperly, whenever a program requires that data be sequenced to perform properly, the program should check that the data is in fact in the expected sequence.

Sequence checking consists of comparing the key field(s) of the record read in with the key field(s) of the previous record. Since reading in a new record destroys the fields from the previous record, the program must save the current key field values somewhere so they are available when the next record is processed.

A special problem is presented when the very first record in the file is processed, for the program logic will try to compare the key field(s) from this first record with some previous values that do not exist. The way around this problem is to initialize the previous key field values to a very small number so that the key field(s) of the first record will be greater than the initial value. (This assumes that the file is supposed to be in ascending order; if the file is to be in descending order, the initial value must be larger than would normally be encountered.) If, for example, we wish to check that an input file is in ascending order by customer number (a field that is always positive), we can initialize the previous customer number field to zeros. Consider the example in Table 3-11. Record 5 is out of sequence, a fact that is very readily picked up by the technique of sequence checking.

Restricted-Value Test

Sometimes the data in a field is restricted to a particular value, or perhaps to one of several values. In other cases a range of possible values might be acceptable. Checking the value of a field to be sure it is acceptable is editing input by means of a *restricted-value test*. The acceptable values must be in memory so that as the data is read in, it can be compared to these values. If the acceptable values are known in advance, they can be built right into the program as *constants* (fields whose values do not change). If these values are subject to change each time the program is run, the program will have to read in the acceptable values prior to processing the data (that is, under the control of module 100). Values acquired in this fashion are referred to as *parameters*. (Parameters may also be used to enable programs to handle a general class of problems. Instead of writing a program to find all males 65 or older, the desired sex and lower age limit could be read in at the start of execution. Then individuals of either sex, greater than or equal to any age, could be located.)

Miscellaneous Other Tests

Depending on the situation, any of a number of other tests may be performed on input data. A field that is supposed to be numeric can be checked to determine if in fact it contains nonnumeric characters. The sign

TABLE 3-11 DETECTING SEQUENCE ERROR

Record	Current customer		Previous customer
1	024758	>	000000
2	038323	>	024758
3	039781	>	038323
4	040406	>	039781
5	040068	<	040406

of a field that is supposed to be positive should be checked. A field that should have something in it can be checked to see if it is blank. In general, if a program will not function properly unless the data in a field meets certain criteria, that field should be tested before the data is used.

Error Routines

What do we do if we find a sequence error or invalid data in a field? Several options are available, depending on the nature of the problem and the type of processing being done:

- Display an error message and terminate processing immediately.
- Display an error message and wait for the operator to take some corrective action.
- Make a record of the error so that it can be corrected later; then continue processing, ignoring the erroneous record.

In all these cases, *error routines* must be included as part of the program to deal with the problems. The first option, termination of the program after displaying an error message, is usually taken when a sequence error is detected, for batch processing normally requires the data to be in the correct sequence. The second option is selected in those cases in which the operator (of either the computer or of a terminal) can correct the data so that processing can continue. The third option might be selected if it is possible to get valid results without using the erroneous data, and this data can be corrected and processed later. Clearly, the appropriate course of action to take in any given situation must be understood before the design of the program can be completed.

Where does the error message go? If data is being entered at a terminal, the error message will be displayed in an area on the CRT screen (usually near the bottom) set aside for this purpose. If a batch of data is being processed and a printed report is being produced, the message may be embedded in the report, or a separate output file may be used just for error messages. The method selected will depend on the type of error and on the capabilities of the computer. If the program should be terminated when a sequence error occurs, the error message may be included at the end of the report so far printed, since the job will have to be rerun. If the output report can be used in spite of the error and if the computer is able to handle multiple printer files, the error message will usually go into a separate file.

DETECTING END OF DATA

In the examples we have examined so far, we have checked for the end of our data directly following a read instruction. We have assumed that the computer will signal an end-of-file condition when it occurs. This technique, or a simple variation of it, is probably the most common one in use today. But the programmer must be prepared for situations in which this technique is not available or not appropriate.

Two other techniques that can be used to detect the end-of-file condition are a sentinel value and a counter.

Sentinel Value

The *sentinel value* is a predetermined value that is placed in a *dummy record* (a record that is not to be processed) at the end of the data file. The sentinel value is usually placed in the key field position in the dummy record. The value selected must be one that would never be found in this field in an actual data record. For example, the sentinel value might be a negative number placed in a field that is known to be always positive, or a string of nines in a customer number field when such a number would never be assigned to a customer. (The use of nines in a key field as a sentinel value has the advantage of ensuring that the dummy record will be at the end of the file when the file is sorted in ascending order.) The program must check the field in question every time a record is read to see if it contains the sentinel value. The DO WHILE loop controlling the reading and processing of the data records would look like this:

DO WHILE key field $\neq$ sentinel value

Counter

The *counter* technique requires that the number of data records to be read be known in advance. This number might be a constant in the program which is made part of the program when it is written. If the number can vary, it will normally be read in as a parameter when the program is run. The program has to maintain a count of the number of records that are read and processed; when the count of the number of records processed equals the number expected, the processing of data records stops. The pseudocode for handling this technique might look like this:

```
read number
move zero to count
DO WHILE count < number
    read data record
    . . .
    add one to count
END DO
```

Note that in this case no priming read is used.

SUMMARY

In this chapter we learned how conditions are used in the loop and selection structures to control processing. We then looked at combinations of conditions, using Boolean algebra and truth tables to better comprehend what happens when conditions are combined. We observed that using combinations of conditions in an IF-THEN-ELSE simplifies the pseudocode for a program.

The use of comparisons was further illustrated by an examination of input editing and the use of a sentinel value or a counter to signal the end of a data file.

KEY TERMS

AND
batch processing
Boolean algebra
compound condition
constant
dummy record
error routine
input editing
NOT

OR
parameter
restricted-value test
sentinel value
sequence checking
simple condition
truth table
variable

EXERCISES

1 A list is to be prepared that will contain the names of any customers whose purchases total at least $10,000 in the current month. Customers will also be included in the list if their purchases so far this year are at least as great as an amount to be read in as a parameter at the time the program is executed. More customers are likely to meet the former criterion than the latter one.

   The input contains the customer name, year-to-date sales, and current monthly sales.

   Execution is to terminate after printing an appropriate error message if a sequence error is detected.

   Documentation for this problem is to consist of the following: structure chart, program flowchart, pseudocode, test input data, and test output data.

2 A list is to be prepared of the item numbers of products to be reordered. An item number will be included in the list if the item has not been flagged as obsolete and if the quantity of the item currently on hand, plus the amount on order, is less than its minimum inventory level. About 5% of the items are considered obsolete (that is, are kept in inventory, but will not be repurchased), and typically 20% of the items are reordered at any one time.

   The input contains the item number, the quantity on hand for the item, the quantity on order, the minimum inventory level, and an obsolete code ('X' if the item is obsolete; a blank if it is not).

   Execution is to terminate after printing an appropriate error message if a sequence error is detected.

   Documentation for this problem is to consist of the following: structure chart, program flowchart, pseudocode, test input data, and test output data.

3 A list is to be prepared of the names of full-time students (students taking 12 or more semester hours or credits) who are 30 years of age or older. If a student appearing on the list is taking more than 20 semester hours, four asterisks are to be placed after the student's name. School records indicate that 60% of the students are full-time and that 30% are 30 years of age or older.

   The input consists of the student's name, the number of semester hours the student is currently taking, and the age of the student.

   Execution of the program is to terminate after printing an appropriate error message if a sequence error is detected.

   Documentation for this problem is to consist of the following: structure chart, program flowchart, pseudocode, test input data, and test output data.

4 Develop truth tables for the following expressions:
   a A AND (NOT B OR C)
   b (A AND NOT B) OR C
   c A OR (NOT B AND C)
   d (A OR NOT B) AND C
   e NOT(A OR B) AND C
   f NOT(A AND B) OR C

CHAPTER 4

COMPLEX COMBINATIONS OF CONDITIONS

OBJECTIVES

Upon completing this chapter the student should be able to:

1 Prepare limited-entry, extended-entry, and mixed-entry decision tables.
2 Prepare structure charts, flowcharts, pseudocode, decision tables, test input data, and test output data for problems involving complex combinations of conditions.
3 Define and use the key terms at the end of the chapter.

INTRODUCTION

In this chapter we will expand on the material of Chapter 3 by considering situations in which complex combinations of conditions must be examined to determine the correct course of action. We will learn to use a new tool—the decision table—for planning how to handle these combinations.

FILE INQUIRY EXAMPLE

Let us review and expand on the concepts presented in the previous chapter by considering an example that involves four conditions that must be met.

Problem Definition

An insurance company wants a list of policy numbers in ascending order for males aged 50 or over with occupation codes of 23 through 27. The input file is supposed to be in ascending order by policy number. End-of-file is signified by a policy number consisting of all nines. The input records contain these fields: policy number, age, sex ('M' or 'F'), and occupation code. We are to prepare the following:

1 Truth table
2 Structure chart
3 Pseudocode
4 Program flowchart
5 Test input data
6 Test output data

From available statistics, we know that our 50,000 policyholders have the following characteristics:

Characteristic	Number	Percent
Age 50 or over	17,500	35
Male	32,000	64
Occupation code < 23	11,000	22
Occupation code > 27	34,500	69

Two things should be immediately obvious:

1 We must do a sequence check.
2 We have to determine the best order for the decisions.

To do a sequence check, we will have to define a field for the previous policy number and initialize it to a small value that could not possibly be a policy number: either a negative number or zeros.

To be included in the list, a policyholder must meet all the criteria. That is, there is an AND relationship between our conditions, so we should try to make our decisions in an order that will exclude as many as possible as soon as possible. The largest number (34,500) can be excluded by checking for an occupation code greater than 27. The next largest number (32,500) will be excluded if we check age. We can exclude 18,000 if we check sex, but only 11,000 if we check for policyholders with occupation codes less than 23. Lacking any additional information about our policyholders, we should examine their characteristics in the order just noted.

Truth Table

The four conditions can be represented as follows:

Condition	
A	Age $\geq$ 50
B	Sex = 'M'
C	Occupation code $\geq$ 23
D	Occupation code $\leq$ 27

The following Boolean expression must be true for a policyholder to be included in the list:

$$A \text{ AND } B \text{ AND } C \text{ AND } D$$

TABLE 4-1 FILE INQUIRY TRUTH TABLE

A	B	C	D	A AND B AND C AND D
T	T	T	T	T
T	T	T	F	F
T	T	F	T	F
T	F	T	T	F
F	T	T	T	F
T	T	F	F	F
T	F	T	F	F
F	T	T	F	F
T	F	F	T	F
F	T	F	T	F
F	F	T	T	F
T	F	F	F	F
F	T	F	F	F
F	F	T	F	F
F	F	F	T	F
F	F	F	F	F

The truth table of Table 4-1 contains 16 rows ($2^4 = 16$). Column 5 shows that only one combination—that in which each simple condition is true—yields a value of "true" for the expression.

Structure Chart

The structure chart of Figure 4-1 shows the functions our program is to perform. Since there is no end-of-file processing required, there is no module 300.

Pseudocode

Figure 4-2 contains the pseudocode for this problem. In this case there are two conditions that can cause the termination of the loop that processes and reads data records: reading a policy number that is all nines or encountering a sequence error. If either of these conditions occurs, we must exit from the DO WHILE loop. The condition controlling the loop is another example of a compound condition. A variable "error" is used to tell us if there has been a sequence error. If error = 'T,' there has been a se-

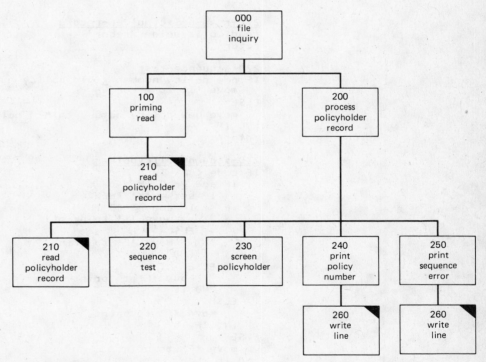

FIGURE 4-1   File Inquiry structure chart.

quence error, so we initialize it to 'F.' The variable "error" is being used as a *program switch*; the switch is on when error equals 'T' and off when it equals 'F.' In module 200 we see that we will continue to process records as long as the following compound condition is true:

(new policy number ≠ all nines) and (error = 'F')

```
000-file-inquiry
set old policy number to zero
set error to 'F'
call 100-priming-read
call 200-process-policyholder-record
stop

100-priming-read
call 210-read-policyholder-record
return

200-process-policyholder-record
DO WHILE (new policy number ≠ all nines) and
                        (error = 'F')
    call 220-sequence-test
    IF error = 'F' THEN
        call 230-screen-policyholder
        IF print = 'T' THEN
            call 240-print-policy-number
        ELSE
            (null)
        END IF
    ELSE
        call 250-print-sequence-error
    END IF
END DO
return

210-read-policyholder-record
read policyholder record
return

220-sequence-test
IF new policy number ≤ old policy number THEN
    move 'T' to error
ELSE
    move new policy number to old policy number
END IF
return

230-screen-policyholder
IF code ≤ 27 THEN
    IF age ≥ 50 THEN
        IF sex = 'M' THEN
            IF code ≥ 23 THEN
                move 'T' to print
            ELSE
                move 'F' to print
            END IF
        ELSE
            move 'F' to print
        END IF
    ELSE
        move 'F' to print
    END IF
ELSE
    move 'F' to print
END IF
return

240-print-policy-number
move policy number to output line
call 260-write-line
return

250-print-sequence-error
move 'SEQUENCE ERROR AFTER' and old policy number
    to output line
```

FIGURE 4-2 File Inquiry pseudocode.

```
call 260-write-line
return

260-write-line
write output line
return
```

FIGURE 4-2   (*Continued*)

Module 220 performs the sequence test. If a new policy number is less than or equal to (policy numbers should be unique) the previous policy number, a 'T' is moved to "error." If there is no error, the new policy number is moved to the old policy number field in preparation for the next sequence test. Upon returning to module 200 the error switch is checked; if the sequence is correct, module 230 will examine the characteristics of the policyholder. If the policyholder meets all the criteria, a 'T' is moved to "print" (another program switch); otherwise, an 'F' is moved. Upon returning from module 230 the contents of "print" is examined. If "print" contains a 'T,' module 240 is called to print the policy number; if it contains an 'F,' nothing more is done.

If there is a sequence error, module 250 is called to print a sequence error message for the operator. To help locate the erroneous record this message includes the previous policy number. (Since not all policy numbers are being printed, locating the error in the input file might be difficult if we printed the number that was out of order.) Since "error" now contains a 'T,' the compound condition for the DO WHILE loop is no longer met, and we exit from the loop.

Figure 4-3 shows three alternatives to module 230 of Figure 4-2. Module 230 of Figure 4-2 shows the AND relationship between the conditions very clearly. So does the first alternative in Figure 4-3, but this alternative simplifies the module by first setting "print" to 'F' and using null ELSEs. The second alternative in Figure 4-3 is a good example of how correct results can be obtained from code that is unsatisfactory; this alternative does not show the relationship between the conditions as clearly as the previous two examples. Finally, the third alternative shows how using compound conditions greatly simplifies the pseudocode. (Note that this degree of simplification cannot be obtained with a program flowchart, where only simple conditions are shown.) The third alternative seems clearly preferable, but it has a major shortcoming. To arrive at a value for the compound condition, all four simple conditions must be examined for each policyholder. We cannot improve our processing efficiency by selecting a particular order for the comparisons.

Program Flowchart

Figure 4-4 shows the program flowchart corresponding to the pseudocode of Figure 4-2. While it is probably easier for a programmer to see what is happening in the flowchart, it must be remembered that a user who knows little about computers will find the pseudocode easier to read. Moreover, the use of compound conditions in a program can be documented more clearly in pseudocode than in a flowchart. Because a data-processing department will normally select one of these planning tools to use in all its documentation, a programmer would not normally prepare both the pseudocode and a program flowchart.

```
230-screen-policyholder
move 'F' to print
IF code ≤ 27 THEN
    IF age ≥ 50 THEN
        IF sex = 'M' THEN
            IF code ≥ 23 THEN
                move 'T' to print
            ELSE
                (null)
            END IF
        ELSE
            (null)
        END IF
    ELSE
        (null)
    END IF
ELSE
    (null)
END IF
return
```

(a) Alternative # 1

```
230-screen-policyholder
IF code > 27 THEN
    move 'F' to print
ELSE
    IF age < 50 THEN
        move 'F' to print
    ELSE
        IF sex = 'F' THEN
            move 'F' to print
        ELSE
            IF code < 23 THEN
                move 'F' to print
            ELSE
                move 'T' to print
            END IF
        END IF
    END IF
END IF
return
```

(b) Alternative # 2

```
230-screen-policyholder
IF (code ≤ 27) and (age ≥ 55) and (sex = 'M')
            and (code ≥ 23) THEN
    move 'T' to print
ELSE
    move 'F' to print
END IF
return
```

(c) Alternative # 3

FIGURE 4-3   Module 230 pseudocode alternatives.

Test Input Data

When preparing test data, the programmer must make sure that all possible conditions of importance are being tested. If a field is being compared on an equal/not-equal basis, data should be included for both the equal and the not-equal conditions. If a field is being compared on a less-than-

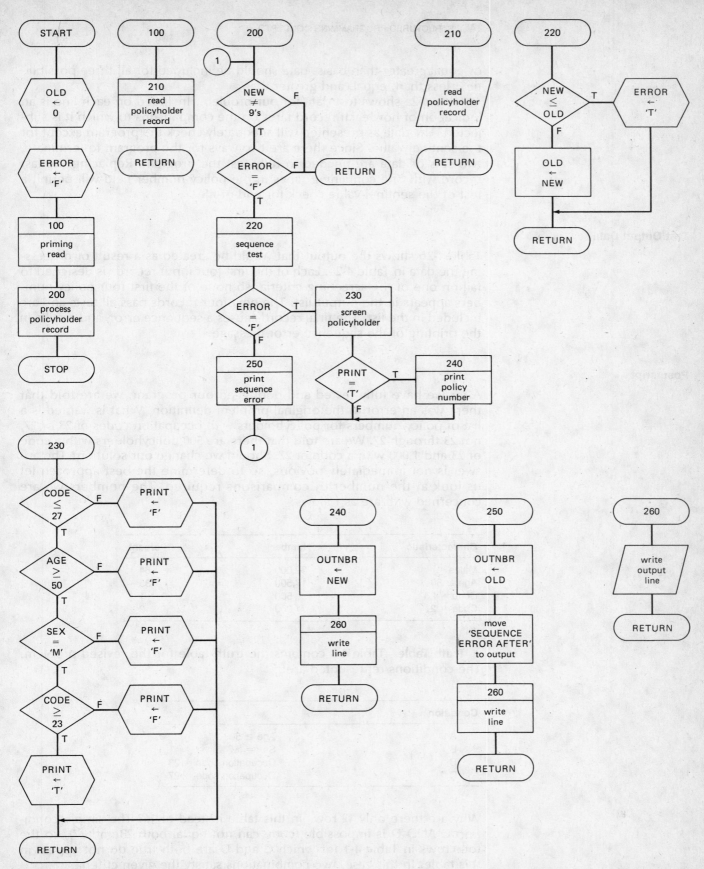

FIGURE 4-4   File Inquiry flowchart.

or-equal/greater-than basis, data should be included for all three possibilities: less than, equal, and greater than.

Table 4-2a shows test data for our problem. Included on each line is an indication of how each record fares on the comparisons to which it is subjected. The data as presented will adequately check the program except for the sentinel value. Since there are two ways for the program to terminate, two sets of data are needed to fully test the program. Replacing the last record with one containing nines in the policy number field will permit a test of the sentinel-value check for end-of-file.

Test Output Data

Table 4-2b shows the output that would be created as a result of processing the data in Table 4-2a. Each of the first four input records is designed to fail on one of the screening criteria, so none of the first four policy numbers appears in the output list. The next four records pass all tests and are included in the list. The final record causes a sequence error, and results in the printing of the sequence error message.

Postscript

After we have fully tested and debugged our program, we are told that there was an error in the original problem definition. What is wanted is a list of policy numbers for policyholders with occupation codes of 23 *or* 27, not 23 through 27. We are told that there are 500 policyholders with a code of 23 and 1,000 with a code of 27. Should we change our solution? The answer is not immediately obvious, so to determine the best approach let us look at the number of comparisons required. The numbers we are concerned with are as follows:

Characteristic	Number	Percent
Males	32,000	64
Age ≥ 50	17,500	35
Code = 23	500	1
Code = 27	1,000	2

Truth Table Table 4-3 contains the truth table for the revised problem. The conditions represented are:

Condition	
A	Age ≥ 50
B	Sex = 'M'
C	Occupation code = 23
D	Occupation code = 27

Why are there only 12 rows in this table instead of 16? The simple condition C AND D is impossible (code can not equal both 23 and 27), so the four rows in Table 4-1 for which C and D are both true do not appear in this table. In this case, two combinations satisfy the given criteria.

TABLE 4-2   FILE INQUIRY TEST DATA   **(a) Input**

Policy number	Age	Sex	Code	Purpose of test data
12345678	50	F	28	Code > 27
23456789	49	M	19	Code < 27, age < 50
34567890	65	F	25	Code < 27, age > 50, sex = 'F'
45678901	51	M	22	Code < 27, age > 50, sex = 'M,' code < 23
56789012	53	M	23	Code < 27, age > 50, sex = 'M,' code = 23
67890123	60	M	24	Code < 27, age > 50, sex = 'M,' code > 23
78901234	50	M	25	Code < 27, age = 50, sex = 'M,' code > 23
89012345	55	M	27	Code = 27, age > 50, sex = 'M,' code > 23
11111111				Sequence error

(b) Output

56789012
67890123
78901234
89012345
SEQUENCE ERROR AFTER 89012345

TABLE 4-3   REVISED FILE INQUIRY TRUTH TABLE

A	B	C	D	A AND B AND (C OR D)
T	T	T	F	T
T	T	F	T	T
T	T	F	F	F
T	F	T	F	F
F	T	T	F	F
T	F	F	T	F
F	T	F	T	F
T	F	F	F	F
F	T	F	F	F
F	F	T	F	F
F	F	F	T	F
F	F	F	F	F

The following Boolean expression states the combination of conditions with which we are concerned:

$$(age \geq 50) \text{ AND } (sex = 'M') \text{ AND } ((code = 23) \text{ OR } (code = 27))$$

This compound condition, if used as the condition in an IF-THEN-ELSE, will be evaluated as follows:

1 Values of "true" or "false" will be assigned to each of the simple conditions.

2 The OR relationship will be evaluated, since it is within parentheses.

3 The leftmost AND relationship will be evaluated, and that result will be ANDed with the result from step 2.

This may not be the most efficient order in which to consider the conditions. Moreover, all four conditions will be evaluated (a total of 200,000 decisions), even if the very first condition is not met. This further illustrates that the advantages to be gained by selecting the most efficient order for the decisions are not available when compound conditions are used.

Order of Comparisons   Let us therefore assume that we will use simple conditions in nested IFs. Since we have no information to the contrary, let us also assume that we are just as likely to find males aged 50 or over, and in the various occupation codes, as we are to find females. Similarly, we have no reason to expect an age bias for the codes. Because there is an OR relationship between the codes, we will be doing the code checks one right after the other; and since a code of 27 is more likely, we will check for that before checking for a code of 23. In addition, we already know that we get better results by checking age before checking sex.

Therefore, we must consider three checking orders:

1 Code = 27, code = 23, age, sex
2 Age, code = 27, code = 23, sex
3 Age, sex, code = 27, code = 23

If we examine the three alternatives in terms of the number of policyholders that must be checked for each criterion, we find the figures given in Table 4-3A.

Alternative 2 is the best one given what we know about the policyholders. A revised flowchart for module 230 of Figure 4-4 is shown in Figure 4-5. Two examples of how this logic can be stated in pseudocode are shown in Figure 4-6. The first example (with just simple conditions) is very awkward. By introducing compounding for the ORed code conditions, we get the simplified second example. This is much easier to understand, but how much less efficient will our processing be if we use a compound con-

TABLE 4-3A   EVALUATION OF THREE ALTERNATIVES

Criterion	Number checked	
Alternative 1		
Code = 27	50,000	
Code = 23	49,000	(50,000 − 1,000)
Age	1,500	(1,000 + 500)
Sex	525	(35% of 1,500)
Total decisions	101,025	
Alternative 2		
Age	50,000	
Code = 27	17,500	(all 50 or over)
Code = 23	17,150	(98% of 17,500)
Sex	525	(3% of 17,500)
Total decisions	85,175	
Alternative 3		
Age	50,000	
Sex	17,500	(all 50 or over)
Code = 27	11,200	(64% of 17,500)
Code = 23	10,976	(98% of 11,200)
Total decisions	89,676	

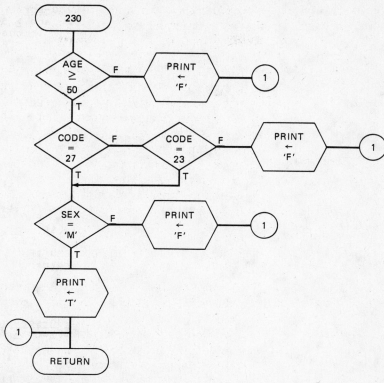

FIGURE 4-5   Revised module 230.

dition? Will the second alternative still be preferred? The following figures tell the story:

Alternative 2		Alternative 3	
Age	50,000	Age	50,000
Code = 27	17,500	Sex	17,500
Code = 23	17,500	Code = 27	11,200
Sex	525	Code = 23	11,200
Total	85,525	Total	89,900

The efficiency is reduced only slightly.

DECISION TABLES

Decision tables are sometimes used to plan and document processing that involves complex combinations of conditions. Table 4-4 contains a decision table for the Screen Employee File problem of Chapter 3. Decision tables show us what is to be done, under what conditions, and in what order. They do not, however, show us the order in which the conditions will be considered. Decision tables can be used to show all the processing required in a program, but this can be awkward and may require the use of go-to instructions. Decision tables are best suited to documenting complex decisions involving combinations of conditions.

```
230-screen-policyholder
IF age > 50 THEN
     IF code = 27 THEN
          IF sex = 'M' THEN
               move 'T' to print
          ELSE
               move 'F' to print
          END IF
     ELSE
          IF code = 23 THEN
               IF sex = 'M' THEN
                    move 'T' to print
               ELSE
                    move 'F' to print
               END IF
          ELSE
               move 'F' to print
          END IF
     END IF
ELSE
     move 'F' to print
END IF
return
```
                         (a) Example # 1


```
230-screen-policyholder
IF age > 50 THEN
     IF (code = 27) or (code = 23) THEN
          IF sex = 'M' THEN
               move 'T' to print
          ELSE
               move 'F' to print
          END IF
     ELSE
          move 'F' to print
     END IF
ELSE
     move 'F' to print
END IF
return
```

FIGURE 4-6   Alternative modules 230.   (b)   Example # 2

TABLE 4-4   SCREEN EMPLOYEE FILE DECISION TABLE 1

Screen employee	1	2	3	4
Sex = 'M'	Y	N	Y	N
Age > 65	Y	Y	N	N
Print employee name	X			
Disregard employee		X	X	X

Components of a Decision Table

Figure 4-7 shows the essential elements of a decision table. The top portion of the table, which is for conditions, is separated by a double line from the bottom portion, which is for actions. The left portion of the table (the *stub*) details what the conditions and actions are; a double line separates it from the right portion which contains entries that show what combinations of conditions will lead to what actions. Thus we have a *condition*

	RULES
CONDITION STUB	CONDITION ENTRIES
ACTION STUB	ACTION ENTRIES

FIGURE 4-7   Decision table format.

stub and *condition entries,* and an *action stub* and *action entries.* The condition stub contains simple conditions. The condition entries consist of a series of *rules,* one for each combination of conditions that must be considered. The order of the rules in the table is not important; the rules will not necessarily be applied in this order. The action stub lists the possible actions in the order that they will be taken. The action entries show for each rule just what actions will be taken.

In Table 4-4 there are two conditions and two actions. The four rules cover all possible combinations of the two conditions. Decision table conventions call for the use of 'Y' and 'N' instead of 'T' and 'F' in the condition entries. While this may seem an unnecessary complication for us, it does make the decision table more acceptable to users, and that is reason enough for us to put up with the notation. Rule 1 states that if sex = 'M' AND age > 65, we will print the employee name. Conditions in the condition stub have an AND relationship. To show an OR relationship, we use multiple rules. Rules 2, 3, and 4 show that we will disregard the employee if sex ≠ 'M' AND age ≥ 65 (rule 2) OR sex = 'M' AND age < 65 (rule 3) OR sex ≠ 'M' AND age < 65 (rule 4).

Redundancy and Contradiction

In creating a decision table, one must be sure that all possible combinations of conditions are included. One must also be sure that for any possible combination, only one rule in the table applies (this is not as easy as it sounds). Finally, one must be alert for two problems: redundancy and contradiction.

Redundancy   *Redundancy* exists when there are more rules than are necessary. We can identify redundancy as follows:

1 Look for two rules that have the same actions.
2 Then if all condition entries but one are exactly the same, there is redundancy between the two rules.

In Table 4-4 there is redundancy between rules 2 and 4 and between rules 3 and 4. In the case of rules 2 and 4, we see an 'N' for the first condition for both rules, but a 'Y' and an 'N' for the second. Therefore, the second condition does not matter; if the first condition is 'N,' regardless of what the second condition is, we want to disregard the employee. In the case of rules 3 and 4, we see that the first condition is immaterial as long as the second condition is 'N.' This might lead us to prepare Table 4-5 as a simplified solution. Can you see what is wrong with Table 4-5? Which rule applies to a female whose age is 31? Either rule 2 or rule 3 could apply, and that violates one of the requirements of a decision table: Only one rule may apply in any situation.

TABLE 4-5   SCREEN EMPLOYEE FILE DECISION TABLE 2

Screen employee	1	2	3
Sex = 'M'	Y	N	—
Age > 65	Y	—	N
Print employee name	X		
Disregard employee		X	X

Where we were lead astray was in trying to eliminate two redundancies at once. We must eliminate redundancies one at a time. If we eliminate the redundancy between rules 2 and 4, we get Table 4-6, where the dash(—) indicates that the condition can be 'Y' or 'N.' This table contains no redundancy, and is therefore an acceptable decision table. The case of the 31-year-old female is covered by rule 2 in this table.

There is another way to simplify the table, however. This is through the use of the ELSE rule. If a number of rules result in the same action, we can lump them together under the heading of ELSE, with no conditions indicated, as in Table 4-7. A table may have only one ELSE rule.

Contradiction   A *contradiction* exists when more than one rule applies in a given situation and the actions under the rules are different. In Table 4-8 there is a contradiction between rules 1 and 2. This may look like a redundancy, but it is not: The *conditions* are the same, but the *actions* are contradictory. Contradictions seem to occur much less often than redundancies in developing decision tables.

TABLE 4-6   SCREEN EMPLOYEE FILE DECISION TABLE 3

Screen employee	1	2	3
Sex = 'M'	Y	N	Y
Age > 65	Y	—	N
Print employee name	X		
Disregard employee		X	X

TABLE 4-7   SCREEN EMPLOYEE FILE DECISION TABLE 4

Screen employee	1	ELSE
Sex = 'M'	Y	
Age > 65	Y	
Print employee name	X	
Disregard employee		X

TABLE 4-8   CONTRADICTORY RULES

Contradiction	1	2	3	ELSE
Condition-A	Y	Y	Y	
Condition-B	N	N	Y	
Condition-C	Y	Y	N	
Action-1	X		X	
Action-2		X		X

Examples of Decision Tables

Let us look now at several more examples of decision tables.

File Inquiry   Table 4-9 is a decision table for the original File Inquiry example of Figure 4-4. Notice how the use of the ELSE rule greatly simplifies this table. Because there are four independent conditions, there could be a total of 16 (2^4) different rules, but 15 of these are included under the ELSE rule.

Table 4-10 shows that when we try to represent the relationships of Figure 4-5, in which there is an OR, we must include another rule. Table 4-10 is interesting because two of the conditions are not independent. If we

TABLE 4-9   FILE INQUIRY **AND** DECISION TABLE

File inquiry	1	ELSE
Code ≤ 27	Y	
Age ≥ 50	Y	
Sex = 'M'	Y	
Code ≥ 23	Y	
Print policy number	X	
Disregard policyholder		X

TABLE 4-10   FILE INQUIRY **OR** DECISION TABLE

File inquiry	1	2	ELSE
Code = 27	Y		
Age ≥ 50	Y	Y	
Sex = 'M'	Y	Y	
Code = 23		Y	
Print policy number	X	X	
Disregard policyholder			X

have a 'Y' for code = 27, we can not have a 'Y' for code = 23. It is not necessary to show an 'N' for code = 23 in the first rule, since it cannot be anything else. The absence of the 'N' for code = 27 in the second rule appears to introduce a redundancy, but the 'N' is unnecessary since if code equals 23 it cannot equal 27. Including an 'N' here would suggest that rule 1 will be examined before rule 2, but the order of rules in the table is not necessarily the order in which they will be considered.

Admittance to Graduate School   A graduate school screens applicants in the following way:

1 A student is admitted who has undergraduate grades of B or better, has an admissions test score over 550, and has an average of B or better for the last two years as an undergraduate.

2 A student with undergraduate grades of less than B, but with a test score over 550 and an average of B or better for the last two years, is also admitted.

3 A student will be admitted on probation if the test score is 550 or under but the undergraduate grade average and the average for the last two years are B or better.

4 A student is also admitted on probation if the average grade for the last two years is less than B but undergraduate grades are B or better and the test score is over 550.

5 A student is also admitted on probation if the undergraduate average is less than B and the test score is less than 550 but the average for the last two years is B or better.

6 All other students are denied admittance.

Table 4-11 restates these criteria in the form of a decision table. This table can be simplified, however, by eliminating the redundancies on the first condition between rules 1 and 2 and between rules 3 and 5. This gives us Table 4-12.

Not only is Table 4-12 simpler, but it can help us in designing our program logic. For example, it would be foolish to start our decision-making process with the undergraduate average grade, for it is a condition in only one of the rules. We should start with one of the conditions that is a factor in all the rules.

Finding the Largest of Three Numbers   Table 4-13 presents rules for determining which of three numbers is the largest. This decision table, though

TABLE 4-11   ADMISSIONS CRITERIA DECISION TABLE 1

Admissions criteria	1	2	3	4	5	ELSE
Undergraduate ≥ B	Y	N	Y	Y	N	
Test score > 550	Y	Y	N	Y	N	
Last 2 years ≥ B	Y	Y	Y	N	Y	
Admit	X	X				
Admit on probation			X	X	X	
Refuse to admit						X

TABLE 4-12   ADMISSIONS CRITERIA DECISION TABLE 2

Admissions criteria	1	2	3	ELSE
Undergraduate $\geq$ B	—	—	Y	
Test score > 550	Y	N	Y	
Last 2 years $\geq$ B	Y	Y	N	
Admit	X			
Admit on probation		X	X	
Refuse to admit				X

TABLE 4-13   FIND LARGEST NUMBER DECISION TABLE 1

Find largest	1	2	3
A $\geq$ B	Y	N	—
A $\geq$ C	Y	—	N
B $\geq$ C	—	Y	N
A is largest	X		
B is largest		X	
C is largest			X

correct, provides no help in planning a program. No condition is a factor in all rules. Table 4-14 also yields correct results, and in this case the first condition is a factor in all the rules and would therefore be a logical first condition to examine in a program. Note that we now have four rules instead of three. Table 4-13 was derived by starting with all possible combinations (there are only six, not eight) and eliminating redundancy. Table 4-14 is what we get if we prepare the flowchart first and then prepare the decision table from the flowchart. This illustrates the fact that although decision tables are not always useful for planning program logic, they do summarize clearly the conditions under which actions will be taken. By

TABLE 4-14   FIND LARGEST NUMBER DECISION TABLE 2

Find largest	1	2	3	4
A $\geq$ B	Y	N	Y	N
A $\geq$ C	Y	—	N	
B $\geq$ C	—	Y		N
A is largest	X			
B is largest		X		
C is largest			X	X

TABLE 4-15 EXTENDED-ENTRY DECISION TABLE

Admissions criteria	1	2	3	ELSE
Undergraduate	—	—	≥B	
Test score	>550	≤550	>550	
Last 2 years	≥B	≥B	<B	
Status	Admit	On probation	On probation	Refused

reading and understanding a decision table, a user can check on whether all combinations of conditions have been included and are being handled properly.

Extended-Entry and Mixed-Entry Tables

The tables discussed above are all examples of limited-entry tables. The condition entries consist of Y's and N's, and the action entries of X's. It is possible to move part of the condition from the condition stub to the condition entries, and part of the action from the action stub to the action entries, as in Table 4-15. Such a table is known as an *extended-entry* decision table. A decision table may also contain a mixture of extended and limited entries, in which case it is a mixed-entry table.

SUMMARY

This chapter expanded on the material of Chapter 3 by combining conditions in more complex ways. We examined in more depth the impact that the order is which comparisons are made has on program efficiency. We also noted that while the use of compound conditions simplifies the pseudocode, it results in a less efficient program because all conditions must be evaluated each time.

The decision table was introduced as a way to summarize and analyze various complex combinations and the actions that should result under different combinations of conditions.

KEY TERMS

action entry   decision table
action stub   program switch
condition entry   redundancy
condition stub   rule
contradiction   stub

EXERCISES

1 A distributor sells to both wholesale (class code = 'W') and retail (class code = 'R') customers. Retail customers get no discount. Wholesale customers who purchase fewer than 10 units also receive no discount. Wholesale customers who purchase 30 or more units receive a 15% discount if they are within 50 miles of the distributor's warehouse; if they are more than 50 miles away, they get only 10%. A 10% discount is also given to wholesale customers who purchase at least 10, but fewer than 30, units and are within 50 miles of the warehouse. If a whole-

sale customer purchases at least 10, but fewer than 30, units and is more than 50 miles away, a 5% discount is allowed.

About 70 percent of the customers are retailers. Of the wholesale purchasers, 60% are within 50 miles of the warehouse. About 20% of wholesale purchases are of 30 or more units, and 55% of 10 to 29 units.

The input consists of a record for each customer purchase containing customer name, class code, and—for a wholesale customer—number of units and distance from the warehouse. The input is in sequence by customer name. End-of-file is denoted by a customer name field filled with Z's. We must create a report that shows the discount that is allowed for each customer.

Execution is to terminate after printing an appropriate error message if a sequence error is found.

Documentation for this problem is to consist of the following: structure chart, program flowchart, pseudocode, decision table, test input data, and test output data.

2 A department store grants credit to a person who has worked in the same job for more than one year, as well as one who is employed and has lived in the same location for at least two years, except that people who owe more than two month's wages in nonmortgage debt or who have more than six children are denied credit. Of the applicants for credit, 95% are employed (75% in the same job for more than one year), 65% have lived at the same address for more than two years, 30% have more than two months' wages in nonmortgage debt, and 3% have more than six children.

The input data includes applicant's name, employment status, years in current job (if any), years at current residence, monthly wages, amount of nonmortgage debt, and number of children. The data is in order by applicant name.

A report is to be produced that will show each applicant's name and whether or not that applicant will be granted credit. Execution will halt after printing an error message if a sequence error is detected.

Documentation for this problem is to consist of the following: structure chart, program flowchart, pseudocode, decision table, test input data, and test output data.

3 A report of commission earnings is to be prepared. The input contains the following fields of interest to us: identification number of salesperson, amount of sale, and product class ('A,' 'B,' or 'C'). There is one record for each sale, and the records are in sequence by salesperson number. Sales are distributed by product class as follows: A, 25%; B, 45%; and C, 30%. Sales of product class A break down as follows: ≤ $1000, 40%; $1001 to 3000, 45%; and > $3000, 15%. Approximately 30% of the sales of product class B are more than $2000.

A printed report is to be produced that will contain a detail line for each sale showing identification number of salesperson, sales amount, product class, and commission earned.

Commissions are determined as follows:

Sale amount	Commission rate, %
Product class A	
≤1,000	5
1,001 to 3,000	7
>3,000	10
Product class B	
≤2,000	4
>2,000	6
Product class C	
Any	5

Execution is to terminate if a sequence error is detected. If a product class other than A, B, or C is detected, ignore the record but continue execution. Print an appropriate error message when either error occurs.

Documentation for this problem is to consist of the following: structure chart, program flowchart, pseudocode, decision table, test input data, and test output data.

CHAPTER 5

CONTROL BREAKS

OBJECTIVES

Upon completing this chapter the student should be able to:

1 Represent the three basic structures in a Nassi-Shneiderman (N-S) flowchart.

2 Prepare a structure chart, a program flowchart, a Nassi-Shneiderman flowchart, and the pseudocode for a control-break problem.

3 Make provisions in structure charts, program flowcharts, and N-S flowcharts for the printing of heading lines and blank lines in reports.

4 Define and use the key terms at the end of the chapter.

INTRODUCTION

A common requirement of many business reports is for the inclusion of various subtotals as well as a final total. For example, a manager using a report that lists each sale of every item in inventory probably would find it convenient to have not only a total of all the sales, but also subtotals of sales by item. The item number field would be the *control field,* since the timing of the printing of the subtotal for each item would be controlled by a change in the item number. This change in the value of the control field is called a *control break.* The input file must be sorted on the item number field so that all records for an item will be grouped together.

Two examples will be developed in this chapter to illustrate the logic and coding used with control-break problems. We will also learn to use the Nassi-Shneiderman (N-S) method of flowcharting for structured programs, a technique that is becoming increasingly popular.

GROSS PAY REVISED

The Gross Pay problem in Chapter 1 required us to produce a report showing earnings for each employee and a final total of all employees' earnings. We assumed that there was one input record for each employee. Management now asks us to revise this program because during a given week an employee may perform different tasks at different hourly pay rates. The input will contain one record for each task an employee performs during a week. The new report is to contain a detail line showing the earnings for each task an employee performs, a total line showing each employee's total earnings for the week, and a final total line to show the earnings of all employees.

Handling the Control Break

Table 5-1 shows some typical input data and the report that should be produced from this data. Each input record contains the employee number, hours worked on a particular job, and the hourly pay rate for the job.

TABLE 5-1   REVISED GROSS PAY INPUT AND OUTPUT

Input		
Employee number	**Hours worked**	**Pay rate**
2345	8	6.00
2345	30	5.50
2345	2	7.50
2453	40	5.00
2534	6	8.00
2534	30	7.00

Output	
EMPLOYEE	GROSS PAY
2345	48.00
2345	165.00
2345	15.00
	228.00*
2453	200.00
	200.00*
2534	48.00
2534	210.00
	258.00*
	686.00**

The output includes something new, a printed *heading line* that identifies the contents of each column. Heading lines may be printed by a program or they may be preprinted on a form. In this case, our program is to print the heading line ("EMPLOYEE" and "GROSS PAY"). It also will print an asterisk to the right of each employee's total earnings, and two asterisks to the right of the final total. We can see from Table 5-1 that employee 2345 performed three different tasks during the week, earning $48.00, $165.00, and $15.00, for a total of $228.00. Employee 2453 worked a single task and earned $200.00. Employee 2534 earned $48.00 and $210.00 for two tasks, for a total of $258.00. The total earnings of the three employees is $686.00 ($228.00 + $200.00 + $258.00).

Notice that all input records for an employee have been grouped together to facilitate the computation of the employee's total earnings. This grouping is accomplished by sorting the file into ascending order by employee number, the control field for this problem. As each record is read in, our program must compare the new employee number to the previous one, not only to confirm that the file is in fact in sequence but also to determine when all records for an employee have been processed. If the employee number in a record is the same as in the previous record, the record is processed immediately by calculating the gross pay, adding it to an earnings total for the employee, and printing a detail line. If the new employee number is smaller then the previous one, we have a sequence error, and the program should halt after printing an error message.

When the new employee number is greater than the employee number from the preceding record—that is, when there is a control break—several things must be done before the record causing the break can be processed:

1 The total earnings of the previous employee must be added to the total being accumulated for all employees.

2 The previous employee's total earnings must be printed.

3 The total earnings field for the employee must be set back to zero so that a total for the new employee can be accumulated.

4 The new employee number must be moved to the old employee number field so sequence checking and control-break checking can take place.

Note that the final total of earnings for all employees is computed as the sum of the total earnings of each employee, not of the earnings for each task. Referring to the input data in Table 5-1 we can see that computing the final total as a sum of the employees' total earnings requires three additions, whereas six would be required if we summed up the earnings for individual tasks.

Special Problems

As we discussed in Chapter 3, sequence checking presents a problem when we process the very first record in the file. To prevent the first employee record from causing a false sequence error, we initialize the old employee number field to zero. Now, however, we are looking not only for sequence errors but also for control breaks. When we process the first record, it will appear that a control break has occurred because the first employee number will be greater than the zero we have placed in the old employee number field. When we get this *false control break,* we do *not* want to print an employee total line and add to the final total, since we have not yet even processed our first record. However, we *do* want to make sure the employee total is zero, and we *do* want to move the employee number from this first record to our previous employee number field. We must have some way to identify the false control break that occurs while processing the very first record in the file if we are to avoid the summing and printing steps that are required when a real control break is encountered.

Encountering the end of our data also presents us with a special problem. We will not know that we have processed all the data for the last employee until we reach the end of the file. At that time we must do the following:

1 Add the total earnings we have accumulated for the last employee to the final total.

2 Print out this employee's total earnings.

3 Print the final total.

4 Terminate program execution.

Note that the first two activities are also performed when we have a control break. For this reason, encountering the end of the data file is regarded as a control break. The difference here is that there is no need to prepare to process another employee (setting the employee total earnings field to zero and moving the new employee number to the old). Instead, we print out the final total and stop.

How we deal with these two problems (the false control break with the first record and processing the last employee's total at end-of-file) will be explained as we develop a solution to the problem.

Structure Chart

Figure 5-1 is a revision of the structure chart of Figure 2-12. The heading line for the report, since it is printed only once, is printed in module

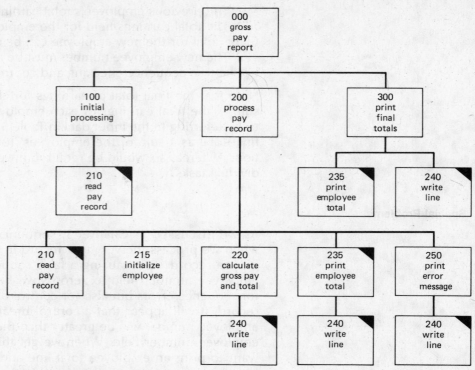

FIGURE 5-1   Revised Gross Pay structure chart.

100, before the first data record is read. The name for module 100 has been changed to reflect the fact that it is now doing more than just a priming read.

A module 215 has been added to handle the initializing steps now required before a new employee record is processed: setting the employee's total earnings to zero and moving the employee's number to the output record and to the field that will be used for sequence and control-break checking. Module 220 will now calculate an employee total instead of a final total; it will also call module 240 to print the employee detail line. In Figure 2-12, module 240 was called by 230 after it moved the employee number to output. Now the moving of the employee number is done in module 215 when we start processing a new employee; the employee number remains in the output record until we move a new one into the same area. This leaves the old module 230 with nothing to do except call module 240, so the call is moved to module 220 and module 230 is eliminated from the structure chart.

Module 235 is added to print the employee total earnings. This module will also accumulate the final total. It is called by module 200 for all but the last employee. Module 235 prints the total earnings for the last employee under the control of module 300 after the end-of-file condition is detected.

Module 250 is new. It will be called to print an error message if a sequence error is detected.

Program Flowchart

Figure 5-2 is a program flowchart for this problem. Unlike Figure 2-11, the flowchart developed for the original Gross Pay problem, this is a structured flowchart.

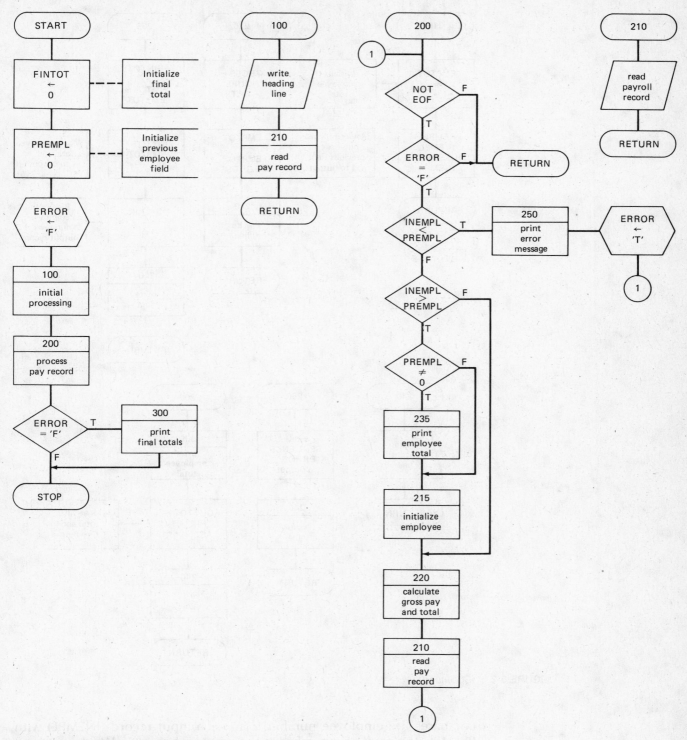

FIGURE 5-2 Revised Gross Pay flowchart.

The main program module initializes the final total (FINTOT), an error switch for sequence errors (ERROR), and a field in which the employee number from the previous record will be saved (PREMPL). The initializing of PREMPL is necessary because the control-break and sequence checking

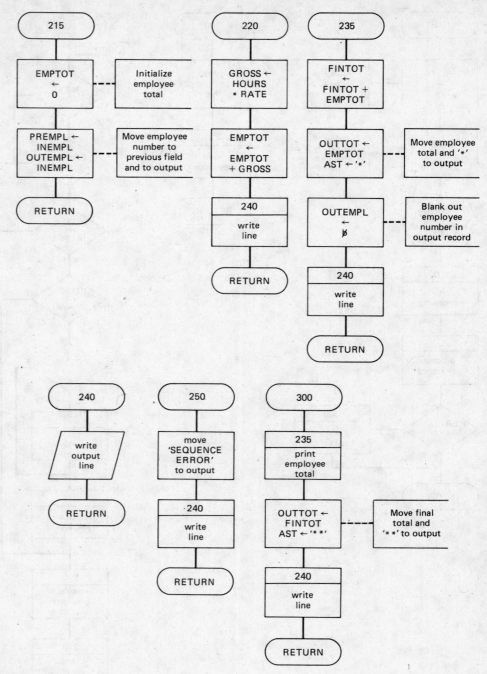

FIGURE 5-2 (*Continued*)

compares the employee number from each input record (INEMPL) with PREMPL (the employee number in the preceding record). We do not want a sequence error to occur when we are processing the first record, so we assign a value of zero to PREMPL. This will result in a false control break when we process the first record; how we cope with that will be discussed shortly. The remainder of the main program module is straightforward, except for the fact that module 300 is called only if there has been no sequence error.

Module 100 now includes the writing of a heading line at the beginning of the report.

Module 200 consists of a loop that is executed as long as neither end-of-file is reached nor a sequence error is detected. If there is a data record, the first thing done in the loop is a check of the sequence. If INEMPL is less than PREMPL, we have a sequence error; we must print an error message and set ERROR to 'T.' We then return to the start of the loop, and, since we can no longer satisfy the condition for the loop, we exit from module 200, returning control to the main program module.

If there is no sequence error, we then determine if we have a control break or another record for the same employee. If INEMPL is greater than PREMPL, we have a control break; however, it might be the false control break that occurs when we process the first record. If the control break is false, we do not want to print an employee total or accumulate the final total. All we want to do is to prepare the first employee for processing by setting the employee total to zero and moving the employee number to the output record and to PREMPL. How do we know if we are processing the first employee record and thus have a false control break? We can use the fact that PREMPL is equal to zero when we start to process the first record. If PREMPL equals zero, we skip the printing step (module 235) and go right to the initializing (module 215). Note that the condition is shown in the decision outline as "$\neq$" instead of "$=$." This is because when one of our alternatives is to do nothing, it must be the false alternative. Expressing the conditions as "PREMPL $\neq$ $\emptyset$" results in a null ELSE.

Module 235 accumulates the final total and prepares the employee total line for printing. The latter requires the moving of the employee total and a single asterisk to the output record, and the blanking out of the employee number in the record.

Whether we have had a control break or simply another record for the same employee, we are now ready to process the input record by calculating the gross pay, accumulating the employee total earnings, and printing the detail line. All this is done in module 220. Then we attempt to read another record (module 210) and execute the loop again.

This flowchart should—of course—be desk-checked. Take the input data of Table 5-1 and process it through the flowchart to see if you get the correct results.

Pseudocode

Figure 5-3 contains the pseudocode corresponding to Figure 5-2. Observe how the care taken in constructing the comparisons in module 200 results in code that is relatively straightforward. A greater appreciation of this will emerge if the student changes the condition, from "$\neq$" to "$=$", for the comparison of the previous employee number with zero. Now try to write the pseudocode for this version of the module.

NASSI-SHNEIDERMAN FLOWCHARTS

One of the problems with using conventional flowcharts in structured programming is the ease with which the programmer can represent a branch. Even a very disciplined programmer may sometimes find it difficult to resist the temptation. An alternative flowcharting method has been developed which makes no provision for branching. With *Nassi-Shneiderman (N-S) flowcharts* there is no way that a branch instruction can be charted.

FIGURE 5-3   Revised Gross Pay pseudocode.

```
000-gross-pay-report
move zero to final total
move zero to previous employee number
set error to 'F'
call 100-initial-processing
call 200-process-pay-record
IF error = 'F' THEN
    call 300-print-final-totals
ELSE
    (null)
END IF
stop


100-initial-processing
write heading line
call 210-read-pay-record
return


200-process-pay-record
DO WHILE not EOF and (error = 'F')
    IF new employee number <
            previous employee number THEN
        call 250-print-error-message
        set error to 'T'
    ELSE
        IF new employee number >
                previous employee number THEN
            IF previous employee number ≠ 0 THEN
                call 235-print-employee-total
            ELSE
                (null)
            END IF
            call 215-initialize-employee
        ELSE
            (null)
        END IF
        call 220-calculate-gross-pay-and-total
        call 210-read-pay-record
    END IF
END DO
return


210-read-pay-record
read payroll record
return


215-initialize-employee
move zero to employee total gross pay
move new employee number to previous employee number
    and to the output record
return


220-calculate-gross-pay-and-total
multiply hours by rate to get gross pay
add gross pay to employee total gross pay
call 240-write-line
return


235-print-employee-total
add employee total gross pay to final total
move employee total and '*' to output record
move blanks to employee number in output record
call 240-write-line
return


240-write-line
write output record
return
```

```
250-print-error-messae
move 'SEQUENCE ERROR' to output record
call 240-write-line
return

300-print-final-totals
call 235-print-employee-total
move final total and '**' to output record
call 240-write-line
return
```

FIGURE 5-3   (*Continued*)

Representing the Three Logical Structures

Program modules are represented in N-S flowcharts by rectangles. Inside these rectangles are other rectangles of various shapes and sizes that represent the three logical structures we examined in Chapter 2: sequence structure, loop structure, and selection structure.

Sequence Structure   A sequence structure is represented by a series of rectangles within a larger rectangle, as shown in Figure 5-4. Each individual instruction is represented by a rectangle, and the five instructions together—which may constitute a module—are represented by the outer rectangle. The instructions are executed in the order in which they appear in the large rectangle.

Loop Structure   The loop structure is also represented by a rectangle, with the extent of the loop indicated by a vertical bar on the left side of the rectangle, as in Figure 5-5. If condition-A is true, the instructions starting with instruction-1 and ending with instruction-n will be executed. These instructions can be any structure, including another loop structure, since the loop structure is, in effect, represented by a rectangle. At least one of the instructions in the loop must alter the condition being tested if the loop is to terminate. When the condition is no longer true, the DO WHILE loop is bypassed and the instruction following it—if any—is executed.

Look back at Figure 2-11. We can represent the logic of this earlier version of the Gross Pay problem with the N-S flowchart of Figure 5-6. Notice

FIGURE 5-4   N-S representation of sequence structure.

| GROSS ← HOURS * RATE |
| TOTAL ← TOTAL + GROSS |
| OUTEMPL ← INEMPL |
| print detail line |
| read employee record |

FIGURE 5-5   N-S representation of loop structure.

DO WHILE condition—A
instruction-1
. . .
instruction-n

| TOTAL ← 0 |
| read record |
| DO WHILE not EOF |
| GROSS ← HOURS * RATE |
| TOTAL ← TOTAL + GROSS |
| OUTEMPL ← INEMPL |
| print detail line |
| read record |
| print total line |

FIGURE 5-6   N-S flowchart for Gross Pay.

how compact the N-S flowchart is. A priming read precedes the DO WHILE loop so that the end-of-file condition will be established before it is checked for the first time. If the not-EOF condition is true, the record just read is processed, a line for the employee is printed, and an attempt is made to read the next data record. The DO WHILE loop ends at this point, so the condition controlling the loop is checked again. If there is another record, the loop is repeated. This continues until all records have been read. Now the not-EOF condition will be false, and the DO WHILE loop will be bypassed. We then encounter the statement for printing out the final total, and the program terminates.

Selection Structure   The N-S representation of the selection structure is shown in Figure 5-7. If condition-B is true, the instructions on the left (under the "T") are executed; if it is false, the instructions on the right (under the "F") are executed. The THEN instructions always appear on the left, and the ELSE instructions on the right. These instructions can include any of the three structures. If no action is to be taken when the condition is false, the space under the "F" is simply left blank. The spaces for the "T" and "F" instructions do not need to be the same width; the available space may be divided as needed.

Other Structures   There are also N-S representations for the other structures introduced in Chapter 2. Figure 5-8 shows how we chart the alternative loop structures, and Figure 5-9 shows the CASE structure. In Figure 5-9a we see the ideal way of charting the CASE structure, with the flow of the logic from top to bottom. If there are many possible alternatives, top-to-bottom representation becomes impractical, because there is too little room across the page for the instructions. Since the CASE structure is most appropriate for situations in which there are many alternatives, the representation in Figure 5-9b is usually used.

Revised Gross Pay Problem

Figure 5-10 is an N-S flowchart for the revised Gross Pay problem. Each module is represented by a separate rectangle. Module 200 is the most in-

FIGURE 5-7   N-S representation of selection structure.

T	condition-B	F
instruction-T	instruction-F	

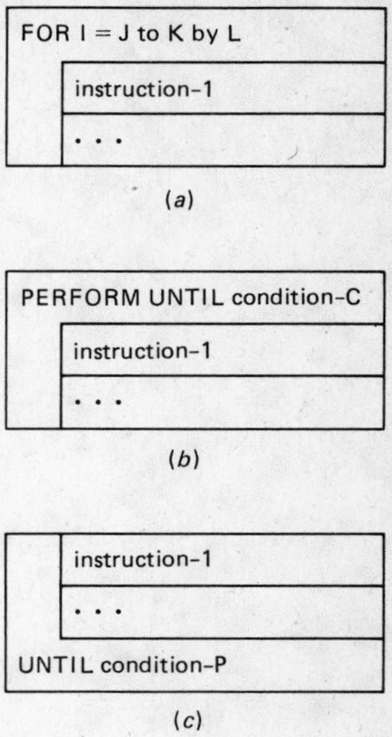

FOR I = J to K by L
instruction-1
. . .

(a)

PERFORM UNTIL condition-C
instruction-1
. . .

(b)

instruction-1
. . .
UNTIL condition-P

(c)

FIGURE 5-8 N-S representations of other loops. (a) FOR loop; (b) PERFORM UNTIL loop; (c) REPEAT UNTIL loop.

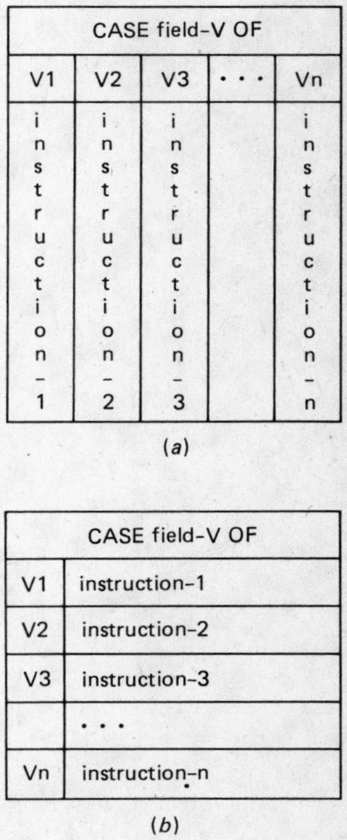

CASE field-V OF				
V1	V2	V3	· · ·	Vn
instruction–1	instruction–2	instruction–3		instruction–n

(a)

CASE field-V OF	
V1	instruction-1
V2	instruction-2
V3	instruction-3
	. . .
Vn	instruction-n

(b)

FIGURE 5-9 N-S representation of CASE. (a) Ideal representation; (b) usual representation.

teresting one to examine, for it is in this module that the bulk of the decision making takes place. The structure of the DO WHILE loop is very clear in the N-S flowchart, and the module logic is documented in a very compact form.

The logical structure of the N-S flowchart is the same as for the program flowchart of Figure 5-2. Notice how similar the N-S flowchart is to the pseudocode of Figure 5-3. However, the N-S flowchart uses actual field

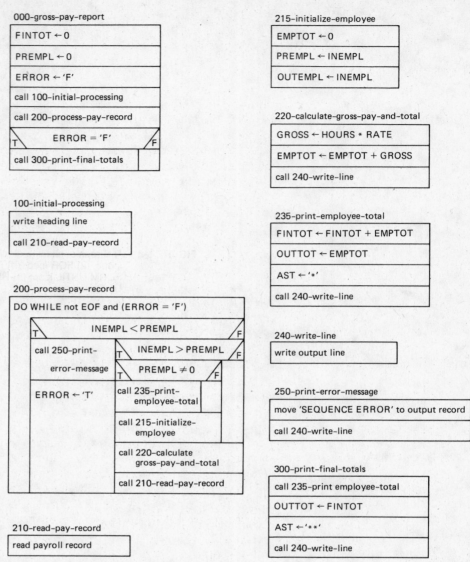

FIGURE 5-10 N-S flowchart for revised Gross Pay.

names, whereas the pseudocode does not. (As you may recall, the decision not to use field names in the pseudocode was made so that it would not resemble actual program instructions too closely.) If field names had been used in the pseudocode, the resemblence to the N-S flowchart would have been even closer.

Actual documentation for a program would not normally include a program flowchart, an N-S flowchart, and pseudocode. The student should recognize that even though in the problems presented in this text, one, two, or even all three of these techniques may be used, a data-processing manager (or instructor) is likely to prefer—and require—the use of just one of these documentation methods.

PURCHASE SUMMARY

Let us look at another control-break problem. While it differs somewhat from the revised Gross Pay problem, what should emerge in working through this problem is a realization of how similar all control-break problems actually are.

Problem Definition

We are to summarize customer purchase data and create a report showing how much each customer purchased as well as the total of all purchases for all customers. There is one record in the input file for every purchase made, containing the customer number and the amount purchased. The data must be in sequence by customer number (the control field); there may be more than one record for a customer.

One obvious difference between the processing required for this problem and for the previous one is the absence of any detail output in this problem. That is, we do not create an output record for every purchase record. Instead, we produce output only when there is a control break.

To enhance the appearance and usability of the report, two heading lines are to be printed. The first heading line will contain a title for the report. It will be followed by two blank lines and then the second heading line, which contains column headings. One blank line will follow the second heading line (see Table 5-2). Not only will these headings appear at the top of the first page, but at the top of all succeeding pages as well. When we reach the bottom of any page, we must skip to the top of the next page and reprint the heading lines. But how do we know that we have reached the bottom of a page?

There are great differences in how this problem is handled by the various languages. We will first determine the number of lines we wish to print on each page (50 in this case). Then as we print the lines, we will increment a counter which will keep track of the number of lines printed. When the counter reaches 50, we will advance to the top of the next page, print the heading lines, and reset the counter to zero.

Some other enhancements will be made to the report. The final total will be separated from the other lines in the report by a blank line, and will have the words "FINAL TOTAL" printed to the left of the amount. The sequence error message will also be preceded by a blank line.

Structure Chart

Figure 5-11 is a structure chart for the Purchase Summary problem. The major differences between this chart and the one in Figure 5-1 are (1) the provisions made in the former for producing the headings and the desired

TABLE 5-2   PURCHASE SUMMARY OUTPUT

PURCHASE SUMMARY	
(blank line)	
(blank line)	
CUSTOMER NUMBER	TOTAL PURCHASES
(blank line)	
123456	2,678.50
124687	11,006.79
125903	397.25
126673	6,498.15
(blank line)	
FINAL TOTAL	20,580.69

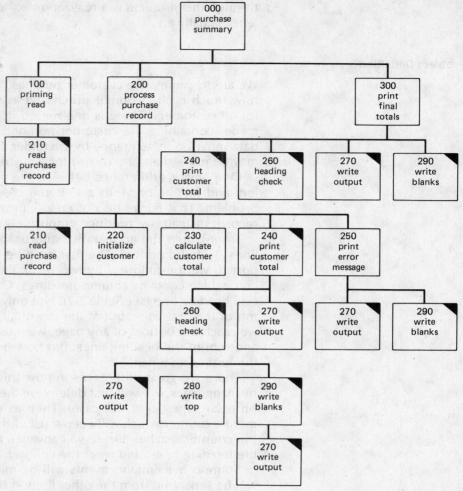

FIGURE 5-11 Purchase Summary structure chart.

spacing of the report and (2) the absence of detail output. Otherwise, as can be seen by the similarity in module names, the same basic functions are being performed by the modules in the two charts.

Since headings will be printed on all pages of the output, module 100 reverts to doing just a priming read. The headings for the first page will be printed when the first customer total line is printed. This is accomplished by initializing the line counter to a value equal to the maximum number of lines allowed on a page. When the line counter is checked just prior to the printing of the first customer total, it will appear that a page has been filled. The program logic will cause a skip to a new page and the printing of the headings.

Module 230 (the equivalent of module 220 in Figure 5-1) will no longer include any printing of detail lines, so it requires no subordinate write module.

Module 240 does the actual printing. This is a more complex output module than any we have encountered in the past, as we can see by its subordinate modules. At the first level of subordination we see module 260, which handles the heading lines, and module 270, which is called to print a customer total line. Subordinate to module 260 are three modules:

1 Module 280 takes care of the first heading line, the one for which we must skip to the top of a new page.
2 Module 290 prints the blank lines, calling module 270 to do the actual printing.
3 Module 260 also calls module 270, to print the second heading line.

Module 250 prints the sequence error message. In addition to calling module 270 to do the actual printing, it calls module 290 to print the blank line that is to precede the message. Note that since no check of the line counter is made before printing the error message, the message could end up being printed on line 51 or 52 of a page. This is a conscious decision; if a sequence error occurs, the report so far produced will have to be discarded, so appearance is no longer a consideration.

Module 300 now has four subordinate modules:

1 Module 240 prints the last customer total.
2 Module 260 prints the headings if they are required.
3 Module 270 prints the final total.
4 Module 290 prints the blank line before the final total if headings have not just been printed.

Note that headings may be printed under the control of module 240 before the last customer total is printed, or—if the last customer total is on line 50—under the control of module 300 before the final total is printed.

Nassi-Shneiderman Flowchart

Figure 5-12 contains an N-S flowchart for the problem. The major changes from Figure 5-10 are—of course—in the logic introduced to print the heading lines and the blank lines.

The handling of the heading lines requires some further explanation. The assumption has been made that, with the exception of the sequence error message, no more than 50 lines of any type (heading, total, or blank) will be printed on any page. When we have 50 lines on a page, it is time to skip to a new page, reprint the headings, and then resume the printing of the total lines. A field called LINES is used to count the number of lines printed on the current page. To get the heading to print on the first page, LINES is initialized to 50. Since LINES is compared with 50 before printing a customer total, the headings will be printed before the total line for the first customer is printed.

We are not going to concern ourselves with exactly how we get to the top of a new page. Different programming languages and different computers accomplish this in different ways. We will just accept the fact that we can print a line after skipping to the top of a new page.

After we print the first heading line, we must advance the paper in the printer in such a way that we will leave two blank lines. Again, different languages and computers accomplish this in different ways. We will assume that in order to leave two blank lines we will actually have to print two blank lines. Module 290 will be used to print the blank lines on the basis of the contents of a field called SPACE. In normal usage, the term *single spacing* refers to printing with no blank lines between report lines, *double spacing* is printing with one blank line between lines, and *triple spacing* is

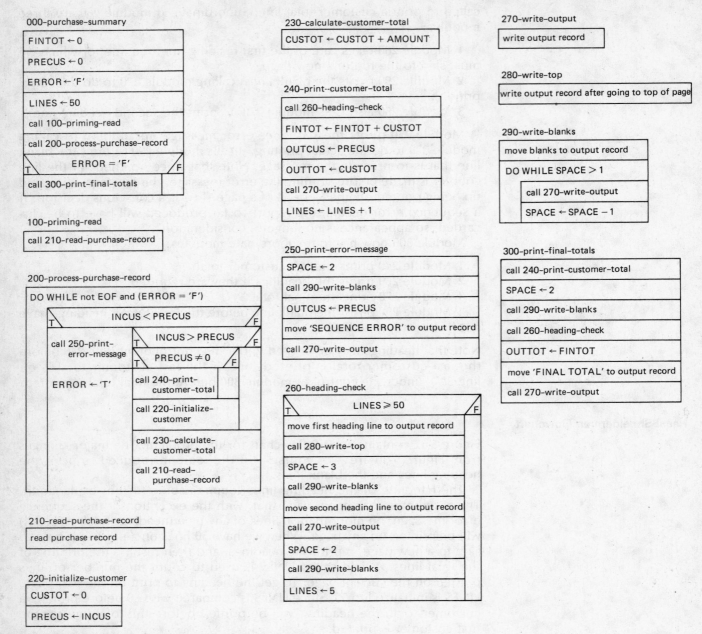

FIGURE 5-12 N-S flowchart for Purchase Summary.

printing with two blank lines between lines of the report. SPACE will therefore contain a value that is one greater than the number of blank lines to be printed. Note how module 290 uses the value in SPACE to print the appropriate number of blank lines.

After printing the first heading line, we move a three into SPACE and call module 290 to give us the desired two blank lines. Then the second heading line is printed, and a value of two is moved into SPACE to provide the single blank line desired between the second heading line and the first customer total line. Module 290 is again called to print this blank line. The line counter field LINES is set to five to account for the two heading lines and the three blank lines that have been printed.

102

Data can not be moved to the output record until after module 260 has been called because this module moves the heading lines into the record area before they are printed. The previous—rather than the new—customer number is moved in module 240 to the output record. When the customer total line is printed, the new and previous numbers are different, and the total being printed is for the previous customer.

Since the customer total lines are to be single-spaced, the only other special spacing requirements are for the final total and the error message to be preceded by a blank line. In both cases, this is accomplished by moving a value of two into SPACE prior to calling module 290 to print the blank line. Note that module 260 is called by module 300 just prior to printing the final total. It is also called by module 240 prior to printing the last customer's total. If the last customer total is printed on line 49 or line 50 of a page, the final total will appear on a page with just the headings.

Pseudocode

Figure 5-13 shows the pseudocode. Again, there is a striking similarity between the pseudocode and the N-S flowchart, with the latter presenting the IF-THEN-ELSEs in a form that is probably easier to visualize. On the other

FIGURE 5-13   Purchase Summary pseudocode.

```
000-purchase-summary
move zero to final total
move zero to previous customer number
set error to 'F'
move 50 to line counter
call 100-priming-read
call 200-process-purchase-record
IF error = 'F' THEN
    call 300-print-final-totals
ELSE
    (null)
END IF
stop


100-priming-read
call 210-read-purchase-record
return


200-process-purchase-record
DO WHILE not EOF and (error = 'F')
    IF new customer number <
            previous customer number THEN
        call 250-print-error-message
        set error to 'T'
    ELSE
    IF new customer number >
            previous customer number THEN
        IF previous customer number ≠ 0 THEN
            call 240-print-customer-total
        ELSE
            (null)
        END IF
        call 220-initialize-customer
    ELSE
        (null)
    END IF
    call 230-calculate-customer-total
    call 210-read-purchase-record
    END IF
END DO
return
```

```
210-read-purchase-record
read purchase record
return


220-initialize-customer
move zero to customer total
move new customer number to previous customer number
return


230-calculate-customer-total
add purchase amount to customer total
return


240-print-customer-total
call 260-heading-check
add customer total to final total
move customer total and previous customer number to
    output record
call 270-write-output
add 1 to line counter
return


250-print-error-message
move 2 to space field
call 290-write-blanks
move previous customer number and 'SEQUENCE ERROR'
    to output record
call 270-write-output
return


260-heading check
IF line counter ≥ 50 THEN
    move first heading line to output record
    call 280-write-top
    move 3 to space field
    call 290-write-blanks
    move second heading to output record
    call 270-write-output
    move 2 to space field
    call 290-write-blanks
    move 5 to line counter
ELSE
    (null)
END IF
return


270-write-output
write output record
return


280-write-top
write output record after going to top of page
return


290-write-blanks
move blanks to output record
DO WHILE space field > 1
    call 270-write-output
    subtract 1 from space field
END DO
return


300-print-final-totals
call 240-print-customer-total
move 2 to space field
call 290-write-blanks
call 260-heading-check
move 'FINAL TOTAL' and final total to output record
call 270-write-output
return
```

FIGURE 5-13   (*Continued*)

hand, a user might—at least initially—find the pseudocode easier to read. Both are presented here to provide additional examples for the student; only one would normally be included in the documentation for a program.

SUMMARY

Many business reports include subtotals. In this chapter we saw how a subtotal can be developed and printed utilizing a control break.

A new flowcharting technique developed especially for structured programming—Nassi-Shneiderman (N-S) flowcharts—was introduced. We learned how to represent the three basic structures using this technique. We observed a striking similarity between pseudocode and N-S flowcharts, and discovered that the format of the latter is both compact and easily understood.

KEY TERMS

control break   heading line
control field   Nassi-Shneiderman flowchart
false control break

EXERCISES

1 A report of customer purchases is to be produced. There is one input record for each purchase made by a customer; each record contains a customer number, item number, quantity purchased, and price per unit. The file is in sequence by customer number.

   The report is to contain a single-spaced line for each customer purchase. This line will show all the input information and the amount purchased (quantity × unit price). Other lines in the report include a line of column headings that is to be printed at the top of every page, a total line for each customer, and a final total line. The total lines contain sums of the amounts purchased. One blank line is to be left after the heading line and before and after a customer total line. A blank line should precede the final total line and the sequence error message. The maximum number of lines of any type that is to be printed on a page is 50.

   Documentation for this problem is to consist of a structure chart, test input and output data, and one of the following: a program flowchart, an N-S flowchart, or pseudocode.

2 A report summarizing students' major fields of study is to be produced. The input file is in sequence by major code. There is a record for each student; it includes a numeric code for the student's major.

   The report will contain a line for each major showing the major code and the total number of students who have selected that major. There will also be a final total count for all students. Three heading lines are to be printed on each page. The first two heading lines describe the report; the third contains column headings. Two blank lines are to be left between the first and second heading lines and between the second and third heading lines. One blank line is to follow the third heading line. The total lines for the various majors are to be double-spaced. Two blank lines are to appear between the last major total and the final count. (If there is no major total on the last page, just the final count, a single blank line is to separate the final count from the last heading line.) A blank line should also precede the sequence error message. Up to a total of 50 lines are to be printed on any page.

   Documentation for this problem is to consist of a structure chart, test input and output data, and one of the following: a program flowchart, an N-S flowchart, or pseudocode.

3 A report of sales by item is desired. The input file contains a record for each sale of an item and is in sequence by item number. There may be more than one record for an item. In addition to the item number, each record contains the amount of the sale.

One line is to be printed for each item showing the total sales of the item. There also will be a final total line showing the total sales for all items. Two heading lines are to be printed at the top of each page, with three blank lines between them. The first heading line describes the report; the second contains column headings. Two blank lines will separate the second heading line from the first item total line on the page. The item total lines will be single-spaced. The final total will be separated from the last item total line (or the heading line, if there is no item total line on the last page) by two blank lines. A blank line should precede the sequence error message. Up to a total of 50 lines are to be printed on any page.

Documentation for this problem is to consist of a structure chart, test input and output data, and one of the following: a program flowchart, an N-S flowchart, or pseudocode.

CHAPTER 6

MULTILEVEL CONTROL BREAKS

OBJECTIVES

Upon completing this chapter the student should be able to:

1 Prepare a structure chart, a program flowchart, an N-S flowchart, and pseudocode for a multilevel control-break problem in which a group-indicated, detail-printed, or group-printed report is to be produced.

2 Prepare a HIPO chart for a program.

3 Define and use the key terms at the end of the chapter.

INTRODUCTION

In Chapter 5 we learned how to produce a report that printed a subtotal whenever there was a control break. In this chapter we will extend this concept to situations in which we wish to have a number of levels of subtotals. Each different level of subtotal will be controlled by a different field; that is, there will be a different control break associated with each level of subtotal. Since control breaks can occur at a number of levels, we naturally speak of *multilevel control breaks*.

We will find that while the logic for multilevel control-break problems is more complex than anything we have previously dealt with, there is a basic pattern to the logic that is repeated for each additional level.

FIELD SALES SUMMARY

The multilevel control-break concept will be illustrated by a problem in which we produce a report that summarizes the sales activities of a field sales force. The sales force is broken down into divisions; the divisions in turn are made up of districts; and the districts are made up of individual salespersons.

Problem Definition

Management wants a report that will include the following:

- Total sales for country
- Total sales for each division
- Total sales for each district
- Total sales for each salesperson
- Detail line for each individual sale

This is a three-level problem: the salesperson is at the lowest level (level-1); at the next level (level-2), we have the district; at the highest level (level-3) is the division. The total for the country will be the final total. We will borrow from RPG a shorthand way of referring to the various levels; L1 will refer to the lowest level, L2 to the next higher level, etc.

Input Table 6-1 shows a sample of the data that is to be processed. Each line represents a record of a sale by a salesperson to a customer. There is one record for every sale each salesperson made. Each record contains the necessary identifying information about the division, district, and salesperson, as well as the amount of the sale. For example, the first two lines show that salesperson 04 in District 1 of Division 1 had two sales—in the amounts of $3000 and $1200.

Notice that in the column headings the division is identified as the *major control field* and the salesperson as the *minor control field*. The terms "major" and "minor" are used in the sorting of a file to identify the most and least significant fields to be used in sequencing the file. The minor field is our L1 field, the lowest-level control field, and the major field is our highest-level control field—in this case L3. District is an *intermediate-level* control field.

To arrange our file for processing, we have to sort by salesperson within district within division. Since division is our major field, all records for a particular division are grouped together. (All Division 1 records precede all Division 2 records.) The next most significant field is district, so within a division, all records for a particular district are grouped together. (Within Division 1, all records for District 1 precede all records for District 2. Note that Division 2 also has Districts 1 and 2, but they are geographically different districts and our sorting keeps them separate.) The least significant field is salesperson. Within each district of a division, all records for a particular salesperson are grouped together. (All records for salesperson 07 in District 1 of Division 1 are grouped together. District 2 also has a salesperson 07, but that person's records are grouped separately as a result of the sort.)

For sorting purposes we can imagine that all three sort fields have been combined into a single field, with the major field in the leftmost (high-order, or most significant) position, down to the minor field in the rightmost (low-order, or least significant) position. Thus the sort field values for the records in Table 6-1 are 1104, 1104, 1107, 1107, 1207, etc. We can see that the records are in ascending order.

TABLE 6-1 FIELD SALES SUMMARY INPUT

Division (major)	District	Salesperson (minor)	Sales amount
1	1	04	3000
1	1	04	1200
1	1	07	2000
1	1	07	1000
1	2	07	3500
1	2	09	2000
1	2	09	1300
2	1	01	2500
2	1	01	1000
2	1	05	1700
2	2	03	2000
2	2	03	1500
2	2	03	2000
2	2	09	3000

As we examine the contents of the control fields in the input file, we see that the major (L3) sort field (division) changes least frequently. The frequency of change increases as we move to lower-level control fields. Salesperson, the minor (L1) field, changes with the greatest frequency.

Output   The type of output that we are to provide to management is illustrated in Table 6-2. This is the output that results from processing the data in Table 6-1. If we look at the right side of the report, we see that each line contains from zero to four asterisks. The number of asterisks helps us to identify what each line records:

Number of asterisks	Type of line
0	Individual sale by a salesperson
1	Total sales for a salesperson
2	Total sales for a district
3	Total sales for a division
4	Total sales for the country

We have three subtotals (1 to 3 asterisks), and for each there will be a control field: salesperson, district, and division, respectively.

Further examination of Table 6-2 reveals that not every detail line (zero asterisks) contains all the division, district, and salesperson information for a sale. In fact, with the exception of the first line, where the values of all three control fields are printed, the value of a control field is printed only

TABLE 6-2   FIELD SALES SUMMARY DETAIL-PRINTED REPORT

DIVISION	DISTRICT	SALESPERSON	SALE AMOUNT	
1	1	04	3000	
			1200	
			4200	*
		07	2000	
			1000	
			3000	*
			7200	**
	2	07	3500	
			3500	*
		09	2000	
			1300	
			3300	*
			6800	**
			14000	***
2	1	01	2500	
			1000	
			3500	*
		05	1700	
			1700	*
			5200	**
	2	03	2000	
			1500	
			2000	
			5500	*
		09	3000	
			3000	*
			8500	**
			13700	***
			27700	****

when it changes. This technique is called *group indication*, a term that probably derives from the fact that we indicate (print) the value of a field used in grouping (sorting) our data only when the value changes. A report is group-indicated to eliminate the repetition of values that have not changed from one detail line to the next. This introduces white space into the report that makes the report easier to read.

Table 6-2 is titled "Field Sales Summary Detail-Printed Report." Table 6-3, also based on the data in Table 6-1, is titled "Field Sales Summary Group-Printed Report." What is the difference? The *detail-printed* report contains detail lines (one line for each input record), whereas the *group-printed* report does not. In the latter report, we group—or accumulate—all data for a salesperson before producing any output. If you refer back to the Purchase Summary problem in Chapter 5, you will note that there too we grouped data; customer purchases were accumulated prior to printing a single line for each customer.

Management has requested the detail-printed report, and we will use group indication to make the report easier for them to use. Later, we will identify what would have to be done differently to produce the group-printed report of Table 6-3.

To keep the logic from becoming any more complex than necessary, blank lines, which normally would be included in the report to make it easier to use, have not been included.

Structure Chart

Figure 6-1 contains a structure chart for this problem.

Module 100 not only does a priming read, it also handles certain initializing steps that are required after the first record has been read.

Module 200 calls certain modules we have encountered before: one to read a record (210), one to print a detail line (220), and one to handle the error message (260). In addition, there is a module for each of the subtotal lines that is to be printed (230, 240, and 250). Because of the many possible places in our processing at which it may be necessary to skip to a new page and write the heading line, a module (270) is introduced that is called for all output except the sequence error message. Module 270 calls module 280, which skips to a new page and prints a heading line if the current page has been filled; it also calls module 290, which handles the printing of the detail and total lines.

TABLE 6-3   FIELD SALES SUMMARY GROUP-PRINTED REPORT

DIVISION	DISTRICT	SALESPERSON	SALE AMOUNT	
1	1	04	4200	*
		07	3000	*
			7200	**
	2	07	3500	*
		09	3300	*
			6800	**
			14000	***
2	1	01	3500	*
		05	1700	*
			5200	**
	2	03	5500	*
		09	3000	*
			8500	**
			13700	***
			27700	****

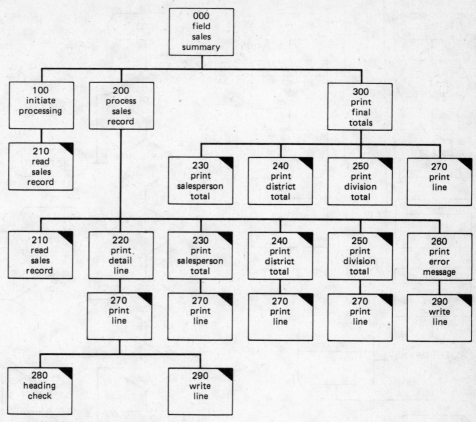

FIGURE 6-1 Field Sales Summary structure chart.

Program Flowchart

A flowchart for this problem is shown in Figure 6-2, but to understand it, we must first define the many field names used in the flowchart. This is done in Table 6-4.

Field Names Because of the large number of field names used in the flowchart, it is important that we devise some system that will enable us to readily recall what a particular name refers to. Examination of Table 6-4 reveals that certain two-letter combinations are used consistently:

DV for division
DS for district
SP for salesperson
AM for amount

TABLE 6-4 FIELD SALES SUMMARY FIELD NAME DEFINITIONS

Input fields	Output fields	Total fields	Checking fields
IDV Division number	ODV Division number	FT Final total	PDV Previous division
IDS District number	ODS District number	DVT Division total	PDS Previous district
ISP Salesperson number	OSP Salesperson number	DST District total	PSP Previous salesperson
IAM Sales amount	OAM Sales amount or total	SPT Salesperson total	
	AST Asterisk field		

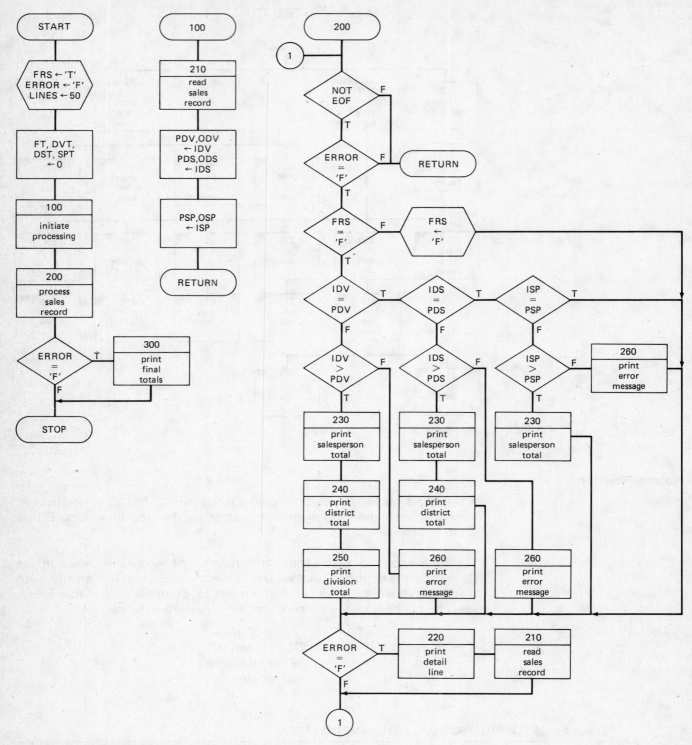

FIGURE 6-2 Field Sales Summary program flowchart.

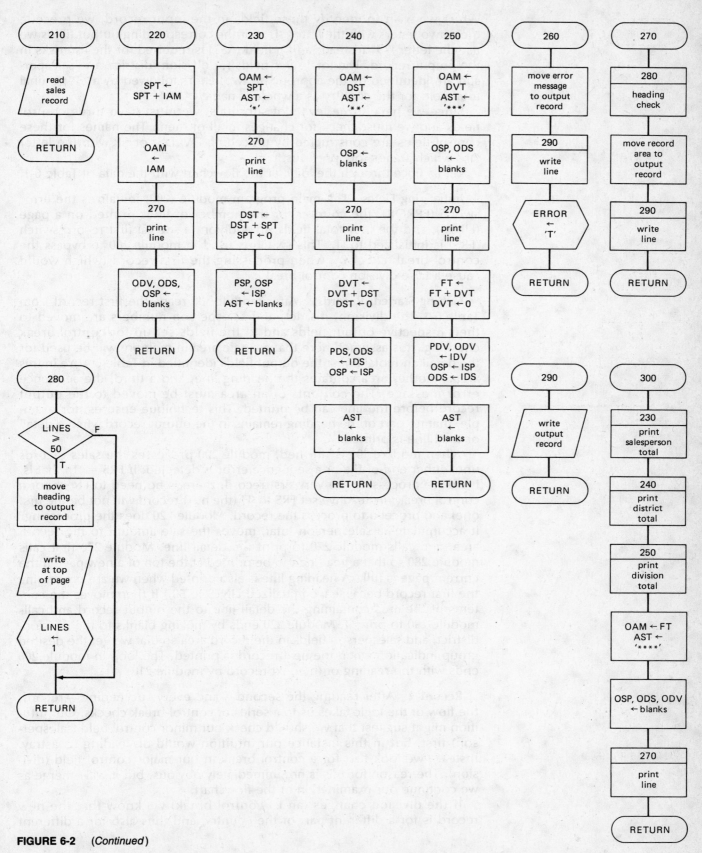

FIGURE 6-2 (Continued)

When we wish to identify these fields in the input record, we precede these two letters with the letter "I." For the corresponding output fields we use the letter "O" instead; a fifth field (AST) is required for the asterisks in the output record. The total sales fields for division, district, and salesperson are identified by the appropriate two letters followed by a "T"; a final total field for the country as a whole is named "FT."

Since we have three levels of subtotals, we must have three control fields and we must check for changes in all of them. The names for these control fields are constructed by preceding DV, DS, or SP with the letter "P," which stands for "previous."

Let us trace through the logic of the flowchart with the data of Table 6-1.

Initializing Fields The main program module (000) initializes the error switch (ERROR), the counter for the number of lines printed on a page (LINES), and the four total fields. In addition, a special first record switch (FRS) is initialized to 'T.' This switch is used in module 200 to bypass the control-break checking when processing the first record (which would cause a false division control break).

Getting Started: Record 1 After module 100 reads the first record from Table 6-1, the division, district, and salesperson numbers are moved to their respective output fields and to the fields set up for control-break checking. It is assumed here that a single area in memory will be used for the detail and total lines; the output fields identified in Table 6-4 are in this area. Another area contains the heading line, and a third, the sequence error message. The contents of an area must be moved to the output record before the line can be printed. This technique ensures, for example, that no part of the heading remains in the output record when a detail or total line is printed.

When module 100 is finished, module 200 processes the sales records until either end-of-file or a sequence error is detected. If FRS = 'T,' that is, if we are processing the very first record, there is no need to check for a control break; instead we set FRS to 'F' (the next record will not be the first one) and proceed to process the record. Module 220 does the processing: it accumulates a salesperson total, moves the sale amount to the record area, and calls module 270 to print the detail line. Module 270 first calls module 280 so that a heading can be printed at the top of a new page if the current page is full. (A heading line is also printed when we are processing the first record because we initialized LINES to 50.) It then moves the contents of the area containing the detail line to the output record and calls module 290 to print it. Module 220 ends by moving blanks to the division, district, and salesperson fields in the record area so that we get the desired group indication when the next record is printed. The loop in module 200 ends with the reading of the next record by module 210.

Record 2 After reading the second—and every succeeding—record, the flow of the logic takes us to a series of control-break checks. Our intuition might suggest that we should check our minor control field (salesperson) first, but in this instance our intuition would be leading us astray. Instead, we look first for a control break in our major control field (division). The reason for this is not immediately obvious, but it will emerge as we continue our examination of the flowchart.

If the division changes (an L3 control break) we know that the new record is for a different part of the country, and thus also for a different district and a different salesperson. Thus, L2 and L1 control breaks also occur when we have an L3 control break. When there is a change in division, we must start accumulating new division, district, and salesperson totals. Before we do this, we must write out the old salesperson, district, and division totals. We must print the total sold by the last salesperson in a district before we print the district total, and the total for the last district in a division before we print the division total. Modules 230, 240, and 250 are called in that order.

If the division is the same but the district (L2) has changed, we know that the salesperson has also changed. An L1 control break occurs when we have an L2 control break. When there is a change in district, we must print out the totals for the previous salesperson and district and then start to accumulate new ones.

If the division and the district are the same but the salesperson (L1) changes, we must print out the previous salesperson's total and begin to accumulate a new one.

Given that these are the activities that must take place at each type of control break, it makes sense to check for a division control break first, for if such a break occurs, we know immediately all the processing that must take place. If we check for a salesperson break first and find that one has occurred, we still have no idea whether a higher-level control break has also occurred. We would have to check for each of the other breaks to get the complete picture. We could even be misled if we checked for a salesperson break first. Look at the fourth and fifth records in Table 6-1. The salesperson numbers are the same, so can we assume that no control break has occurred? If we look closer, we will see that there has in fact been a district break, and when there is a district break there is also a salesperson break. The salesperson number is the same, but since the district is different, we have a new salesperson. We must accumulate a new total for this salesperson. By starting with the major field when checking for control breaks and working down to the minor field, as soon as a break is detected, the programmer knows that all lower-level control fields also have breaks. However, if the programmer starts with the minor field, the complete picture does not emerge until all control fields up to and including the major have been checked.

Before we digressed to discuss the proper order in which to check for control breaks, we were preparing to process the second record in Table 6-1. When the input division (IDV) and the previous division (PDV) are compared, they are found to be equal, so the flow takes us to a comparison of the input district (IDS) and the previous district (PDS). These also are the same, so we look for a salesperson control break. Since there is no salesperson control break either, we call module 200 to process the record. When the detail line for the second record is printed, it contains only the amount field because the division, district, and salesperson fields were blanked out after printing the detail line for the first record. Blanks are again moved into these fields in the record area in order to blank out any fields that may have been nonblank because of a control break. In this case this is an unnecessary operation, but it is faster just to move these blanks than to try to determine if the blanks actually need to be moved.

Record 3 Again the loop in module 200 ends with the reading of another record. As we work our way down through the control-break checks for the third record, we find that the salesperson number has changed; we have an L1 control break. We therefore print out a salesperson total by calling module 230. This module moves the salesperson total and an asterisk to the record area and calls module 270 to print the record. Then the salesperson total is added to the district total, and the salesperson total is set to zero so that a total for the new salesperson can be accumulated. The new salesperson number is moved to the previous salesperson field in preparation for control-break checking and to the output salesperson field so that the new number will print on the next detail line. Finally, the asterisk in the asterisk field is blanked out.

Having completed the control-break processing, the record causing the control break is now processed by module 220. We start to accumulate a sales total for the new salesperson. A detail line — including the new salesperson number but no asterisk — is then printed. Blanks are then moved to the division, district, and salesperson fields; as a result, the new salesperson number will not print in the next detail line. Again the loop ends with the reading of another record.

Record 4   The fourth record contains another sale for the same salesperson, so it is processed by module 220 and a detail line containing only a sales amount is printed.

Record 5   The fifth record in Table 6-1 causes a district break. And, of course, the district break also results in a salesperson break. We first call module 230 to print the total for the last salesperson in the district. Then module 240 is called to print the district total. In module 240, the district total (DST) is moved into the output amount field, and two asterisks are moved to the asterisk field. Because the processing of the salesperson control break ended with the movement of the new salesperson number into the record area, it must be blanked out before the district total is printed.

After the district total is printed, it is added to the division total and then set back to zero so that a new district total can be developed. The new district number must be moved to the previous district number field so that control-break checking can be performed. It must also be moved to the record area so that it will be group-indicated on the next detail line. We must also put the new salesperson number back into the record area, so that it too will print on the next detail line. Finally, the asterisks in the asterisk field are blanked out. This completes the district control-break processing, so the record causing the control break can now be processed by module 220.

When the detail line is printed, it contains the new district and salesperson numbers, but these are blanked out right after the line is printed.

Record 6   The sixth record causes a salesperson control break, so the processing is the same as for the third record. A salesperson total is printed. The next detail line contains the new salesperson number, which is blanked out after the line is printed.

Record 7   The seventh record causes no control breaks and is processed as the second and fourth ones were.

Record 8   Record 8 causes a division break, and therefore also district and salesperson breaks. The salesperson-break processing is performed first, followed by the district-break processing, as we observed with record 5. After the salesperson and district total lines are printed, the division-break processing is performed. The division total and three asterisks are moved to the output record. Before printing the division total, the new salesperson and district numbers must be blanked out in the record area. After the division total is printed, it is added to the final total and set back to zero. The new division number is moved to the previous division field and to the division field in the output record. The new salesperson and district numbers are moved back into the output record. Finally, the asterisks in the asterisk field are blanked out. Then the record causing the division control break is processed.

When the detail line for this record is printed, it contains new division, district, and salesperson numbers. These are blanked out before the next record is read.

End-of-File   The processing continues in this way until we run out of data. The output created up to the time end-of-file is detected stops with the detail line for the last record in the file. At EOF we must complete our report by printing:

- Total for the last salesperson
- Total for the last district
- Total for the last division
- Final total

In a multilevel control-break problem, EOF is regarded as the highest-level control break, and thus all other control breaks are assumed to have occurred also. Under the control of module 300, modules 230, 240, and 250 are called to print the first three totals. Then the final total and four asterisks are moved to the record area. The division, district, and salesperson numbers (which were moved into this area by module 250) are blanked out, and the final total is printed.

Sequence Errors   We have so far ignored the logic that handles a sequence error. There are three ways that a sequence error can occur during the control-break checking that takes place:

1 If the new division (IDV) is less than the previous division (PDV)

2 If IDV equals PDV, but the new district (IDS) is less than the previous district (PDS)

3 If IDV equals PDV, and IDS equals PDS, but the new salesperson (ISP) is less than the previous salesperson (PSP)

Note that it is not a sequence error for a new control-field value to be less than the previous value for that control field if a higher-level control break has occurred. In fact, this is what we would expect to see. Verify this by referring to Table 6-1 again.

Decision Table for Module 200

The logic of module 200 is difficult to grasp because it is so complex. Decision tables are intended for situations like this. Table 6-5 presents the logic of module 200 in a concise form. It also illustrates two additional features of decision tables: *call* and *go-to* actions. As in subroutines and modules, the call action represents a temporary transfer of control to another module (or decision table, in this case). When the called decision table has

TABLE 6-5 DECISION TABLE FOR MODULE 200

Module 200	1	2	3	4	5	6	7	8	9	10
EOF	F	F	F	F	F	F	F	F	F	T
ERROR	F	F	F	F	F	F	F	F	T	
FRS	T	F	F	F	F	F	F	F		
IDV : PDV		=	=	=	=	=	>	<		
IDS : PDS			=	=	=	>	<			
ISP : PSP			=	>	<					
FRS ← 'F'	X									
call module 230			X		X		X			
call module 240					X		X			
call module 250							X			
call module 260				X		X		X		
ERROR ← 'T'				X		X		X		
call module 220	X	X	X		X		X			
call module 210	X	X	X		X		X			
go to module 200	X	X	X	X	X	X	X	X		
return									X	X

completed its processing, control returns to the next indicated action following the call. The go-to action is a permanent transfer of control, and we have made an effort to avoid using it. It is required here, however, to accomplish the looping that takes place in module 200. It does this by transferring control back to the start of the very same decision table in which it is used.

Pseudocode

Figure 6-3 contains the pseudocode for this problem. It is derived from the structure chart of Figure 6-1 and the program flowchart of Figure 6-2. Note in module 200 how the checking for the salesperson control break and a

FIGURE 6-3 Field Sales Summary pseudocode.

```
000-field-sales-summary
set first record switch to 'T'
set error to 'F'
move 50 to line counter
move zero to final total, division total, district
    total, and salesperson total
call 100-initiate-processing
call 200-process-sales-record
IF error = 'F' THEN
        call 300-print-final-totals
ELSE
    (null)
END IF
stop
```

```
100-initiate-processing
call 210-read-sales-record
move division number from input record to output
    division and to previous division
move district number from input record to output
    district and to previous district
move salesperson number from input record to output
    salesperson and to previous salesperson
return

200-process-sales-record
DO WHILE not EOF and (error = 'F')
    IF first record switch = 'F' THEN
        IF input division = previous division THEN
            IF input district = previous district THEN
                IF input salesperson >
                                    previous salesperson THEN
                    call 230-print-salesperson-total
                ELSE
                    IF input salesperson <
                                    previous salesperson THEN
                        call 260-print-error-message
                    ELSE
                        (null)
                    END IF
                END IF
            ELSE
                IF input district > previous district THEN
                    call 230-print-salesperson-total
                    call 240-print-district-total
                ELSE
                    call 260-print-error-message
                END IF
            END IF
        ELSE
            IF input division > previous division THEN
                call 230-print-salesperson-total
                call 240-print-district-total
                call 250-print-division-total
            ELSE
                call 260-print-error-message
            END IF
        END IF
    ELSE
        set first record switch to 'F'
    END IF
    IF error = 'F' THEN
        call 220-print-detail-line
        call 210-read-sales-record
    ELSE
        (null)
    END IF
END DO
return

210-read-sales-record
read sales record
return

220-print-detail-line
add input sales amount to salesperson total
move input sales amount to output sales amount
call 270-print-line
move blanks to output division, district, and
    salesperson
return

230-print-salesperson-total
move salesperson total to output sales amount
move '*' to asterisk field
```

FIGURE 6-3 *(Continued)*

```
call 270-print-line
add salesperson total to district total
move zeros to salesperson total
move new salesperson number to output salesperson
    and to previous salesperson
move blanks to asterisk field
return


240-print-district-total
move district total to output sales amount
move '**' to asterisk field
move blanks to output salesperson
call 270-print-line
add district total to division total
move zeros to district total
move new district number to output district
    and to previous district
move new salesperson number to output salesperson
move blanks to asterisk field
return


250-print-division-total
move division total to output sales amount
move '***' to asterisk field
move blanks to output salesperson and output
    district
call 270-print-line
add division total to final total
move zeros to division total
move new division number to output division
    and to previous division
move new salesperson number to output salesperson
move new district number to output district
move blanks to asterisk field
return


260-print-error-message
move sequence error message to output record
call 290-write-line
set error to 'T'
return


270-print-line
call 280-heading-check
move record area to output record
call 290-write-line
return


280-heading-check
IF line counter > 50 THEN
    moving heading to output record
    write output record at top of page
    move 1 to line counter
ELSE
    (null)
END IF
return


290-write-line
write output record
return


300-print-final-totals
call 230-print-salesperson-total
call 240-print-district-total
call 250-print-division-total
move final total to output sales amount
move '****' to asterisk field
move blanks to output salesperson, output district,
    and output division
call 270-print-line
return
```

FIGURE 6-3   (*Continued*)

salesperson sequence error have been altered from the logic of Figure 6-2. For the division and district we test the most likely condition (=) first. This cannot be done with the salesperson because when the new salesperson number is the same as the previous one, no total or error message is printed. The pseudocode logic forces this null alternative into the last ELSE for the salesperson checking. If the equal condition is handled in any other way, we have a null THEN, and this is not acceptable in our pseudocode.

Nassi-Shneiderman Flowchart of Module 200

As has been noted in earlier chapters, the pseudocode and N-S flowchart for a problem are very similar. There is something to be learned from examining the N-S flowchart of module 200 in Figure 6-4, however. It is fortunate that the rectangle used in N-S flowcharts to represent modules can be of any size and shape, for this module requires a very broad rectangle indeed. Even so, there is not enough room for the full module names, so only the module numbers are used. Deeply nested IFs present problems in N-S flowcharts, but, on the other hand, the structure of the nesting is revealed more clearly than in pseudocode.

Alternative Handling of Output

The flowchart in Figure 6-2 is based on the use of a single record area for the detail and total lines. If storage is not at a premium, the programmer can simplify the coding and speed up execution by defining multiple record areas. Two options are available:

1 Use two record areas, one for the detail line and one for the total lines.

2 Use one record area for the detail line and a separate one for each total line; in this case that would be five record areas.

Both these options eliminate the necessity for blanking out and moving in control fields in modules 230, 240, and 250. The second option also eliminates the moving in and blanking out of asterisks for the total lines and allows the various totals to be accumulated in the respective total record areas.

The use of multiple areas necessitates some other changes, however. The various record areas must be moved to the output record prior to

FIGURE 6-4   N-S flowchart of module 200.

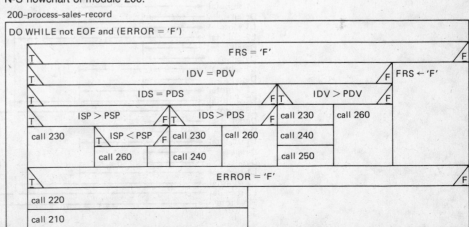

calling a module that simply prints the contents of the output record. (Modules 270 and 290 are replaced by a single module that prints the output record.) Before the contents of a record area are moved, the heading check must be performed because the output record is also used for the heading line.

Accumulating and Printing Totals

Figure 6-5 summarizes the technique for accumulating and printing three levels of subtotals. This technique can be readily extended to any number of levels. The time at which a total is accumulated is related to the time at which a particular type of line is printed. The final total is the result of accumulating the highest-level (L3) subtotals whenever an L3 subtotal is printed. The L3 subtotals are the result of accumulating the next-lower-level (L2) subtotals whenever an L2 subtotal is printed. The L2 subtotals are accumulated from the L1 subtotals whenever an L1 subtotal is printed, and the L1 subtotals are accumulated when detail lines are printed (or—in the case of a group-printed report—when detail records are processed). All subtotals except the lowest-level (L1) subtotals are accumulated from the next-lower-level subtotals because this is more efficient than accumulating them from the detail records. (In Chapter 5, the L1 subtotals were accumulated from the detail records also, and—since we had only one level of subtotal—the final total was accumulated from the L1 subtotals.)

A different field will control the calculation and printing of each level of subtotal. Thus, we accumulate an L1 subtotal while the contents of the L1 control field remain unchanged. When there is a change (an L1 control break), the L1 subtotal is printed, added to the L2 subtotal, and then set back to zero. An L2 subtotal is accumulated from L1 subtotals until the contents of the L2 control field changes (an L2 control break). When there is an L2 control break, the L2 subtotal is printed, added to the L3 subtotal, and reset to zero. The final total, in turn, is accumulated when there is a control break at the highest level (L3 in this case).

FIGURE 6-5   Accumulating and printing totals.

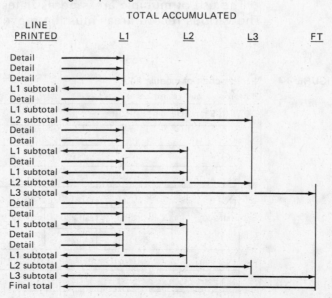

Group-Printed Field Sales Summary Report

If a company has a large field sales organization, management may decide that there is too much detail in a detail-printed report such as Table 6-2. Instead of getting information about every sale a salesperson made, management might prefer only the salesperson, district, division, and final totals, as illustrated by Table 6-3. What would we have to change in Figures 6-2 and 6-3 to produce this group-printed report? It turns out that very little has to be changed:

- Module 220 is reduced to merely accumulating the salesperson total.
- At the end of module 230, blanks are moved to the output division and district to get the desired group indication.
- The asterisk field is not set to blanks in modules 230, 240, and 250.

It is left to the student to verify that these changes will in fact produce the output of Table 6-3.

HIPO CHARTS

Preparing a *HIPO chart* (hierarchical input-process-output chart) is another way to document structured programs. HIPO charts combine structure-chart and pseudocode techniques, adding some elements to describe in more detail what happens in each module. (You may recall from Chapter 2 that a structure chart is sometimes referred to as a hierarchy (hierarchical) chart. The structure chart we have learned to prepare is the first component of HIPO.)

A page (an IPO chart) is prepared for each module. It shows what data is used by the module (what is input to the module), the processing steps performed by the module (represented in pseudocode), and the fields changed or records written by the module (what is output).

There is no standard for HIPO, so there is much variation in what is deemed essential for a HIPO chart. What is presented here is a modest subset of what is possible. This version of HIPO is quite simple, yet it demonstrates the advantages (and disadvantages) of the technique.

Preparing a HIPO Chart

The first step in preparing a HIPO chart is to develop a structure chart. Since we are experienced in this area, no further comment is needed. The structure chart becomes a cover page for the rest of the documentation.

The remaining components are recorded in a form like the one in Figure 6-6. IPO forms and templates are available for their preparation. The pseudocode is prepared next and entered in the middle part of the form. We also are experienced in preparation of pseudocode, so what remains for us to examine is the definition of the input and output components, along with two minor enhancements.

From the pseudocode it is possible to determine what items of data must be available to the module. Fields used by a module and records read by it are identified in the input section. Any field that can be altered by the module, or any output record created, is identified in the output section.

This is the minimum found in a HIPO chart, but two additional elements make the chart even more useful. Between the input and process sections we can record the numbers of any module that can call the module being documented, and between the process and output sections we can record the numbers of any modules called by this module.

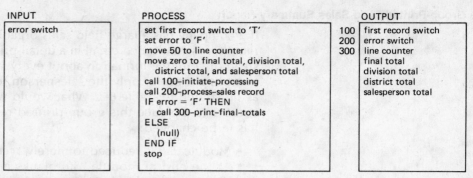

INPUT	PROCESS		OUTPUT

error switch	set first record switch to 'T'
	set error to 'F'
	move 50 to line counter
	move zero to final total, division total,
	   district total, and salesperson total
	call 100-initiate-processing
	call 200-process-sales record
	IF error = 'F' THEN
	   call 300-print-final-totals
	ELSE
	   (null)
	END IF
	stop
		100
		200
		300
			first record switch
			error switch
			line counter
			final total
			division total
			district total
			salesperson total

FIGURE 6-6   IPO diagram for module "000 field sales summary."

Figure 6-6 contains a chart for the main program module (000) of the Field Sales Summary problem. The pseudocode comes directly from Figure 6-3. This module checks the error switch (ERROR), so it is included in the input section. This module also initializes a number of fields: first record switch, error switch, line counter, final total, division total, district total, and salesperson total. These fields are all listed as output of module 000. Module 000 calls modules 100, 200, and 300, so they are listed between the process and output sections. Since this is the main program module, it is called by no other module and so there is no entry between the input and process sections.

Figure 6-7 shows the IPO chart for module 100, and Figure 6-8, for module 200. Note in particular the entries in the input and output sections, as well as the module numbers between the input and process sections and between the process and output sections. Verify that these are correct. To complete the HIPO documentation of the program, we would have to prepare similar charts for each module.

Advantages and Disadvantages of HIPO

There is more work involved in preparing a HIPO chart than in preparing the other forms of documentation we have been using. Such charts, however, provide more information. For one thing, the input and output for each module are clearly identified. We can also determine very easily what modules call the module being examined.

The main disadvantage of HIPO is that the documentation for a program gets to be rather bulky: there is a page for each module regardless of the actual size of the module.

FIGURE 6-7   IPO diagram for module "100 initiate processing."

INPUT		PROCESS		OUTPUT
input division input district input salesperson	000	call 210-read-sales-record move division number from input record to output division and to previous division move district number from input record to output district and to previous district move salesperson number from input record to output salesperson and to previous salesperson return	210	output division previous division output district previous district output salesperson previous salesperson

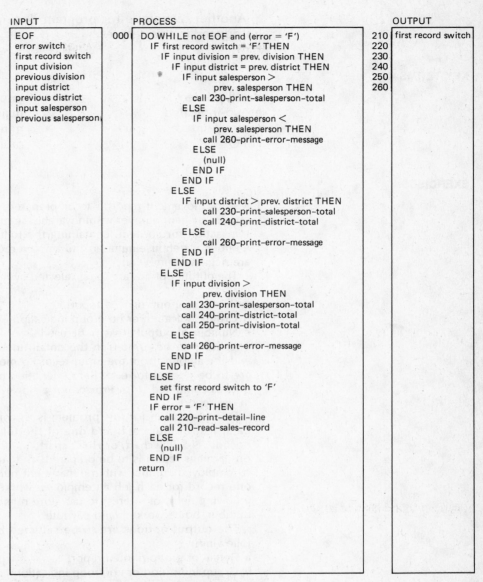

INPUT	PROCESS	OUTPUT

EOF
error switch
first record switch
input division
previous division
input district
previous district
input salesperson
previous salesperson
	000 DO WHILE not EOF and (error = 'F')
	   IF first record switch = 'F' THEN
	     IF input division = prev. division THEN
	       IF input district = prev. district THEN
	        IF input salesperson >
	           prev. salesperson THEN
	          call 230–print-salesperson-total
	        ELSE
	         IF input salesperson <
	           prev. salesperson THEN
	          call 260–print-error-message
	         ELSE
	          (null)
	        END IF
	       END IF
	      ELSE
	       IF input district > prev. district THEN
	        call 230–print-salesperson-total
	        call 240–print-district-total
	       ELSE
	        call 260–print-error-message
	       END IF
	      END IF
	     ELSE
	      IF input division >
	        prev. division THEN
	       call 230–print-salesperson-total
	       call 240–print-district-total
	       call 250–print-division-total
	      ELSE
	       call 260–print-error-message
	      END IF
	     END IF
	    ELSE
	     set first record switch to 'F'
	    END IF
	    IF error = 'F' THEN
	     call 220–print-detail-line
	     call 210–read-sales-record
	    ELSE
	     (null)
	    END IF
	  return
		210 first record switch
		220
		230
		240
		250
		260

FIGURE 6-8   IPO diagram for module "200 process sales record."

HIPO charts are not as widely used as structure charts and pseudocode, but they are a required form of documentation in some computer installations.

SUMMARY

We now are able to include any number of subtotals in a report. Implementing multilevel control breaks requires much more complex programming logic than we have dealt with before, but there is a pattern to this logic which makes it relatively easy to design a program to handle any number of levels.

We learned how to make reports easier to read by using group indication and how to reduce the size and complexity of a report by group-printing it.

Another technique for program documentation, the HIPO chart, was introduced in this chapter.

detail-printed	intermediate control field
group-indicated	major control field
group-printed	minor control field
HIPO	multilevel control break

1 A stock movement report is to be prepared. The input consists of records in sequence by item number within warehouse number. There is one record for each transaction for an item, containing the following fields of interest to us: item number, warehouse number, and amount received or disbursed. (Disbursements are negative numbers.)

The output options are to be selected by the instructor from among the following:

a Detail- or group-printed report

b Group indication or no group indication

c Number of output areas to be used

The fields to be printed in the detail line are warehouse and item numbers and the amount from the input record. Amount totals (showing net movement) are to be printed for each item (identified by *), warehouse (**), and all warehouses combined (***). Provide for a single heading line, but ignore blank lines in the report.

Documentation for this problem is to consist of: structure chart, test input data, test output data, and one of the following: program flowchart, pseudocode, N-S flowchart, or HIPO chart.

2 An earnings report is to be prepared. The input consists of records in sequence by employee number within department number within store number. There is one record for each job an employee worked during the week, containing the following fields of interest to us: store number, department number, employee number, hours worked, and pay rate.

The output options are to be selected by the instructor from among the following:

a Detail- or group-printed report

b Group indication or no group indication

c Number of output areas to be used

The fields to be printed include the store, department, and employee numbers; if the report is detail-printed, hours, rate, and earnings (where earnings = rate × hours) are to be printed for each job. Totals of hours and earnings are to be printed for each employee (identified by *), department (**), store (***), and all stores combined (****). Provide for a single heading line, but ignore blank lines in the report.

Documentation for this problem is to consist of structure chart, test input data, test output data, and one of the following: program flowchart, pseudocode, N-S flowchart, or HIPO chart.

3 A report that shows the total number of students by geographic area is to be produced. The input consists of records in sequence by zip code within county within state. There is one record for each student enrolled, containing the following fields of interest to us: student number, county code, state code, and zip code.

The output options are to be selected by the instructor from among the following:

a Group indication or no group indication
b Number of output areas to be used
The fields to be printed are zip code, county, and state numbers, and the number of students in the geographic area. The totals will be identified as follows: zip code, no asterisks; county, (*); state, (**); and country, (***). Provide for a single heading line, but ignore blank lines in the report.

Documentation for this problem is to consist of: structure chart, test input data, test output data, and one of the following: program flowchart, pseudocode, N-S flowchart, or HIPO chart.

CHAPTER 7

TABLES

OBJECTIVES

Upon completing this chapter the student should be able to:

1 Flowchart and code the loading and searching of discrete and segmented tables that are fixed or variable in size.

2 Choose the order for an argument table that will make searching most efficient.

3 Discuss the pros and cons of (a) declaring tables and using table files, and (b) sequential and binary searches.

4 Describe circumstances and techniques for using direct table addressing.

5 Use a table to accumulate the results of processing.

6 Load, search, and reference a two-dimensional table.

7 Define and use the key terms at the end of the chapter.

INTRODUCTION

The *table* (known as an *array* in some languages) is one of the most powerful programming tools available. It provides the programmer with a way to organize a collection of homogeneous data items that facilitates processing. Data items are considered to be homogeneous when they are the same type (for example, numerics, alphabetics, records) and the same length. Tables can be used to hold information that is required in processing and also to store the results of processing.

In this chapter, we will develop a vocabulary for working with tables. We will examine techniques for creating tables in the computer's memory and for retrieving information from a table and we will learn how a table can be used to store the results of processing.

TERMINOLOGY

Before proceeding further, let us look at some terms that are used to describe tables.

Single and Paired Tables

Table 7-1 illustrates the difference between single and paired tables. The *single table* of Table 7-1a provides us with a list of salesperson numbers. This table can be used in the editing of salesperson numbers in input records to verify that they are valid. We place in the table all valid salesperson numbers, and then as each transaction record is read, we check its salesperson number against the table. Any number that cannot be found in the table is flagged as an error.

Two tables with the same number of elements (though not necessarily the same type of elements) and some logical relationship are called *paired tables*. Most tables used in business applications are paired. For example,

TABLE 7-1   SINGLE AND PAIRED TABLES

(a) Single	(b) Paired	
Salesperson number	Salesperson number	Salesperson name
03	03	D Dingbat
05	05	P Perhaps
06	06	A Axlegrease
09	09	F Farout
14	14	M Maybe
16	16	B Boo
21	21	G Glutz
22	22	Q Quicksand
29	29	N Numbskull
33	33	I Iconoclast

the salesperson number table can be paired with another table, as in Figure 7-1b, to enable us to find the name corresponding to each salesperson number. When we determine where in the number table a salesperson number appears, we can retrieve the name from the corresponding position in the name table. In this way, a report of sales by a salesperson can include both the names and the numbers of the salespeople. Of course, instead of using a table to get a salesperson's name we could put it in the transaction record, but this would require extra keying and additional space in the record. Use of a paired table allows us to put just the salesperson number in the record. It should be noted that the number table of the pair can also be used by itself (that is, as a single table) to edit the salesperson number field in a transaction record.

Argument and Function Tables

Table 7-2 contains two additional examples of paired tables. The table of Table 7-2a could very well have been used in the Gross Pay problems we looked at in previous chapters. Instead of having the pay rate in the input record, we could have a job code. We would have to locate this job code

TABLE 7-2   ADDITIONAL PAIRED TABLES

(a)		(b)	
Job code	Pay rate	Argument	Function
2	8.25	1	January
3	6.37	2	February
5	5.95	3	March
7	7.75	4	April
10	6.37	5	May
13	9.40	6	June
14	7.10	7	July
15	6.80	8	August
17	8.62	9	September
		10	October
		11	November
		12	December

in the first table and then use the pay rate from the corresponding position in the second table to calculate the gross pay. You might wonder why anyone would want to go to all this trouble; it would seem to be much easier just to put the pay rate in the record. The table affords some conveniences that make the extra effort worthwhile. For one thing, it eliminates the possibility that an incorrect pay rate might be entered. Also, when pay rates need to be revised, the changes can be made quickly and uniformly simply by replacing the table.

The job code table of Table 7-2a is referred to as the *argument table*, and the pay rate table as the *function table*. As in mathematical functions, for every argument (job number) there will be one function (pay rate). We say that the pay rate is a function of the job code argument. The job number that we look for in the argument table is called the *search argument*. We perform a *table search*, starting with the first argument entry and looking for a matching entry in the argument table so that we may retrieve the desired function value.

Table 7-2b further illustrates these concepts. Months are usually identified by number rather than by name because the number is shorter. However, in some cases it may be desirable to use the name of a month in a report. Given the number of a month, we can easily retrieve the corresponding name from the function table. There actually is no need for an argument table in this case, for the month number tells us which month name we want. Accessing a function table directly without first searching an argument table is known as *direct table addressing*. With this technique we can have a function table with no corresponding argument table.

The single table of Figure 7-1a, on the other hand, is an argument table; it has no corresponding function table.

Discrete and Segmented Argument Tables

An argument table is either discrete or segmented. The tables we have looked at so far have all been examples of *discrete tables*. In all these cases, we looked for a particular value in the argument table that *equaled the search argument*. Table 7-3a is another example of a discrete table. The discount rate to be applied to a purchase is a function of the quantity purchased. For each quantity (up to a maximum of 99), there is a discount rate that can be applied; but note that more than one quantity can have the same discount rate. For example, whether the quantity is 6, 7, 8, 9, or 10, the discount rate is 5 percent.

We can segment the argument table so that each discount rate appears in the function table only once, as in Table 7-3b. Now we have a *segmented argument table* consisting of a series of ranges for each of which there is a corresponding function value.

The form of the segmented argument table shown in Table 7-3b contains more information than is needed to determine the appropriate discount rate. All we really need is the upper limit of each segment, as in Table 7-3c. To find the appropriate discount rate, we look for the first table argument that is *greater than or equal to the search argument*. With a search argument of 12, we search the argument table until we get to the fourth line, where 15 > 12. We then retrieve the fourth discount rate from the function table for use in our processing. The lower limit for a segment is assumed to be 1 greater than the upper limit of the preceding entry, except for the first entry, where the lower limit is assumed to be 1. Thus, the implied

TABLE 7-3   DEVELOPMENT OF SEGMENTED TABLE

Quantity purchased	Discount rate, %
(a) Discrete	
1	0
2	0
3	3
4	3
5	3
6	5
7	5
8	5
9	5
10	5
11	8
12	8
13	8
14	8
15	8
16	12
17	12
18	12
19	12
20	12
21	15
22	15
.	.
.	.
.	.
99	15
(b) Segmented	
1–2	0
3–5	3
6–10	5
11–15	8
16–20	12
21–99	15
(c) Segmented for computer	
2	0
5	3
10	5
15	8
20	12
99	15

lower limit for the third entry is 6, one more than the previous argument entry (5).

ORDER OF TABLE ARGUMENTS

The way we search the argument table is affected by how its entries are ordered. If we look back at the argument tables we have examined so far, we note that they are all in ascending order. Argument tables may also be in descending order, or—in the case of discrete tables—in neither ascending nor descending order.

Ascending Order

Argument tables are usually in ascending order simply because people are used to working with information organized in this way.

Discrete   If we think about the process of searching a discrete argument table when the search argument value is not in the table, we realize that there is an advantage to having the table in ascending order: We do not have to search the entire table. When we find a table argument that is *greater than* the search argument, we know that there is no match and we can stop the search.

There is no advantage to having the table in ascending order if there is a match between the search argument and a table argument. On the average, assuming that all table arguments are equally likely to be used, we will have to examine half of the entries before we find the one that matches.

Segmented   We have already examined the process for searching a segmented argument table in ascending order. This search ends when we find a table argument greater than or equal to the search argument. There is normally no problem with missing table arguments. If the data has not been edited, however, and if it is possible that a search argument may be less than the implied lower limit for the table (1 in the case of Table 7-3c), or greater than the upper limit, then the search argument should be compared with these limits before the table is searched.

Descending Order

There may be situations in which we would like to have the argument table entries in descending order. For example, if the larger entries are the ones searched for more often, we can shorten the searching time by arranging entries in descending order.

Discrete   In the case of a discrete argument table, we know that we are not going to find a match when we encounter a table argument that is *less than* our search argument. The table search is halted at that point. If all table entries are equally likely to be sought, we will have to examine half of the entries before we find the one that matches.

Segmented   A segmented argument table in descending order consists of entries that are the lower limits of the segments. The discount rate table of Table 7-3b could be set up as the descending argument table of Table 7-4. The search ends when a table entry is found that is *less than or equal to* the search argument. If most purchases are of more than 10 items, this is a logical way to set up the table.

TABLE 7-4   DESCENDING SEGMENTED TABLE

Quantity	Rate, %
21	15
16	12
11	8
6	5
3	3
1	0

When the segmented argument table is in descending order, the entries consist of lower limits and the implied upper limit for each segment is just one less than the previous entry. Thus, the implied upper limit for the third entry is 15, one less than 16. It appears that the first entry has no upper limit, but a limit is in fact imposed by the size of the argument field. Since the argument is a two-digit number, the implied upper limit for the first entry is 99. If this implied upper limit is unacceptable, the search argument will have to be compared to the acceptable upper limit before the table is searched. If it is possible for the search argument to be less than the last entry, the search argument should be compared with this limit before searching the table.

Neither Ascending nor Descending

It is possible for a discrete argument table to be set up in neither ascending nor descending order, but an unordered segmented table is impractical.

Discrete   If a discrete argument table is in no particular order, we will have to search the entire table before we know that there is no table argument to match our search argument. This is a disadvantage of using unordered argument tables as compared with tables that are in ascending or descending order. If there is a table argument that matches the search argument and if all table arguments are used with the same frequency, we will have to search half the argument entries, on average, before we find the match. Thus, when search arguments are known to be valid and all table arguments are sought equally, it makes no difference whether the table is in order or not.

We sometimes know that certain entries in a table are used much more frequently than others. There is an *80-20 rule* which—if applicable—says that 80 percent of our searches will be satisfied by 20 percent of our table arguments. If we put the table in order by probability that an entry will be referenced, with the highest probabilities first and the lowest last, we can reduce the time required for a search when there is a match. On the average, we have to search less than 20 percent of the table. In those cases in which the search argument is invalid, we have to search the entire argument table before we can be certain that there is no match. If the 80-20 rule is indeed applicable and if there is little or no chance of an invalid search argument, then ordering the argument table by probability that an entry will be used will significantly reduce the time needed to search the table.

Segmented   In searching the segmented table of Table 7-3c, we look for the first quantity that is greater than or equal to our search argument. Our search argument will only occasionally actually equal this quantity. Because the search argument so seldom equals the table argument, searching a segmented argument table that is not in order is a very involved process. Consider the unordered argument table shown in Table 7-5. How do we search this table with a search argument of 12? If we stop at the first entry that is greater than or equal to 12, we will stop at the second entry (20), but the one we really want is the sixth entry. The only way we can search this table and find the right argument is to search the entire table, keeping track of the position in the table—and the value—of the argument closest to, and greater than or equal to, the search argument. This is a very ineffi-

TABLE 7-5   UNORDERED SEGMENTED TABLE

10	5
20	12
5	3
2	0
99	15
15	8

cient searching procedure. The only practical way to search a segmented argument table is to have it in either ascending or descending order.

Postscript

If an argument table is supposed to be ordered, it may be necessary to include a sequence check when the table is being loaded into the computer's memory. We know how to do sequence checks when the order is supposed to be ascending, but how do we verify that the order of an argument table is descending?

If a table is changed with almost every use, the sequence checking can be built into the program using the table. Otherwise, it is probably more efficient to run a special program just to check the sequence of the argument table whenever it is changed.

TABLES IN MEMORY

A table must be placed in the computer's memory before we can retrieve information from it. We will look at two ways to get the table data into memory, but first let us settle on a way to refer to individual table entries.

Referencing Table Entries

To refer to an entry in a table, we must specify the name of the table and we must indicate the specific entry in some way. An individual table entry is specified by an *index* (or *subscript*) enclosed in parentheses following the table name. For example, to refer to the third entry in Table 7-2*b*, we write

month name (3)

We can refer to the *n*th month name (where n has a value between 1 and 12) by writing

month name (n)

Getting the Tables into Memory

Table data may be defined as constants within a program or read from a file.

Defining Table Data as Constants   The data in Table 7-2*b* could be defined as constants in a program because the data in this table will never change. We could code 12 instructions to store the names:

```
move 'January   ' to month name (1)
move 'February  ' to month name (2)
                •
                •
                •
move 'December  ' to month name (12)
```

Notice that blanks have been added to the month names to make them all nine characters long, the length of the longest month name. All table entries must be the same size. Alphabetic entries are left-justified and padded with blanks on the right as necessary; numeric entries are right-justified and padded on the left with zeros.

How we actually define constant table entries varies greatly depending on the programming language being used. The process is relatively easy in COBOL, RPG, FORTRAN, and assembler, and somewhat tedious in BASIC and Pascal.

Reading a Table from a File   Defining table values as constants in a program is not recommended if the table contents change frequently. For example, the discount rates in Table 7-3c are likely to change over time, particularly when the company runs special sales promotions. If the tables are defined as constants in the program, the program has to be changed every time the rates change. Whenever we change a program, there is a risk that we will inadvertently introduce errors, and so the program must be retested before it can be used with confidence.

For a table that is subject to change it is better to read data from a file. In this way the *table file* can be changed without affecting the integrity of the program. The table is loaded into the computer's memory as the first step in the execution of the program.

Most tables from which we wish to retrieve information are subject to change and therefore are read into memory from a file.

Organizing the Table File

Paired tables are usually placed in a table file with a single argument and its corresponding function in a record. This organization makes it easy to change the file. For example, it can be expected that the pay rates in Table 7-2a will change periodically. We are more likely to make a pay rate change to the right job number if both items are in the same record.

If the size of a table can vary (a subject discussed later in this chapter), adding or removing pay classes is facilitated by having a single class and rate in each record. If there are multiple pairs in a record, the insertion or deletion of a class may require a significant amount of shifting of table data within the file. On the other hand, if the number of pairs of entries in the table is not going to change, putting multiple pairs in a table file record reduces the number of records in the file and the time required to load the table into memory.

Reading the Table File

A table must be stored in the computer's memory before it can be used in the processing of data records. The storing of the table is therefore done by modules subordinate to module 100, which handles the processing that takes place prior to the processing of the data records.

Let us assume that the data for Table 7-6 is organized in a table file with one argument-function pair per record. Let us also assume that the argument table is supposed to be in ascending order. Since the table-searching instructions will be based on this assumption, if the arguments are in fact not in ascending order, the program will produce invalid results when the customer purchases are processed.

Figures 7-1 and 7-2 show the steps that must be included in the program to provide for the loading of the table. Module 000 sets an error switch to 'F' and calls module 100. If when control is returned to module 000 by module 100 the error switch still has the value 'F,' the processing of customer purchases may proceed. If it has the value 'T,' however, there has been an error in the sequence of arguments and processing must halt.

Module 100 initializes the field that is used for checking the sequence of the arguments. After a priming read of the table file, module 100 transfers control to module 110. In the latter module, as long as the sequence is correct and the end of the table file has not been reached, the argument and function from each table record are moved into the table in memory.

It is left to the student to determine how Figures 7-1 and 7-2 have to be modified if the argument table is in descending order, if it is unordered, or if it is known to be in the proper order.

SEARCHING A DISCRETE TABLE

Searching a table is also sometimes referred to as doing a *table lookup.* The objective in searching a single table is to determine if the search argument is in the table. In the case of paired tables, the objective is usually to retrieve from a function table a value that corresponds to the search argument. The searching is done in conjunction with the processing of the transaction data (that is, in a module that is subordinate to module 200).

Sequential Search

The *sequential search* is the most commonly used algorithm for searching an argument table. The search starts with the first table argument and takes each succeeding argument in turn until a match is found or—in the case of a sequenced discrete table—a missing table argument is detected. The logic for a sequential search of the product code table of 10 entries is shown in Figures 7-3 and 7-4.

TABLE 7-6 PRODUCT CODE–SELLING PRICE TABLE

Product code	Selling price
02	13.67
05	4.29
06	11.07
09	3.69
14	1.84
16	5.70
21	8.36
26	15.87
29	3.91
30	3.69

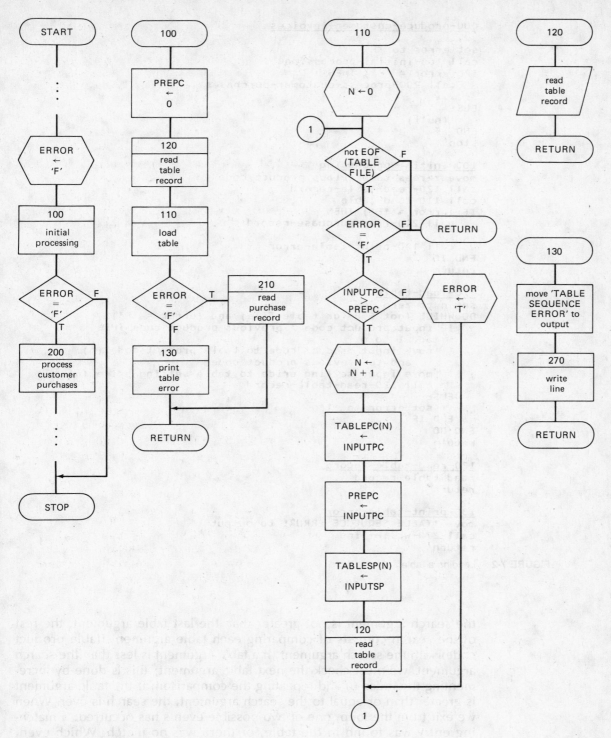

FIGURE 7-1   Loading a table.

The search argument is first compared with the last table argument to identify erroneous search arguments that would otherwise cause the search to extend beyond that last valid argument entry. Given that

```
000-produce-customer-invoices
   •••
set error to 'F'
call 100-initial-processing
IF (error = 'F') THEN
    call 200-process-customer-purchases
   •••
ELSE
    (null)
END IF
stop


100-initial-processing
move zeroes to previous product code
call 120-read-table-record
call 110-load-table
IF (error = 'F') THEN
    call 210-read-purchase-record
ELSE
    call 130-print-table-error
END IF
return


110-load-table
set n to zero
DO WHILE (not EOF for table file) and (error = 'F')
    IF input product code > previous product code THEN
        add 1 to n
        move input product code to table product code (n)
            and to previous product code
        move input selling price to table selling price (n)
        call 120-read-table-record
    ELSE
        set error to 'T'
    END IF
END DO
return


120-read-table-record
read table record
return


130-print-table-error
move 'TABLE SEQUENCE ERROR' to output
call 270-write-line
return
```

FIGURE 7-2   Loading a table.

the search argument is not greater than the last table argument, the rest of the search consists of comparing each table argument (table product code) with the search argument. If a table argument is less than the search argument, we must check the next table argument; this is done by incrementing the index (i) and repeating the comparison. If the table argument is greater than or equal to the search argument, the search is over. When we exit from the loop, one of two possible events has occurred: a matching entry was found in the table, or there was no match. Which event occurred is determined by comparing the ith product code and the search argument. If they are equal, a match was found and selling price (i) can be used in subsequent processing. If they are unequal, no match was found and the error switch is set to 'T.' Subsequent processing will cause an error message to be printed and — at the very least — the processing of the current transaction to be abandoned.

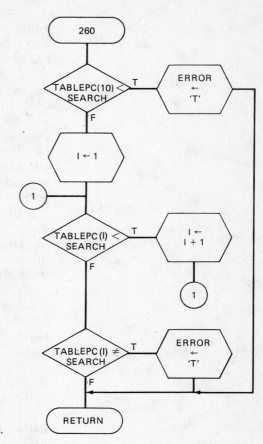

FIGURE 7-3   Searching a discrete table.

```
260-search-table
IF table product code (10) < search argument THEN
    set error to 'T'
ELSE
    set i to 1
    DO WHILE (table product code (i) < search argument)
        add 1 to i
    END DO
    IF table product code (i) ≠ search argument THEN
        set error to 'T'
    ELSE
        (null)
    END IF
END IF
return
```

FIGURE 7-4   Searching a discrete table.

Binary Search

All the searches we have considered so far have been sequential. This simple technique works very well with relatively small tables. For large tables, however, sequential searching can be quite time-consuming. For example, if we have a table of 500 entries, all equally likely to be sought, the average match will require the examination of 250 argument entries.

The *binary search* is a more efficient searching technique for large tables. When the binary search is used, the argument table *must* be in either ascending or descending order. The description that follows is for a binary search of a discrete argument table in ascending order. Only minor changes are needed if the table is in descending order. Binary searches are used mostly with discrete tables. They can also be used with segmented tables, but extensive modifications are required.

In a binary search, the search argument is first compared with the argument entry in the middle of the argument table. If there is no match, the comparison will reveal in which half of the table the matching entry should be. (If the middle entry is greater than the search argument, the matching entry should be in the first half of the table; otherwise, it should be in the second half.) The search argument is then compared with the entry in the middle of that half of the table where the matching entry should be. If there is no match, the comparison will reveal in which half of the half the matching entry should be, that is, in which quarter of the table it should be. The next comparison is then made with the entry in the middle of that quarter. The binary search continues in this fashion, successively halving the portion of the table being searched until a match is found or it can be determined that there is no match.

Clearly a binary search is much more difficult to program than is a sequential search, but it is very efficient for large tables. For example, with a table of 500 entries, an average of eight comparisons is needed to locate a match. The first comparison accesses the middle entry; the second could access the middle entry in either quarter; and so on. Table 7-7 reveals that the eighth comparison can access any one of 128 different entries in a table. The preceding seven comparisons combined could have accessed any of 127 different entries, for a total of 255 entries by the eight comparisons. One more comparison could access any of 256 entries, bringing to 511 the number of entries that could have been accessed by the nine comparisons.

While the sequential search requires as many as 500 comparisons to find a match, only 9 are required with the binary search. If the maximum number of comparisons needed is designated by n and the number of entries by E, then n is the smallest integer for which $2^n > E$ ($2^9 = 512 > 500$). The average number of comparisons is $n - 1$, or in this case 8; this compares favorably with the average of 250 required for a sequential search. The exact breakeven point between binary and sequential searches (the number of argument entries for which the binary and sequential searches are equally good) is a function of the computer and programming language being used.

TABLE 7-7 ENTRIES ACCESSED DURING BINARY SEARCH

Comparison number	Potential number of entries accessed	Total potential entries accessed
1	1	1
2	2	3
3	4	7
4	8	15
5	16	31
6	32	63
7	64	127
8	128	255
9	256	511

Because a sequential search is much easier to program than a binary search, it is tempting for the programmer to use the former. It was perhaps with this in mind that some versions of COBOL provide the programmer with two search routines, one sequential and one binary. The programmer can easily use the one that is more appropriate.

Figure 7-5 contains the program flowchart for a binary search, and Figure 7-6, the pseudocode. In Figure 7-5 "FIRST" and "LAST" are indexes marking the first and last entries in the portion of the table currently being

FIGURE 7-5   Binary search flowchart.

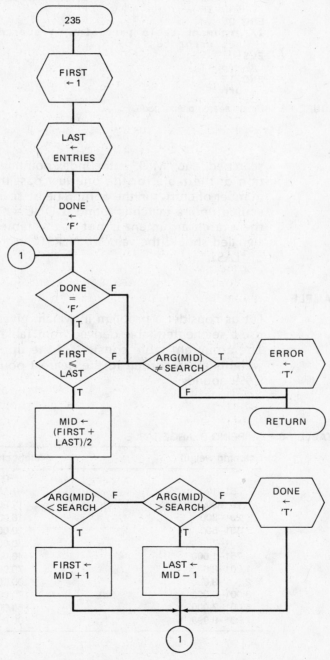

```
235-binary-search
move 1 to first
move number of entries in table to last
set done to 'F'
DO WHILE (done = 'F') and (first < last)
    calculate midpoint as (first + last)/2 rounded
        to integer
    IF argument table (midpoint) < search argument THEN
        move midpoint + 1 to first
    ELSE
        IF argument table (midpoint) > search argument THEN
            move midpoint - 1 to last
        ELSE
            set done to 'T'
        END IF
    END IF
END DO
IF argument table (midpoint) ≠ search argument THEN
    set error to 'T'
ELSE
    (null)
END IF
return
```

FIGURE 7-6   Binary search pseudocode.

searched, and "MID" is the index pointing to the middle entry in this portion of the table (or the one just past the middle if there are an even number of entries in the portion being searched). The searching loop is executed until a match is found (DONE = 'T') or it can be determined that the search argument is not in the table. This latter condition will be signaled should the value of "FIRST" ever become greater than the value of "LAST."

SEGMENTED TABLE EXAMPLE

Let us consider a problem in which, given the weight of a shipment, we use a segmented table derived from Table 7-8 to retrieve a freight charge. The argument table consists of the upper limits of each segment. All weights are recorded to the nearest pound, and no weight can exceed 9,999 pounds.

TABLE 7-8   SHIPPING CHARGE TABLE

Shipping weight	Freight charge
1–50	5.00
51–100	7.50
101–200	12.50
201–300	16.00
301–500	20.00
501–750	30.00
751–1,000	40.00
1,001–2,000	70.00
2,001–3,000	100.00
3,001–5,000	175.00
5,001–7,000	250.00
7,001–9,999	300.00

Getting the Table into Memory

As with the discrete table, module 100 controls the loading of the table. The underlying logic of Figures 7-1 and 7-2 works for the loading of this table as well. Only the names of the argument ("shipping weight" instead of "product code") and function ("freight charge" instead of "selling price") change.

Searching the Table

The logic for sequentially searching a segmented table is much simpler than the logic for sequentially searching a discrete table, as can be seen by comparing Figures 7-7 and 7-8 with Figures 7-3 and 7-4. As the module number indicates, the search module is subordinate to module 200, the one controlling the processing of the transaction records. No error arises as a result of the search, but this is because it is assumed that no input weight (the search argument) can be more than four digits long (that is, 9,999) and that the transaction data has previously been checked so that no weight will be less than one. If either assumption is incorrect, each transaction weight should be checked before the table is searched.

When the search is over, freight charge (i) can be used in subsequent processing.

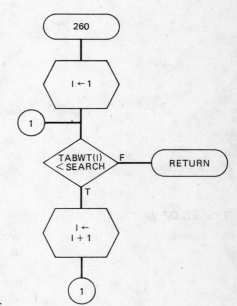

FIGURE 7-7 Searching a segmented table.

```
260-search-table
set i to 1
DO WHILE table weight (i) < search argument
    add 1 to i
END DO
```

FIGURE 7-8 Searching a segmented table.

USING A TABLE TO ACCUMULATE RESULTS OF PROCESSING

We have seen that tables can be used to retrieve information required in processing. In addition, they may be used to store the results of processing. For example, let us assume that we wish to develop a table of total sales by day of the month and that we have a file that contains a record for each sale made during a month. We could sort the file by day and produce a group-printed report, but we can also develop the desired information without sorting.

We define in memory a table of 31 entries, in each of which a total for a day of the month can be accumulated. The day portion of the date in each sales record indicates the entry in the table to which a sales amount should be added. As each sales record is processed, the amount can be added to the appropriate position in the table. At EOF the table will contain the total sales for each day of the month. If "sales table" is the name of the table, "day" is the day portion of the date, and "sales amount" is the amount of a sale, the pseudocode for accumulating the totals can be expressed as:

add sales amount to sales table (day)

This is another example of direct table addressing.

Here are a few other examples of the use of a table to accumulate the results of processing:

• Counting the number of A's, B's, C's, D's, and F's in a class. The argument table consists of the letter grades, and the function table is used to accumulate the counts. When a search of the argument table produces a match, the corresponding position in the function table is incremented by one.

• Recording number of employees by weight category (for example, <100 pounds, 100–109 pounds). Here we have a segmented argument table that must be searched for the appropriate weight category; once again, the function table is used to accumulate counts.

• Computing average income by employee class. A discrete function table is required for the employee class information. Two function tables are required: one to accumulate the income for each class, and the other the number of employees in each class.

TABLES OF VARIABLE SIZE

We have assumed that we know in advance how many entries there will be in a table and that this number will never change. There are some situations, however, in which these assumptions cannot be made. When the number of entries in a table can vary, we must reserve storage for the largest number that we expect. We use a sentinel value to mark the end of the argument table, both in the table file and in memory. The code for loading the table has to include a check to be sure that no attempt is made to load more entries into the table than we have reserved space for in the program.

Discrete

If we have a discrete argument table in ascending order, we can use an argument entry of nines (as many of them as there are positions in the search argument) as a sentinel value to mark the end of the argument table in the file and in memory. If the search argument can never be all nines, any search argument that is greater than the last valid table argument will be identified as invalid because the nines entry will be greater than the search argument.

Similarly, if the table is in descending order, the last argument entry must be chosen so that it will be less than any valid search argument. Negative nines (or zeros if the search argument is positive) work nicely. Any search argument that is less than the last valid table argument will be identified as invalid because the last actual table argument (negative nines) will be less than the search argument.

The product code–selling price table (Table 7-6) is an example of a discrete table that could change in size. We assumed that there were exactly 10 entries in this table, but it would have been better to allow for fluctuation in its size as new products are added and others dropped. If an argument entry of 99 marks the end of the table, the initial comparison of the last table argument with the search argument can be eliminated from Figures 7-3 and 7-4.

Segmented

A nines argument can also be used to mark the end of a segmented argument table that is in ascending order, as we saw in Tables 7-3c and 7-8. In these cases, however, the nines are not sentinel values but valid argument entries.

Should a search argument of nines be invalid, the program will have to compare the search argument with the largest valid table argument before doing the table search. This upper limit for valid arguments should be read in as a parameter before the transactions are processed. We could also use the highest valid argument entry to mark the end of the argument table. If it is possible for a search argument to be larger than this last entry (that is, the data has not previously been edited), a comparison of the search argument with this limit will be necessary before the table is searched.

If the table is in descending order, our last argument entry will be the lowest valid search argument. If we are not sure that the search argument will be greater than or equal to the lowest valid argument, the search argument should be compared with the lowest valid argument before the table is searched. If this lower limit can change, it should be read in as a parameter.

DIRECT TABLE ADDRESSING

We have not discussed the technique of direct table addressing, although we have seen two examples of its use:

1 We can retrieve a month name given the number of a month by using the month number as an index.

2 We can accumulate sales by day of the month simply by using the day as the index to the appropriate entry in a table in which totals are accumulated.

An advantage of direct table addressing is that function entries can be accessed without having to search an argument table.

Determining the Index of the Function

For the month name table the index varied from 1 to 12; for the total table it varied from 1 to 31. In general, if an argument table consists of consecutive integers starting with one, we can dispense with the argument table and use the search argument as an index to go directly to the appropriate function entry. In fact, if the argument table consists of consecutive integers but does not start with one, direct table addressing can still be used. The index of a function entry can be calculated as

$$index = (search\ argument - first\ argument + 1)$$

Additional Examples of Direct Addressing

Table 7-9 shows two additional examples of direct addressing. Both the argument table and the function table are shown, although only the function table is actually placed in the computer's memory.

The first example is similar to the month name table. It is used to convert a date to a form in which it is written "yyddd," where yy is the last two digits of the year and "ddd" is the number of the day within the year. (For January 1, ddd = 001; for December 31, ddd = 365, or 366 in a leap year.) The month number can be used as an index to retrieve from the function table the total number of days accumulated during the year up to the start of the month. To this amount we add the day portion of the date to get the ddd of the date. For example, April 15, 1986, is 86105 (90 + 15). This way of representing dates makes it easier to determine the number of days between two dates, something that banks must do regularly.

Table 7-9*b* illustrates another situation in which direct table addressing can be used. Note that while the arguments are consecutive, they do not start with one; the index to the pay rate table is calculated as

$$jobcode - 20$$

(The first argument is 21, so the index is calculated as "jobcode − 21 + 1.") Note that some job codes in the sequence are not actually required. If we are going to use direct table addressing, we can omit no integers in the sequence, so there must be entries in the function table for job codes 26 and

TABLE 7-9   ADDITIONAL EXAMPLES OF DIRECT TABLE ADDRESSING

| (a) | | (b) | |
Month	Accumulated days	Job code	Pay rate
1	0	21	8.75
2	31	22	7.46
3	59	23	10.25
4	90	24	9.45
5	120	25	8.50
6	151	26	not used
7	181	27	9.25
8	212	28	11.00
9	243	29	not used
10	273	30	8.35
11	304		
12	334		

29. We therefore put in the sixth and ninth positions of the function table a value that can immediately be recognized as invalid, such as zero or a negative number. After we retrieve a pay rate, we must check it to be sure that it is valid (that is, not zero or negative) before using it.

MULTIDIMENSIONAL TABLES

The function tables from which we have so far retrieved data are referred to as *one-dimensional tables*. The value to be retrieved is a function of a single search argument, or—to put it another way—only one index is needed to retrieve the function. In some business applications and in many mathematical and scientific applications, there is a need for *multidimensional tables*: two or more search arguments (or indexes) are used to retrieve a function value.

Table 7-10 is an example of a two-dimensional table. The freight charge for a shipment is a function of two arguments: shipping weight and shipping zone (geographic area). Any one of five freight charges may apply to a particular shipping weight, depending on the zone to which the shipment is delivered. Conversely, any one of 12 freight charges may apply in a particular zone, depending on the weight. We can think of this as a 12 × 5 table, a table with 12 rows and 5 columns. We refer to an element of this table by specifying two indexes:

freight charge (row, column)

We could add a third dimension to the table if the shipping charge was also a function of the material being shipped. We could have one function table such as we see in Table 7-10 for grain, another for steel, a third for liquids, and so on. Three-dimensional tables are difficult for many people to visualize, and tables of more than three dimensions present insurmountable problems for just about everyone. Fortunately, most business data-processing applications can be handled with one- or two-dimensional tables.

Some programming languages, particularly those designed for mathematical applications, handle multidimensional tables very easily, but there is considerable variation from language to language (and even for the same language on different computers) with regard to maximum number

TABLE 7-10   FREIGHT CHARGES BY SHIPPING ZONE

Shipping weight	Shipping zone				
	1	2	3	4	5
1–50	2.50	5.00	7.50	10.00	15.00
51–100	3.75	7.50	11.25	15.00	22.50
101–200	6.25	12.50	18.75	25.00	37.50
201–300	8.00	16.00	24.00	32.00	48.00
301–500	10.00	20.00	30.00	40.00	60.00
501–750	15.00	30.00	45.00	60.00	90.00
751–1,000	20.00	40.00	60.00	80.00	120.00
1,001–2,000	35.00	70.00	105.00	140.00	210.00
2,001–3,000	50.00	100.00	150.00	300.00	300.00
3,001–5,000	87.50	175.00	262.50	350.00	525.00
5,001–7,000	125.00	250.00	375.00	500.00	750.00
7,001–9,999	150.00	300.00	450.00	600.00	900.00

of dimensions allowed. Other programming languages (for example, assembler and RPG II) accommodate more than one dimension in a process that amounts to converting a multidimensional table into a series of one-dimensional tables.

We will not explore multidimensional tables in depth, but we will discuss loading, searching, and referencing two-dimensional tables; the techniques can be extended to tables of more than two dimensions if desired. Then we will develop a simple algorithm for using a two-dimensional table in RPG II, a language that was designed to handle only one-dimensional tables.

Two-Dimensional Tables

The ways in which two-dimensional tables are loaded varies considerably from one language to another. Figures 7-9 and 7-10 show the module 110 that can be used with Figures 7-1 and 7-2 to load the table data of Table 7-10. It is assumed that each record in the table file contains the upper limit of a weight range and the five corresponding freight charges and that the table file is known to be correct.

To retrieve the proper shipping charge from Table 7-10, we must find the proper row (shipping weight range) and column (shipping zone). The shipping weight and zone arguments would be derived from input data. Given the shipping weight, the row can be determined by searching the one-dimensional weight table, as in Figures 7-11 and 7-12. The result of the search will be the index value (i) for the proper row in the freight charge table. The proper column is provided directly by the shipping zone number. Here we have a table search to determine one index and direct table addressing for the other. Following this search, the appropriate shipping charge can be retrieved by specifying

freight charge (i, input shipping zone)

(It is assumed that the input weight and shipping zone are valid.)

Let us consider two other ways in which the arguments might be expressed:

1 The columns could be identified as shipping zones, as in Table 7-10, and the rows could be identified as weight categories with a number between 1 and 12.

2 The rows could be identified as a range of weights, as in Table 7-10, and the columns as ranges of miles (for example, ≤ 100, 101–500, 501–1,000, 1,001–2,000, and 2,001–9,999).

For the first alternative, no argument table searching is required. Direct table addressing can be used with both the row and the column to retrieve the appropriate freight charge:

freight charge (weight category, shipping zone)

For the second alternative, two argument tables have to be searched. In addition to searching the weight table to get an index i to the proper row, a search also has to be made of a distance table (using mileage from the input as a search argument) to get an index j to the proper column.

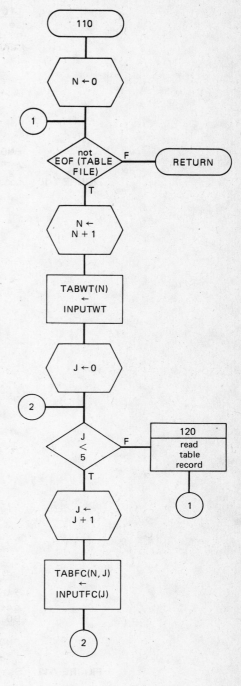

FIGURE 7-9 Loading a two-dimensional table.

Figures 7-13 and 7-14 show the algorithm for this search. Following the searches, the shipping charge can be retrieved by specifying:

freight charge (i, j)

Multidimensional tables can also be used to accumulate the results of processing. Instead of determining total sales simply by day of the month,

```
110-load-table
set n to zero
DO WHILE (not EOF for table file)
   add 1 to n
   move input weight to table weight (n)
   set j to 0
   DO WHILE j < 5
      add 1 to j
      move input freight charge (j) to
            table freight charge (n, j)
   END DO
   call 120-read-table-record
END DO
return
```

FIGURE 7-10 Loading a two-dimensional table.

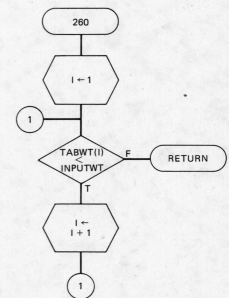

FIGURE 7-11 Searching a weight table.

```
260-search-table
set i to 1
DO WHILE table weight (i) < input weight
   add 1 to i
END DO
return
```

FIGURE 7-12 Searching a weight table.

we might want to look at sales by customer class by day of the month. Our table would then consist of 31 rows and as many columns as there are customer classes. For example, if there are seven classes numbered 1 to 7, the class would serve as the column index using direct table addressing. If some other classification scheme were used, a search could be made of a classification table to determine the column index.

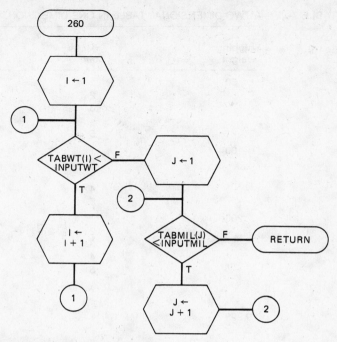

FIGURE 7-13   Searching both argument tables.

```
260-search-table
set i to 1
DO WHILE table weight (i) < input weight
   add 1 to i
END DO
set j to 1
DO WHILE table mileage (j) < input mileage
   add 1 to j
END DO
return
```

FIGURE 7-14   Searching both argument tables.

Two-Dimensional Tables in One Dimension

RPG II provides for only a single index in referencing tables (actually called arrays in RPG). How then can we accommodate a table such as Table 7-10? We can visualize this table as a large one-dimensional table composed of 12 subsidiary tables, each containing five elements, as in Table 7-11. Whereas the search of the weight table provided an index i to the proper row when we were working with a two-dimensional table, the same search now tells us which of the 12 subtables we want. The shipping zone then tells us which entry in the designated subtable is the appropriate shipping charge. We can derive a single index value j that will tell us which of the 60 entries in this one-dimensional table we want by performing the following calculation:

$$j = 5(i - 1) + \text{shipping zone}$$

The rightmost column of Table 7-11 shows these index values.

TABLE 7-11 A TWO-DIMENSIONAL TABLE IN ONE DIMENSION

Shipping weight	Zone	Freight charge Value	Index
50	1	2.50	1
	2	5.00	2
	3	7.50	3
	4	10.00	4
	5	15.00	5
100	1	3.75	6
	2	7.50	7
	3	11.25	8
	4	15.00	9
	5	22.50	10
200	1	6.25	11
	2	12.50	12
	3	18.75	13
	4	25.00	14
	5	37.50	15
.	.	.	.
.	.	.	.
.	.	.	.
9,999	1	150.00	56
	2	300.00	57
	3	450.00	58
	4	600.00	59
	5	900.00	60

Let us assume that we are looking for the correct charge for a shipment of 175 pounds to zone 2. The search of the weight table reveals that we want the third subtable ($i = 3$). Substituting 3 for i and 2 for the shipping zone in the above expression yields a value for j of 12:

$$5(3 - 1) + 2$$

The twelfth entry in Table 7-11 is for a shipment of 101 to 200 pounds to zone 2.

Let us now generalize this algorithm for converting two indexes into one. Given

      j = index of desired element in one-dimensional table
      n = number of elements in each subtable
      i = index of desired subtable
      k = index of desired element in subtable

we have

$$j = n(i - 1) + k$$

In the example considered above, there were 5 elements corresponding to the 5 shipping zones in each of the 12 subtables ($n = 5$); a search of the weight subtable revealed that we wanted the third subtable ($i = 3$); in this case $k = 2$, the shipping zone.

This technique can be extended to handle three-dimensional arrays as well. It can also be used in any programming language to allow for more dimensions than are provided for in the design of the language.

SUMMARY

This chapter introduced a powerful programming tool, the table. The table provides us with a very convenient way of organizing similar data items so that we may access them more readily. We saw that there is a great deal of variety in the types of tables and how they are used. Tables may be single or paired, argument or function, discrete or segmented. Argument tables may be in ascending order, descending order, or no order at all. We learned how to get table information into memory (read it from a file, define it as constants, or develop it as the result of processing data), how to retrieve information from tables (search an argument table or use direct table addressing), and how to cope with tables that change in size. We also took a brief look at multidimensional tables and how they can be accessed.

KEY TERMS

argument table	search argument
array	segmented table
binary search	sequential search
direct table addressing	single table
discrete table	subscript
function table	table
index	table file
multidimensional table	table lookup
one-dimensional table	table search
paired table	

EXERCISES

1 A payroll register is to be produced. The transaction records are in order by employee number within department number. Each record contains the following fields: department number, employee number, job number, and hours worked. There is one record for each job an employee performed during the week.

Each record in a table file contains a job number and a pay rate. There may be up to 100 records in the table file, which is in sequence by job number. A job number of 999 is used as a sentinel value to mark the end of the table file; there is no job with a number of 999. Assume that the table file is correct.

The output is to consist of a detail-printed report. Each detail line will contain the department, employee, and job numbers, the hours worked, the pay rate, and earnings. Total earnings are to be printed for each employee, each department, and all departments combined.

Documentation for this problem is to consist of the structure chart, the program flowchart and pseudocode for the processing that takes place prior to the transaction processing, and the program flowchart and pseudocode to search the table and use the data retrieved (including the calling of the modules in which these activities take place).

2 A tax report is to be prepared. The input consists of records in sequence by employee number. Each record contains the employee number and the employee's taxable income. There is one record for each employee.

A printed report is to be produced that will contain a detail line for each employee, showing employee number, income, and tax. A final total of all income and taxes is also printed.

Taxes are to be computed using a table similar to the following:

Taxable income	Tax due
0–15,000	20% of taxable income
15,000–29,999	$3,000 + 30% of amount > 15,000
30,000–49,999	$7,500 + 40% of amount > 30,000
50,000–74,999	$15,500 + 50% of amount > 50,000
75,000–99,999	$28,000 + 75% of amount > 75,000

The income ranges and tax rates are subject to change, so that tax information is read from a table file. Each record in this file contains a lower income limit (for example, 30,000), an upper income limit (for example, 49,999), a base tax for the range (for example, 7,500), and a tax rate for the range (for example, 40). The number of entries in the tax table may change, but no more than 10 entries are expected. Assume that the table file is correct.

Hint: Think of the table file as containing one argument table and three function tables.

Documentation for this problem is to consist of the structure chart, the program flowchart and pseudocode for the processing that takes place prior to the transaction processing, and the program flowchart and pseudocode to search the table and use the data retrieved (including the calling of the modules in which these activities take place).

3 A company that is concerned about the physical condition of its employees wants a report that will show how many employees of each sex fall into various weight categories. Records in the personnel file contain weight and sex ("M" or "F") fields.

A table file is to be used for the weight categories so that the categories may be changed as needed. As many as 25 different categories should be provided for. Each record in the table file is to contain both the lower and upper limits of a range. The table file records will be in order by weight, and the last upper limit will be 999. Assume that the table file is correct.

The output is to consist of a listing in which each line contains a weight range and the corresponding counts of female and male employees in the range.

Documentation for this problem is to consist of the structure chart, the program flowchart and pseudocode for the processing that takes place prior to the transaction processing, and the program flowchart and pseudocode to accumulate and print the results. (Ignore headings and spacing.)

CHAPTER 8

MULTIFILE PROCESSING: SEQUENTIAL ACCESS

OBJECTIVES

Upon completing this chapter the student should be able to:

1 Prepare documentation for programs that create, update, or maintain sequential files on magnetic tape or magnetic disk.

2 Explain how activity and volatility rates affect the choice between magnetic tape and magnetic disk for master files to be processed sequentially.

3 Define and use the key terms at the end of the chapter.

INTRODUCTION

Much of business data processing is concerned with keeping information in files current. For example, an inventory file that records how much of each item is on hand needs to be changed to

- Increase the balance on hand when a shipment is received from a supplier or merchandise is returned by a customer
- Reduce the balance on hand when merchandise is sold to a customer or returned to a supplier
- Add a new item to the file
- Delete an item from the file that is no longer to be kept in stock
- Correct an error in a record

In this chapter we will examine techniques for changing master files stored on magnetic tape and disk. These techniques are also useful in making changes to the table files discussed in Chapter 7.

TERMINOLOGY

The discussion of file processing in this and the following chapter will require the use of some new terms.

Master and Transaction Files

The inventory file that is to be altered is an example of a *master file*. While the number of records in the file and the contents of specific records will change, the inventory file will be retained for an indefinite period of time. Information about the changes to be made is found in a *transaction file,* a file that is retained for only a short time. As the title for this chapter suggests, we are going to be examining situations requiring more than one input file. Programs will be developed that read both a master file and a transaction file; both files will be accessed (read) sequentially.

Sequential and Serial Access

The terms "sequential" and "serial" are similar, but they are not synonymous. Sequential access is actually one form of serial access. *Serial access* refers to a method of reading or writing a file in which the first record in the file is processed first, then the second record is processed, and so on until the last record has been processed. The records are not necessarily in any particular order. *Sequential access* differs from serial access in that the records being processed are in the file in a sequence that is based on the value in a field in each record called the *key field*.

When information in a transaction file is to be used to alter a master file, having both files in sequence on the same key field greatly facilitates the processing. Unless both files are similarly sequenced, the search for the master record to be changed (that is, the one with the same key field value as in the transaction record) must start with the first record in the master file for each new transaction record. When the master and transaction files are in sequence on the same key field, the matching process is much more efficient. Finding the match for the first transaction requires searching from the beginning of the master file; however, the search for the matching master record for each subsequent transaction can begin with the last master record that matched. This will be illustrated in several examples very shortly.

Batch processing is used with sequential files. That is, a batch of transactions is accumulated, and then at some predetermined time (for example, daily or weekly), the batch is used as input to a processing run.

Maintaining, Updating, and Referencing

File-processing activities can be categorized as maintaining, updating, or referencing. In this text, the terms are used as follows:

Maintaining refers to any activities that change the number of records in a master file. Adding records to and deleting records from a master file are the most common maintenance activities. We can also consider as maintenance the initial creation of the master file and its elimination (scratching or purging) when the file is no longer needed.

Updating a master file changes the content of one or more records in the file but does not alter the number of records. Updating is considered by some to be just one type of file maintenance activity, but we will treat updating and maintaining as separate activities.

Referencing a file changes nothing in the file; it merely extracts information from the file. Producing a report from information in a master file is an example of referencing a file. In previous chapters we have for the most part been referencing files. In this and the following chapter, our concern will be with maintaining and updating master files.

FILE MEDIA FOR SEQUENTIAL FILES

The problems we have considered in previous chapters have typically involved reading records from an input file and creating output on a printer. Our input has been in a serial file; often the file has been organized sequentially. Our output file (the collection of records sent to the printer) has also been a serial file.

In the discussion that follows, we will be unconcerned about the source of our transaction data; it could be on punched cards, magnetic tape, magnetic diskette, or magnetic disk, and it even could be entered from an online terminal. In whatever form the transaction data exists, batch processing will be used. The transaction data will have been accumulated and sorted prior to our processing run. For reasons that will emerge later in the chapter, it will not be entered from an online terminal.

We will consider two forms of media for our master files: magnetic tape and magnetic disk. There are other media that can be used for master files that are to be accessed sequentially, but disk and—to a lesser extent—tape are the most common.

MAGNETIC TAPE

Magnetic tape was widely used for master files in the early 1960s. Its use for master files has declined, however, as the costs of magnetic disks have been reduced and their access speed and capacity have been increased. Tape is used today primarily as a medium for *backing up* (making a copy of) files that are stored on disk, for archiving (long-term storage) of transaction data, and for transferring data and programs from one computer to another. Since magnetic tape is conceptually simpler than disk, we will start our discussion with this medium.

Tape is strictly a serial medium, for the processing of a file on tape starts with the very first record. If we want to access a particular record in a tape file, we must read all the records that precede it. The computer is unable to go directly to a specific record stored on tape.

Creating a Master File

Magnetic tapes can be read and written only by machines. If a master file is to be stored on a reel of magnetic tape, a program must be written to read the necessary information and write it on the tape. As the structure chart of Figure 8-1, the program flowchart of Figure 8-2, and the pseudocode of Figure 8-3 illustrate, this can be a very simple program. It is assumed that the master file is to be created from records that are in sequence on a key field, so a sequence check is included in the program. Note that the check prevents records with identical keys from being written to the master file. Records in a master file must have unique keys.

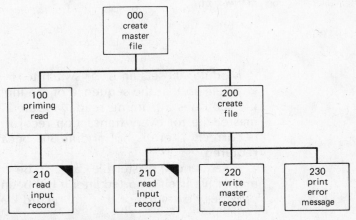

FIGURE 8-1   Creating master file (structure chart).

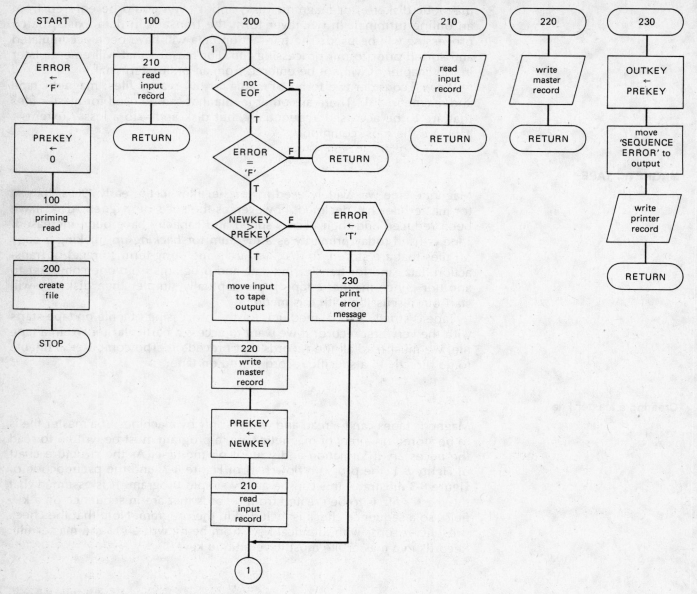

FIGURE 8-2 Creating master file (program flowchart).

Module 000 sets an error switch to 'F' and moves zeros into a previous key field so that the sequence of the input records can be checked. Module 100 does a priming read. Module 200 simply writes a record to the master file for every transaction record read in, as long as the sequence is correct. There is no module 300 because no end-of-file processing is required.

A sequenced master file can also be created from unsorted input if the master file itself is sorted after it has been created; however, this approach provides no assurance that the record keys are unique.

```
000-create-master-file
set error to 'F'
move zeroes to previous key field
call 100-priming-read
call 200-create-file
stop

100-priming-read
call 210-read-input-record
return

200-create-file
DO WHILE not EOF and (error = 'F')
    IF new key field > previous key field THEN
        move input to tape output area
        call 220-write-master-record
        move new key field to previous key field
        call 210-read-input-record
    ELSE
        set error to 'T'
        call 230-print-error-message
    END IF
END DO
return

210-read-input-record
read input record
return

220-write-master-record
write master record
return

230-print-error-message
move previous key field and 'SEQUENCE ERROR'
    to printer output area
write printer record
return
```

FIGURE 8-3   Creating master file (pseudocode).

Updating a Master File

When a sequential master file is updated, the transactions are placed in the same order as the records in the master file. Each transaction record contains the key of the record to be updated and the information necessary to do the updating. The updating structure chart is shown in Figure 8-4.

Figure 8-5 contains the program flowchart for updating a sequential tape file and Figure 8-6 contains the pseudocode. It is important to realize that the new file is not written on top of the old file on the same reel of tape. The updating produces a completely new master file on a different reel of tape.

An Overview   Module 000 initializes a switch named "DONE" to 'F.' This switch is used to control the loop in module 200 that oversees all the processing. Its use will be clarified in the discussion that follows.

Module 100 must do two priming reads, one for each file. There is no module 300 because there is no processing required at end-of-file.

As is usually the case, module 200 is the most interesting module. It is executed until the ends of both the transaction file and the master file have been reached.

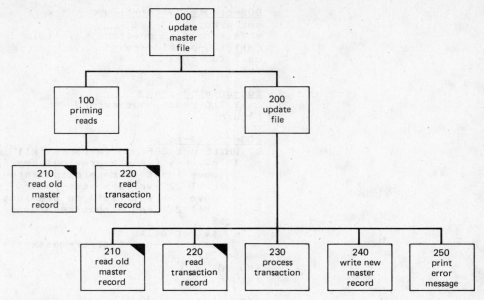

FIGURE 8-4 Updating tape master file.

A module 300 is not required; if present, it would handle processing required after EOF has been reached on both files.

Locating the Master Record to Update The processing in module 200 begins with a comparison of the keys of the transaction and master records. For any master record, there may be any number of transactions, including none. If the master key is less than the transaction key, there are no transactions for the master record, so it is simply copied to the new reel of tape. Module 240 writes a "new" master record in the sense that the record is written to the new master file. Another master record is read from the old master file, and its key is compared with the transaction key. The process described in this paragraph is repeated until a master record with the same key value as the transaction key is read.

Updating the Master Record If the keys of the master and transaction records are the same, the master record is updated from information in the transaction record. (The details of the processing are relatively unimportant; our concern is with the logic for processing the two files.) After the transaction has been processed, another transaction record is read. The flow returns to the start of the DO WHILE loop, and the new transaction key is compared with the key of the same master record. If they are equal, the master record is updated again with information from this new transaction. All transactions with the same key field must be processed before the corresponding master record is completely updated. In the case of an inventory file, all receipts and issues for an item must be processed before the current quantity on hand for that item can be determined.

How will we know that we have processed all transactions for an item? Since the transactions are in ascending order, when a transaction record for a different item is read, the key of the master record being updated will be less than the key of the new transaction record. When this happens, the updated record is written to the new master tape and another master

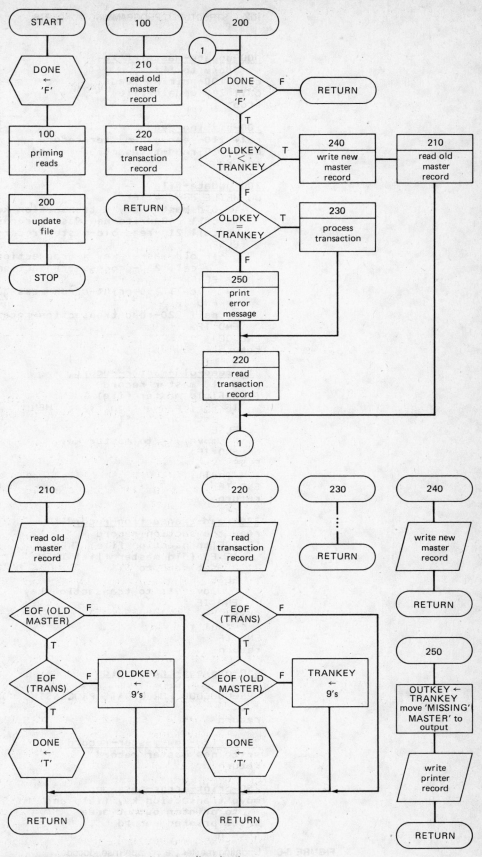

FIGURE 8-5   Updating master file on tape (program flowchart).

```
000-update-master-file
set done to 'F'
call 100-priming-reads
call 200-update-file
stop

100-priming-reads
call 210-read-old-master-record
call 220-read-transaction-record
return

200-update-file
DO WHILE done = 'F'
   IF old master key < transaction key THEN
       call 240-write-new-master-record
       call 210-read-old-master-record
   ELSE
       IF old master key = transaction key THEN
          call 230-process-transaction
       ELSE
          call 250-print-error-message
       END IF
       call 220-read-transaction-record
   END IF
END DO
return

210-read-old-master-record
read old master record
IF EOF(old master file) THEN
   IF EOF(transaction file) THEN
      set done to 'T'
   ELSE
      move 9's to master key
   END IF
ELSE
    (null)
END IF
return

220-read-transaction-record
read transaction record
IF EOF(transaction file) THEN
   IF EOF(old master file) THEN
      set done to 'T'
   ELSE
      move 9's to transaction key
   END IF
ELSE
    (null)
END IF
return

230-process-transaction
 ...
 PSEUDOCODE FOR UPDATE PROCESSING GOES HERE
 ...
return

240-write-new-master-record
write new master record
return

250-print-error-message
move transaction key field and 'MISSING MASTER'
   to printer output area
write printer record
return
```

FIGURE 8-6   Updating master file on tape (pseudocode).

record is read from the old master file. The flow again returns to the start of the loop, where the key of this master record is compared with the key of the transaction record waiting to be processed. If the transaction and master record keys are the same, the master record is updated. If the master key is less than the transaction key, the master record is copied to the new master file.

Error Handling If the key of the record from the old master file is greater than the key of the transaction record waiting to be processed, there is no master record with the desired transaction key in the master file. For any transaction there should be a corresponding master record, but an update program must provide for the possibility that there is no matching master record in the file. When this occurs, the transaction cannot be processed.

Why might we have a transaction with no matching master record? There may be an error in the transaction key field. It is possible that a record with that key should have been added to the master file, but was not included in a maintenance run. Or we may have a transaction for a master record that has been removed from the file. Since the transaction cannot be processed, an error message is printed (by module 250). This error will not normally interfere with subsequent processing, so a new transaction record is read and the flow returns to the start of the loop. Note that a new transaction record is read whenever the old master key is greater than or equal to the transaction key.

Terminating Processing The updating continues in this fashion. For every record read from the input master file there will be a record written to the output master file. Those records from the old master file for which there are transactions will be updated; the others will simply be copied to the new file.

We must reach the end of both the transaction and master files before our processing is "done." That is, all transactions must be processed and all records in the input master file must be written—changed or not—to the new master file. If we reach the end of the transaction file first (that is, the key of the last transaction is less than the key of the last master record), we must copy all remaining records from the input master file to the output file. If we reach the end of both files at the same time (that is, the last records in both files have the same key), we must write the updated version of the last master record to the output file. If we reach the end of the master file before we reach the end of the transaction file (that is, the key of the last transaction record is greater than the key of the last master record), the remaining unprocessed transactions have no corresponding master record; an error message is printed for each transaction.

The way in which we control the end-of-file processing is rather simple: we use the transaction key field (hereafter referred to as TKEY) and the master key field (MKEY) as switches. When the end of one file is detected, a check is made to see if the end of the other file has also been encountered. If the end of the other file has not been reached, the key field for the file that has ended is set to all nines and processing resumes. If we reach the end of the transaction file first, we move the nines to TKEY. If we reach the end of the master file first, the nines are stored at MKEY. If the end of the other file has already been reached, the DONE switch is set to 'T' so that when control returns to the start of the loop, the condition controlling the loop will no longer be true and the module 200 — and thus the program — will be finished.

For example, let us assume that we reach the end of the transaction file first. When that happens in module 220, we set TKEY to nines and return to compare the keys. Since there is no master record for which MKEY is equal to nines, the less-than condition will be detected, causing the current master record to be written to the new master file by module 240. The next master record is read, and since its key will also be less than nines, it too is copied to the output file. This continues until the end of the input master file is finally reached in module 210. When this happens, a check is made to see if TKEY equals nines (if all transactions have been processed). Since we assumed that we had previously reached the end of the transaction file and had set TKEY to nines, the DONE switch is set to 'T.' Note that the end of the transaction file is encountered first whenever the key of the last transaction record is less than or equal to the key of the last master record.

If the end of the master file is reached first, MKEY is set to nines. Since no transaction will have a key of nines, all subsequent comparisons of keys will result in the greater-than condition, with module 250 being called to print an error message for each remaining transaction. When the end of the transaction file is reached in module 220, we check, by comparing MKEY to nines, to see if all master records have also been processed. Since MKEY was set to nines, the DONE switch is set to 'T' and module 200 and the program are finished.

An Example Table 8-1 illustrates the processing steps involved in updating a master file on tape. Three situations are presented:

1 The key of the last master record is greater than the key of the last transaction record.
2 The keys of the last master and transaction records are the same.
3 The key of the last master record is less than the key of the last transaction record.

At the top of the table we see the keys of the records in each file for each situation. The master file is the same for all three situations; only the contents of the transaction file change.

In the processing steps, "M(1)" refers to the master record with a key of 1 and "T(5)" refers to a transaction record with a key of 5. Steps 1 to 33 are the same for the first two situations. For the second situation, steps 34 to 42 are changed, and four more steps are added. Steps 1 to 37 are the same for the second and third situations, but for the third situation steps 38 to 46 change and four steps are added. At the bottom of the figure we see for each situation the keys of the records written to the new master file. Note that all records in the input master file — and only those records — are included in the output file. Some have been updated, and the others have simply been copied.

This example illustrates how sequencing both files on the same key field facilitates the matching of transaction and master records. It is not necessary to start searching with the first master record whenever a new transaction record is read.

Adding Records to a File

Figure 8-7 contains the structure chart for adding records to a sequential file on tape. It is similar to Figure 8-4, except in this case module 230 is

TABLE 8-1   UPDATING MASTER FILE ON TAPE

Situation 1		_Situation 2_		_Situation 3_	
Master	Trans.	Master	Trans.	Master	Trans.
1	1	1	1	1	1
3	5	3	5	3	5
5	5	5	5	5	5
6	7	6	7	6	7
8		8	8	8	8
					10

```
PROCESSING STEPS

 1. Read M(1)
 2. Read T(1)
 3. DONE = 'F'
 4. M(1) = T(1)
 5. Process T(1)
 6. Read T(5)
 7. DONE = 'F'
 8. M(1) < T(5)
 9. Write M(1)*
10. Read M(3)
11. DONE = 'F'
12. M(3) < T(5)
13. Write M(3)
14. Read M(5)
15. DONE = 'F'
16. M(5) = T(5)
17. Process T(5)
18. Read T(5)
19. DONE = 'F'
20. M(5) = T(5)
21. Process T(5)
22. Read T(7)
23. DONE = 'F'
24. M(5) < T(7)
25. Write M(5)*
26. Read M(6)
27. DONE = 'F'
28. M(6) < T(7)
29. Write M(6)
30. Read M(8)
31. DONE = 'F'
32. M(8) > T(7)
33. Missing M(7)
34. EOF(T)          34. Read T(8)
35. MKEY ≠ 9's      35. DONE = 'F'
36. TKEY <- 9's     36. M(8) = T(8)
37. DONE = 'F'      37. Process T(8)
38. M(8) < T(9's)   38. EOF(T)          38. Read T(10)
39. Write M(8)      39. MKEY ≠ 9's      39. DONE = 'F'
40. EOF(M)          40. TKEY <- 9's     40. M(8) < T(10)
41. TKEY = 9's      41. DONE = 'F'      41. Write M(8)*
42. DONE <- 'T'     42. M(8) < T(9's)   42. EOF(M)
                    43. Write M(8)*     43. TKEY ≠ 9's
                    44. EOF(M)          44. MKEY <- 9's
                    45. TKEY = 9's      45. DONE = 'F'
                    46. DONE <- 'T'     46. M(9's) > T(10)
                                        47. Missing M(10)
                                        48. EOF(T)
                                        49. MKEY = 9's
                                        50. DONE <- 'T'


MASTER FILE OUTPUT

  1* 3 5* 6 8        1* 3 5* 6 8*        1* 3 5* 6 8*

* Updated master record
```

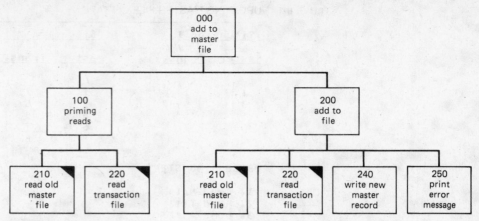

FIGURE 8-7 Adding records.

omitted because no update processing is required. The transaction records contain the same fields that were in the records from which the file was originally created.

The program flowchart and the pseudocode for adding records are very similar to their updating counterparts. In addition to eliminating module 230, we must alter the code for modules 000, 200, and 250. (Note that modules 100, 210, and 220 do not change.) The revised modules are shown in Figures 8-8 and 8-9. The revisions include new names for the main program module and for module 200, and a different error message to be printed by module 250.

Additional, more significant, changes are made to module 200. If we examine the actions taken after the keys are compared, we see that when MKEY < TKEY we write the master record to the output file and read in a new master record, just as we did when updating the file. The actions taken when the other two conditions are encountered, however, are different.

When MKEY > TKEY, we know that we have found the place to insert the new record in the file. The new master record is written, and then a new transaction record (for another record to be added) is read. No master record is read because there already is a master record in memory waiting to be written to the output file.

MKEY should never equal TKEY when records are being added. If it does, we are trying to duplicate a record key, as the error message (ALREADY IN FILE) indicates.

Table 8-2 (see p. 169) shows the processing steps involved in adding records to a tape file. The same three end-of-file situations as in Table 8-1 are examined with the same master files but with different transaction files. Note that when an attempt is made to add a record with a key that is already in the master file, the old record, not the new one, is written to the output file.

Deleting Records from a File

The structure chart of Figure 8-7 applies to deleting records as well as to adding them. Only the names of modules 000 and 200 need to be changed to reflect the deletion, rather than the addition, of records. The only information needed in a transaction record is the key of the record to be deleted.

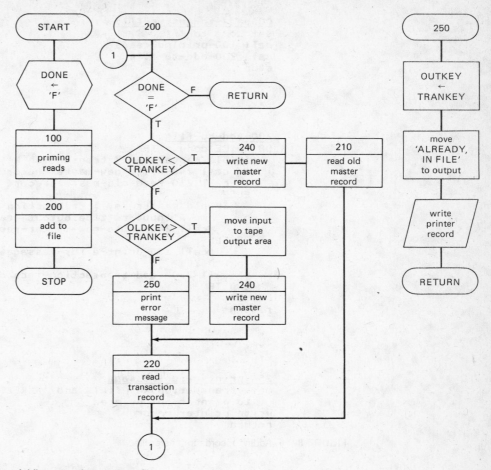

FIGURE 8-8   Adding records to master file.

The program flowchart and the pseudocode for modules 000, 200, and 250 of Figures 8-8 and 8-9 must be revised as shown in Figures 8-10 and 8-11. The changes to modules 000 and 250 are again very minor. What changes in module 200 is the processing that takes place when MKEY = TKEY and when MKEY > TKEY. The processing is unchanged when MKEY < TKEY.

When MKEY = TKEY, we have found the record to be deleted. A record is deleted by not writing it to the output file, so on the equal condition, a new master record and a new transaction record (containing the key of the next record to be deleted) are read.

If MKEY > TKEY, we have been unable to find a master record that matches the transaction key; that is, there is no record to delete. The error message printed (NOT IN MASTER) indicates this fact. The processing continues with the reading of another transaction.

Table 8-3 (see p. 172) contains an example of a run to delete records from a tape file.

In some cases, it may be necessary to retain in a master file records that are no longer "active." For example, for tax-reporting purposes the payroll master records for employees who have left a company must be retained until the end of the year. This can be done by just marking the records as deleted while keeping them in the file. A special delete code field is required, and this field must be checked by all programs using the file to ensure that a deleted record is not processed by mistake.

```
000-add-to-master-file
set done to 'F'
call 100-priming-reads
call 200-add-to-file
stop

   .
   .
   .

200-add-to-file
DO WHILE done = 'F'
   IF old master key < transaction key THEN
      call 240-write-new-master-record
      call 210-read-old-master-record
   ELSE
      IF old master key > transaction key THEN
         move input to tape output area
         call 240-write-new-master-record
      ELSE
         call 250-print-error-message
      END IF
      call 220-read-transaction-record
   END IF
END DO
return

   .
   .
   .

250-print-error-message
move transaction key field and 'ALREADY IN FILE'
   to printer output area
write printer record
return
```

FIGURE 8-9   Adding records to master file.

A Combined Add and Delete Run

There is no reason why additions and deletions cannot be taken care of in the same processing run, but there must be a code in each transaction record to differentiate between the two types of transactions. (In our example, a code of "A" in a transaction record identifies an addition, and "D" a deletion.) The structure chart of Figure 8-7 can be used again, with new names for modules 000 and 200.

Minor revisions in the program flowchart of Figure 8-8 and the pseudocode of Figure 8-9 for modules 000 and 250 are again required, as shown in Figures 8-12 and 8-13. The significant changes appear in module 200. The logic for doing the necessary code and key checking is more complicated than the logic for doing additions and deletions separately.

As might be expected, the processing performed in module 200 when MKEY < TKEY has not changed.

If MKEY > TKEY, we should have reached the place where we add a new master record to the file, but the transaction code is checked to confirm that this is in fact what we are trying to do. If the code is "A," the new record is added to the file and a new transaction is read. If the code is not "A," we may have an erroneous deletion or a code error. If the code is "D," we are attempting to delete a record that is not in the file, and an error message is written by first moving an appropriate message into the printer output area. If the code is not "D," we have an error in the code

TABLE 8-2   ADDING RECORDS TO MASTER FILE

Situation 1		Situation 2		Situation 3	
Master	Trans.	Master	Trans.	Master	Trans.
1	3	1	3	1	3
3	7	3	7	3	7
5		5	8	5	8
6		6		6	10
8		8		8	

PROCESSING STEPS

```
 1. Read M(1)
 2. Read T(3)
 3. DONE = 'F'
 4. M(1) < T(3)
 5. Write M(1)
 6. Read M(3)
 7. DONE = 'F'
 8. M(3) = T(3)
 9. Duplicate (3)
10. Read T(7)
11. DONE = 'F'
12. M(3) < T(7)
13. Write M(3)
14. Read M(5)
15. DONE = 'F'
16. M(5) < T(7)
17. Write M(5)
18. Read M(6)
19. DONE = 'F'
20. M(6) < T(7)
21. Write M(6)
22. Read M(8)
23. DONE = 'F'
24. M(8) > T(7)
25. Write M(7)*
```

```
26. EOF(T)              26. Read T(8)
27. MKEY ≠ 9's          27. DONE = 'F'
28. TKEY <- 9's         28. M(8) = T(8)
29. DONE = 'F'          29. Duplicate (8)
30. M(8) < T(9's)       30. EOF(T)                   30. Read T(10)
31. Write M(8)          31. MKEY ≠ 9's               31. DONE = 'F'
32. EOF(M)              32. TKEY <- 9's              32. M(8) < T(10)
33. TKEY = 9's          33. DONE = 'F'               33. Write M(8)
34. DONE <- 'T'         34. M(8) < T(9's)            34. EOF(M)
                        35. Write M(8)               35. TKEY ≠ 9's
                        36. EOF(M)                   36. MKEY <- 9's
                        37. TKEY = 9's               37. DONE = 'F'
                        38. DONE <- 'T'              38. M(9's) > T(10)
                                                     39. Write M(10)*
                                                     40. EOF(T)
                                                     41. MKEY = 9's
                                                     42. DONE <- 'T'
```

MASTER FILE OUTPUT

```
1 3 5 6 7* 8        1 3 5 6 7* 8            1 3 5 6 7* 8 10*
```

* Added to master file

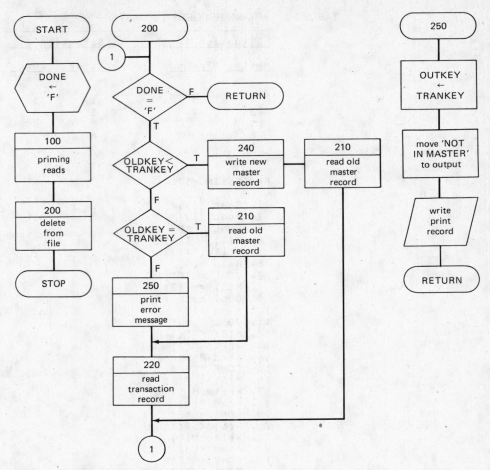

FIGURE 8-10 Deleting records from master file.

field and another appropriate message is moved into the printer output area. After the error message is printed by module 250, another transaction is read.

If MKEY = TKEY, we should be processing a deletion. We should not assume that we are, however. Instead, we check the code to be sure that the master file record with the given key is to be deleted. If the code is "D," we simply read new transaction and master records. If the code is not "D," there is a problem. If it equals "A," we are attempting to duplicate a key in the master file; otherwise, we simply have a code error. In either case, an appropriate error message is moved to the printer output area, the error message is printed, and a new transaction is read.

You will note that module 250 has been altered to handle a variety of error messages. When an error is detected, an error message is moved to the printer output area prior to the calling of module 250. Module 250 then moves the key of the transaction record being processed to this area and prints the message. Processing resumes with the reading of another transaction.

Table 8-4 (see p. 175) illustrates how a program that does both additions and deletions processes the files in the three situations previously examined.

```
000-delete-from-master-file
set done to 'F'
call 100-priming-reads
call 200-delete-from-file
stop

      •
      •
      •

200-delete-from-file
DO WHILE done = 'F'
   IF old master key < transaction key THEN
      call 240-write-new-master-record
      call 210-read-old-master-record
   ELSE
      IF old master key = transaction key THEN
         call 210-read-old-master-record
      ELSE
         call 250-print-error-message
      END IF
      call 220-read-transaction-record
   END IF
END DO
return

      •
      •
      •

250-print-error-message
move transaction key field and 'NOT IN MASTER'
   to printer output area
write printer record
return
```

FIGURE 8-11   Deleting records from master file.

Combining Updating and Maintenance

Since both updating and maintenance runs produce a new master tape, it is possible to consolidate these activities into a single program. These activities are frequently kept separate, however, because this provides better control of the master file. If they are combined, it is essential that each transaction record contain a code to identify the type of processing to be done. The transaction file is usually sorted so that a master record is added before any updating transactions with the same key are processed, and updating transactions are processed against a master record before it is deleted.

Backup for Tape Files

Master files are usually critical to the ongoing operation of a business. It is essential that there be some way to re-create a master file if it is lost or damaged. The processing steps outlined above automatically provide for the backup of tape master files. If we are updating an inventory file daily, we have the situation depicted in Figure 8-14. On Monday, master file A and transaction file A are processed by the update program to produce the updated master file B. On Tuesday, master file B and transaction file B are processed to produce master file C. Master file C will be processed on

TABLE 8-3 DELETING RECORDS FROM MASTER FILE

Situation 1		_Situation 2_		_Situation 3_	
Master	Trans.	Master	Trans.	Master	Trans.
1	3	1	3	1	3
3	4	3	4	3	4
5		5	8	5	8
6		6		6	10
8		8		8	

PROCESSING STEPS

```
 1. Read M(1)
 2. Read T(3)
 3. DONE = 'F'
 4. M(1) < T(3)
 5. Write M(1)
 6. Read M(3)
 7. DONE = 'F'
 8. M(3) = T(3)
 9. Read M(5)
10. Read T(4)
11. DONE = 'F'
12. M(5) > T(4)
13. Missing M(4)
14. EOF(T)             14. Read T(8)
15. MKEY ≠ 9's         15. DONE = 'F'
16. TKEY <- 9's        16. M(5) < T(8)
17. DONE = 'F'         17. Write M(5)
18. M(5) < T(9's)      18. Read M(6)
19. Write M(5)         19. DONE = 'F'
20. Read M(6)          20. M(6) < T(8)
21. DONE = 'F'         21. Write M(6)
22. M(6) < T(9's)      22. Read M(8)
23. Write M(6)         18. DONE = 'F'
24. Read M(8)          24. M(8) = T(8)
25. DONE = 'F'         25. EOF(M)
26. M(8) < T(9's)      26. TKEY ≠ 9's
27. Write M(8)         27. MKEY <- 9's
28. EOF(M)             28. EOF(T)          28. Read T(10)
29. TKEY = 9's         29 MKEY = 9's       29. DONE = 'F'
30. DONE <- 'T'        30. DONE <- 'T'     30. M(9's) > T(10)
                                           31. Missing M(10)
                                           32. EOF(T)
                                           33. MKEY = 9's
                                           34. DONE <- 'T'
```

MASTER FILE OUTPUT

```
  1 5 6 8          1 5 6          1 5 6
```

Wednesday to produce yet another version of the master file. If something should happen to master file C before Wednesday, we can repeat Tuesday's processing to re-create master file C, *if* we have retained master file B and transaction file B. Moreover, if when we attempt to re-create master file C we discover a problem with master file B, we can always redo Monday's run *if* we have kept master file A and transaction file A. This method of providing backup for master files is referred to as the *grandfather-father-son* method: C is the son; B is the father; and A is the grandfather. Of course, to provide full backup, we also need to retain the source for the transaction records in case something happens to a transaction file.

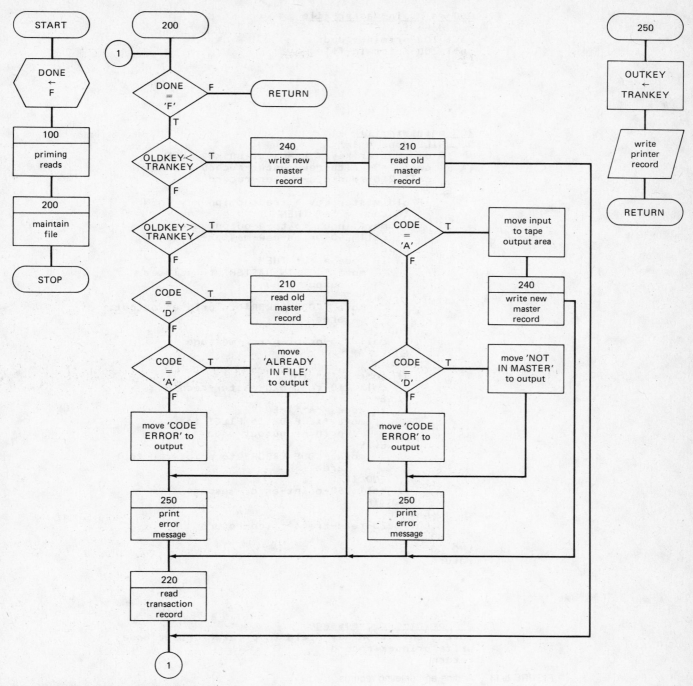

FIGURE 8-12 Adding and deleting records.

After Wednesday's run produces master file D, master file A and transaction file A can be scratched (purged). Only three generations of master and transaction files are kept. While this method is not foolproof, with reasonable care it does provide a way to re-create master tape files.

The grandfather-father-son method is also used when maintenance is performed on a file. That is, the transaction file used to add or delete

```
000-maintain-master-file
set done to 'F'
call 100-priming-reads
call 200-maintain-file
stop


    •
    •
    •


200-maintain-file
DO WHILE done = 'F'
    IF old master key < transaction key THEN
        call 240-write-new-master-record
        call 210-read-old-master-record
    ELSE
        IF old master key > transaction key THEN
            IF code = 'A' THEN
                move input to tape output area
                call 240-write-new-master-record
            ELSE
                IF code = 'D' THEN
                    move 'NOT IN MASTER' to printer
                        output area
                ELSE
                    move 'CODE ERROR' to printer output
                        area
                END IF
                call 250-print-error-message
            END IF
        ELSE
            IF code = 'D' THEN
                call 210-read-old-master-record
            ELSE
                IF code ='A' THEN
                    move 'ALREADY IN FILE' to
                        printer output area
                ELSE
                    move 'CODE ERROR' to printer output
                        area
                END IF
                call 250-print-error-message
            END IF
        END IF
        call 220-read-transaction-record
    END IF
END DO
return


    •
    •
    •


250-print-error-message
move transaction key field to printer output area
write printer record
return
```

FIGURE 8-13   Adding and deleting records.

records must be retained, along with the version of the file on which the maintenance was performed, as one generation for backup purposes.

MAGNETIC DISK

One of the reasons magnetic disk has supplanted tape for master files is that we are able to go directly to any record stored on the disk, a capability

TABLE 8-4 ADDING AND DELETING RECORDS

Situation 1		Situation 2		Situation 3	
Master	Trans.	Master	Trans.	Master	Trans.
1	3A	1	3A	1	3A
3	4D	3	4D	3	4D
5	7A	5	7A	5	7A
6		6	8D	6	8D
8		8		8	10S

PROCESSING STEPS

```
 1. Read M(1)
 2. Read T(3A)
 3. DONE = 'F'
 4. M(1) < T(3)
 5. Write M(1)
 6. Read M(3)
 7. DONE = 'F'
 8. M(3) = T(3)
 9. COD ≠ 'D'
10. COD = 'A'
11. Duplicate (3)
12. Read T(4D)
13. DONE = 'F'
14. M(3) < T(4)
15. Write M(3)
16. Read M(5)
17. DONE = 'F'
18. M(5) > T(4)
19. COD ≠ 'A'
20. COD = 'D'
21. Missing M(4)
22. Read T(7A)
23. DONE = 'F'
24. M(5) < T(7)
25. Write M(5)
26. Read M(6)
27. DONE = 'F'
28. M(6) < T(7)
29. Write M(6)
30. Read M(8)
31. DONE = 'F'
32. M(8) > T(7)
33. COD = 'A'
34. Write M(7)*
```

```
35. EOF(T)            35. Read T(8D)
36. MKEY ≠ 9's        36. DONE = 'F'
37. TKEY <- 9's       37. M(8) = T(9)
38. DONE = 'F'        38. COD = 'D'
39. M(8) < T(9's)     39. EOF(M)
40. Write M(8)        40. TKEY ≠ 9's
41. EOF(M)            41. MKEY <- 9's
42. TKEY = 9's        42. EOF(T)
43. DONE <- 'T'       43. MKEY = 9's
                      44. DONE <- 'T'
```

```
                                          42. Read T(10S)
                                          43. DONE = 'F'
                                          44. M(9's) > T(10)
                                          45. COD ≠ 'A'
                                          46. COD ≠ 'D'
                                          47. Code error T(10)
                                          48. EOF(T)
                                          49. MKEY = 9's
                                          50. DONE <- 'T'
```

MASTER FILE OUTPUT

```
   1 3 5 6 7* 8          1 3 5 6 7*          1 3 5 6 7*
```

* Added to master file

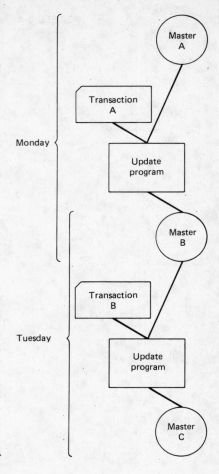

FIGURE 8-14 Backup for tape files.

that will be examined in the next chapter. Magnetic disk is also used for sequential files, however, and that is the concern of this chapter.

The handling of sequential files stored on magnetic disk differs in one major way from the handling of these files on tape: a record that has been read from a disk file can be written back to the same location on disk from which it came.

Creating a Master File

The structure chart of Figure 8-1, the program flowchart of Figure 8-2, and the pseudocode of Figure 8-3 are also applicable to the creation of sequential disk files. The only change needed is to replace references to "tape" with references to "disk." The earlier comments concerning the creation of a master file on tape are equally applicable when the file is on disk.

Updating a Master File

When a sequential disk file is updated, it is not necessary to create a completely new copy of the master file. The updated file will be in the same location on disk as the previous master file. Changed records replace the original versions. While each record in the master file must be read, only those records that are updated need to be written back to the disk. Master records for which there are no updating transactions will not change, and since they already appear in the disk file, we can omit writing these records back to the disk.

We write only those records that are updated, and we write an updated record only when we have processed all transactions for the item (that is, when the new transaction key is greater than the master key). Therefore, when MKEY < TKEY, we must be able to determine if the master record currently in memory has been updated. (The "MKEY < TKEY" condition occurs whether there are transactions for a master record or not.)

The structure chart for updating a sequential disk file is shown in Figure 8-15. It differs slightly from Figure 8-4 (the structure chart for updating a sequential tape file) because of the way the end-of-file processing is handled.

Rather extensive revisions of the program flowchart and the pseudocode are required, as we can see in Figures 8-16 and 8-17. An UPDATE switch is used to tell us whether a master record has been updated. This switch is initialized to 'F' in module 000. Whenever a master record is updated in module 230, the UPDATE switch is set to 'T.' When MKEY < TKEY, we check the switch to see if the current master record has been updated. If the switch equals 'T,' we have an updated master record that is written back to the disk; the UPDATE switch is then set back to 'F.' If when MKEY < TKEY the UPDATE switch equals 'F,' the master record currently in memory was not updated so it is not written back to the disk and the UPDATE switch does not need to be reset. In either case, a new master record is read.

If MKEY > TKEY, we are attempting to update a record that does not exist, and this error is handled in the same way it is with tape.

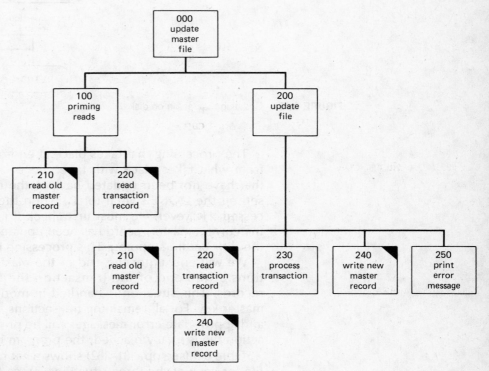

FIGURE 8-15   Updating disk master file.

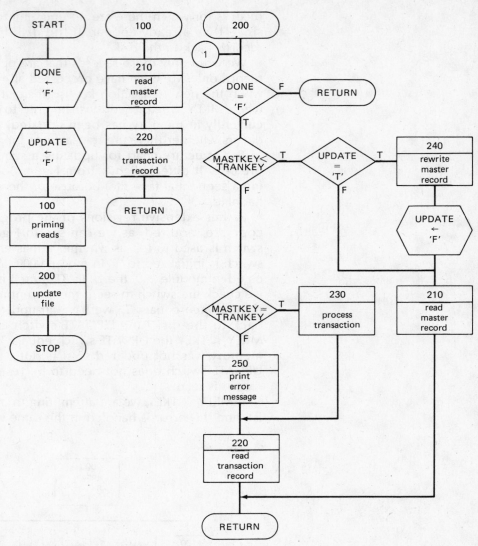

FIGURE 8-16   Updating master file on disk.

The processing that takes place at end-of-file with disk is quite different from what takes place with tape. Since we do not need to write records that have not been updated back to the disk, the program may stop (by setting the DONE switch to 'T') when the last transaction has been processed. However, we must first check the UPDATE switch to determine if the current master record has been updated. If so, we must write it back to the disk before stopping. This processing is shown in module 220.

We will encounter the end of the master file only if there are transactions at the end of the transaction file for which there are no master records. This situation is handled in module 210 by moving nines to the master key. For all remaining transactions, MKEY will be greater than TKEY, and appropriate error messages will be printed. When the end of the transaction file is finally reached, the program halts.

Table 8-5 (see pp. 181–182) shows what happens in the updating of a disk file for each of the three situations. Trace through the processing, particularly the steps taken when the end-of-file conditions are detected.

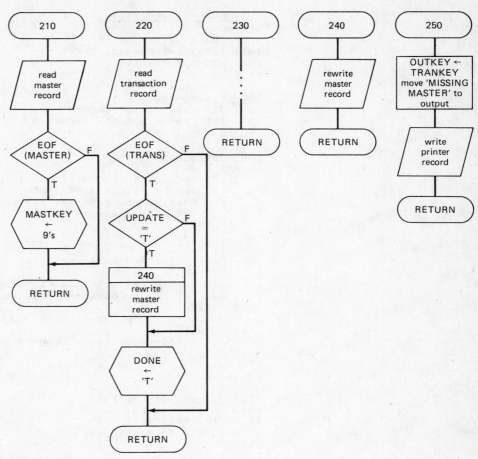

FIGURE 8-16   (Continued)

Adding Records

Since adding records to a sequential disk file changes the size of the file, a completely new version of the file must usually be created. The processing required to do this is the same as for adding records to a tape file, so Figures 8-7, 8-8, and 8-9 can be used with disk files simply by changing the tape I/O operations to disk I/O operations. The example in Table 8-2 also works for disk.

In some cases, records may be added to the end of a file (a *piggyback file*) if the keys of all records to be added are larger than the last key in the master file and space has been reserved for additional records at the end of the file. This special case will not be discussed here.

Deleting Records

Deleting records from a disk file changes the number of records, so Figures 8-10 and 8-11 and Table 8-3 are applicable to disk also. However, it is possible with disk to merely insert a code in a record on disk to show that it has been deleted. This saves having to re-create the file somewhere else on disk if no additions are being made. If this technique is used, update processing must check the deletion code field before a record is updated.

Deletions can be combined with additions, as in Figures 8-12 and 8-13 and Table 8-4.

```
000-update-master-file
set done to 'F'
set update switch to 'F'
call 100-priming-reads
call 200-update-file
stop

100-priming-reads
call 210-read-master-record
call 220-read-transaction-record
return

200-update-file
DO WHILE done = 'F'
   IF master key < transaction key THEN
      IF update switch = 'T' THEN
         call 240-rewrite-master-record
         set update switch to 'F'
      ELSE
         (null)
      END IF
      call 210-read-master-record
   ELSE
      IF master key = transaction key THEN
         call 230-process-transaction
      ELSE
         call 250-print-error-message
      END IF
      call 220-read-transaction-record
   END IF
END DO
return

210-read-master-record
read master record
IF EOF(master file) THEN
   move 9's to master key
ELSE
   (null)
END IF
return

220-read-transaction-record
read transaction record
IF EOF(transaction file) THEN
   IF update switch = 'T' THEN
      call 240-rewrite-master-record
   ELSE
      (null)
   END IF
   set done to 'T'
ELSE
   (null)
END IF
return

230-process-transaction
...
  PSEUDOCODE FOR UPDATE PROCESSING GOES HERE
...
return

240-rewrite-master-record
rewrite master record
return

250-print-error-message
move transaction key field and 'MISSING MASTER'
   to printer output area
write printer record
return
```

FIGURE 8-17 Updating master file on disk.

TABLE 8-5   UPDATING MASTER FILE ON DISK

_Situation_1_		_Situation_2_		_Situation_3_	
Master	Trans.	Master	Trans.	Master	Trans.
1	1	1	1	1	1
3	5	3	5	3	5
5	5	5	5	5	5
6	7	6	7	6	7
8		8	8	8	8
					10

PROCESSING STEPS

```
1.  Read M(1)
2.  Read T(1)
3.  DONE = 'F'
4.  M(1) = T(1)
5.  Process T(1)
6.  UPS <- 'T'
7.  Read T(5)
8.  DONE = 'F'
9.  M(1) < T(5)
10. UPS = 'T'
11. Rewrite M(1)*
12. UPS <- 'F'
13. Read M(3)
14. DONE = 'F'
15. M(3) < T(5)
16. UPS = 'F'
17. Read M(5)
18. DONE = 'F'
19. M(5) = T(5)
20. Process T(5)
21. UPS <- 'T'
22. Read T(5)
23. DONE = 'F'
24. M(5) = T(5)
25. Process T(5)
26. UPS <- 'T'
26. Read T(7)
27. DONE = 'F'
28. M(5) < T(7)
29. UPS = 'T'
30. Rewrite M(5)*
31. UPS <- 'F'
32. Read M(6)
33. DONE = 'F'
34. M(6) < T(7)
35. UPS = 'F'
36. Read M(8)
37. DONE = 'F'
38. M(8) > T(7)
39. Missing M(7)
40. EOF(T)
41. UPS = 'F'
42. DONE <- 'T'
```

```
40. Read T(8)
41. DONE = 'F'
42. M(8) = T(8)
43. Process T(8)
44. UPS <- 'T'
45. EOF(T)
46. UPS = 'T'
47. Rewrite M(8)*
48. DONE <- 'T'
```

```
45. Read T(10)
46. DONE = 'F'
47. M(8) < T(10)
48. UPS = 'T'
49. Rewrite M(8)*
50. UPS <- 'F'
51. EOF(M)
52. MKEY <- 9's
53. M(9's) > T(10)
54. Missing M(10)
```

TABLE 8-5   (*Continued*)

```
                                                          55. EOF(T)
                                                          56. UPS = 'F'
                                                          57. DONE <- 'T'
        MASTER FILE OUTPUT

          1* 5*                    1* 5* 8*              1* 5* 8*


        * Updated master record
```

Combining Updating and Maintenance

Updating and maintenance are less likely to be combined when a sequential file is stored on disk, because adding and deleting records usually require the creation of a new file in a different location on the disk, whereas updating does not.

Backup for Disk Files

Because the updated disk file overlays the previous master file, we do not have backup versions created as a normal course of our updating. Even when maintenance is performed and a new version is created, the space previously occupied by the old version is usually made available for use by other files. (More than one file is usually kept on a disk, whereas a reel of tape normally contains a single file.)

We cannot use the grandfather-father-son method for backing up our disk files, so a different technique must be employed. The usual method is to copy files from the disk to another medium — usually tape or diskette — on a regular basis and to retain this copy in case something happens to the file on disk. In addition to keeping the copy, all transactions processed since the copy was made must be retained. The master file can be re-created by restoring the earlier version of the file from the tape or diskettes and processing all transactions that have occurred since the copy was made. Master files are normally backed up at the end of a day in which updating or maintenance has taken place. Clearly, many files must be backed up each business day.

ACTIVITY AND VOLATILITY

The *activity rate* for a master file is a measure of the relative number of records in the file that are altered in an updating run. The *volatility rate* is a measure of the relative amount of change in the number of records in a master file, that is, the amount of maintenance required on a file. Activity and volatility are important factors to consider in selecting a storage medium for a file. In the next chapter, we will see how they also affect the choice of a way to organize data in a master file.

If we are trying to decide whether to put a sequential master file on tape or disk, the activity rate for the file is of primary interest. Updating a tape file requires that all master records be read from the old file and written to the new file, regardless of the activity rate (the number of records actually updated). When the master file is kept on disk, only those records actually updated need to be written, and once the last transaction has been processed, the remaining master records (for which no updating is required) need not be read.

If a sequential file has a low activity rate, there is an advantage to storing it on disk simply because fewer I/O operations are required. With a low activity rate, most records are not changed. If disk is used, these unchanged records do not need to be written. If tape is used, all records—whether updated or not—must be written to the new file. As the activity rate increases and more records need to be written, tape becomes a more viable alternative. Of course, there are other factors, such as cost and I/O speed, to be weighed in choosing a storage medium.

Volatility is a significant consideration in selecting a file medium for a sequential file only if deletions are not actually removed from a disk file. Since they usually are removed, the entire old file must be read and the entire new file must be written whether the file is stored on disk or tape.

POSTSCRIPT

To update and maintain sequential files in most programming languages, a programmer must, essentially, utilize the logic presented in this chapter. One notable exception is RPG II, in which a technique called *matching records* provides a simple method for handling the sequential processing of multiple input files.

SUMMARY

Much of business data processing is concerned with keeping information in files current. This involves creating files, adding and deleting records, and changing the contents of records. In this chapter we considered files which are kept in order by a key field and which are processed starting with the first record in the file. The sequential files we considered are stored on magnetic tape or magnetic disk, and we saw how the various types of processing are affected by the storage medium used.

KEY TERMS

activity rate
backing up
grandfather-father-son backup
key field
maintaining
master file
piggyback file

referencing
sequential access
serial access
transaction file
updating
volatility rate

EXERCISES

1 Prepare a structure chart, a program flowchart, and the pseudocode for a program that both updates and maintains a sequential master file on magnetic tape. Assume that update records contain a code of "C," addition records a code of "A," and deletion records a code of "D." This code field becomes the minor sort field so that for any key, additions precede updating transactions, which in turn precede deletions.

2 Prepare a structure chart, a program flowchart, and the pseudocode for a program that both updates and maintains a sequential master file on magnetic disk. Assume update records contain a code of "C," addition records a code of "A," and deletion records a code of "D." This code field becomes the minor sort field so that for any key, additions precede updating transactions, which in turn precede deletions. All master records are active.

3 A savings account master file on disk is to be updated. The master file records contain the account number, the balance forward, and a deletion code (0 = active, 9 = deleted). The transaction file contains three types of records:

a Deposit records contain the account number, the amount of a deposit, and a record code of "D."

b Withdrawal records contain the account number, the amount of a withdrawal, and a record code of "W."

c Interest records contain the account number, the amount of interest earned, and a record code of "I."

There is a deposit record for each deposit a customer made, a withdrawal record for each withdrawal, and an interest record if interest was credited during the period. Both files are in sequence by account number.

The output required is an updated master file and an error report. The updating process consists of adding all deposits and interest to the balance forward and subtracting all withdrawals.

Documentation for this problem is to consist of a structure chart, a program flowchart, and the pseudocode.

4 An accounts receivable master file on tape is to be updated. Each record in the master file contains the customer number, the balance forward, and the credit limit. The transaction file contains two types of transactions:

a Sales records that contain the customer number, the amount of a sale to the customer, and a record code of "2."

b Payment records that contain the customer number, the amount of a payment by the customer, and a record code of "3."

Both files are in sequence by customer number.

The output is to include an updated master file and a printed report. The updating consists of adding all sales to the balance forward and subtracting all payments. In addition, if after processing all transactions for a customer, the new balance forward exceeds the customer's credit limit, the customer number and name are to be printed, along with the credit limit and the new balance. Error messages are also part of this report. Heading and blank lines are not required.

Documentation for this problem is to consist of a structure chart, a program flowchart, and the pseudocode.

CHAPTER 9

MULTIFILE PROCESSING: DIRECT ACCESS

OBJECTIVES

Upon completing this chapter the student should be able to:

1 Prepare structure charts, program flowcharts, and the pseudocode for programs to create, update, and maintain indexed and random files.

2 Discuss the relative merits of sequential, indexed, and random file organizations.

3 Discuss the relative merits of three methods of indexing: the indexed sequential-access method (ISAM), the virtual-storage access method (VSAM), and the full index.

4 Define and use the key terms at the end of the chapter.

INTRODUCTION

If a sequential master file has a low activity rate, updating it involves a lot of unnecessary reading and—in the case of tape—writing of records that are not changed. For example, if the activity rate for a tape file is 5 percent, 95 percent of the I/O operations involve records that are not updated. Using disk for the file eliminates the writing of these unneeded records and possibly the reading of some records at the end of the file.

In this chapter we will examine some techniques that provide *direct access* to records, that is, the ability to retrieve a specific record from a file without having to first read all preceding records. Because the master file is not being accessed sequentially, the transactions do not have to be sorted prior to processing. They do not even have to be batched, but can instead be processed by means of an online system in which transactions to update or maintain a file are entered at terminals.

We will consider several methods that use indexes to access records directly, and then we will look at a method in which the location of the record on a disk is derived from the record key. As we examine these techniques, compare the logic for processing a file directly with the logic for doing the same processing sequentially and note how much simpler the direct-accessing logic is.

Before we can discuss the indexing techniques, we must understand more about how data is stored on a *direct-access storage device (DASD)*. Magnetic disk is the most widely used DASD, and it is the one we will consider.

STORING DATA ON DISK

Disks are round, rigid, flat surfaces on which data is recorded magnetically. The data is recorded in *tracks*, which are concentric rings on the surface of the disk. Figure 9-1 shows a surface containing 500 tracks; the tracks are numbered starting with zero for the track farthest from the center of the disk. The number of tracks on a disk varies with different disk systems.

Disks may be fixed (permanently part of the disk drive that does the reading and writing) or removable. In either case, there normally are a number of disks mounted together as a unit, as shown in Figure 9-2. Data is read or written by read/write heads mounted on an accessing mechanism that is capable of moving to any track on the surface of a disk. Although an accessing mechanism may have the ability to read more than one track on a side from a given position, the discussion that follows will assume the simpler situation, in which only a single track can be accessed.

When a read/write head is positioned at a particular track on the surface of a disk, all read/write heads on the accessing mechanism are positioned at the same track number on the surfaces from which they read and to which they write. This collection of tracks of the same number, all of which

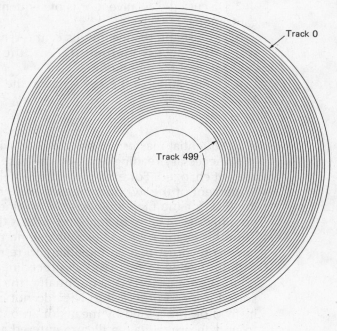

FIGURE 9-1   Surface of a disk.

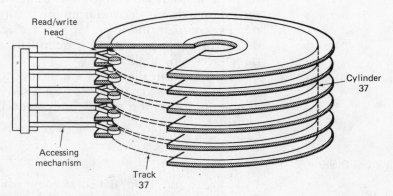

FIGURE 9-2   Disk pack showing cylinder.

can be accessed with a single positioning of the accessing mechanism, is known as a *cylinder*. Considering this collection of tracks in isolation from all other tracks on the disk, we can visualize it as being like the surface of a cylinder (for example, the rounded surface of a tin can).

Data is recorded on a disk by cylinder rather than by surface. A file that is stored starting with track 37 of side 0 (sides are also numbered starting with zero) continues on track 37 of side 1, then track 37 of side 2, and so on until cylinder 37 has been filled. Then side 0 of cylinder 38 is used. Cylinders are used in this way because a single positioning of the accessing mechanism provides access to all tracks in the cylinder, although to only one side at a time. With the disk in Figure 9-2, 10 tracks can be accessed without moving the accessing mechanism. (The upper surface of the top disk and the lower surface of the bottom disk are not used.) Ten tracks of a file can be processed before the relatively slow operation of moving the accessing mechanism to the next cylinder is performed.

INDEXED FILES

Imagine how difficult it would be to find information about "group indication" in this text if you had to start at the beginning and go through it page by page until you happened on what you needed. It is much easier to turn to the back of the book and consult the index. The index is arranged alphabetically, so we can quickly find the "G" entries. We then search these entries until we find the one for "group indication," which gives the number of the page in the text where the concept is explained. We turn to that specific page and examine its contents until we find the needed information.

A record can be retrieved from an *indexed file* in a similar way. Indexes provide the location of a record, and the system can go directly to that location to retrieve that specific record.

Indexed files provide not only direct access to records, but sequential access as well. It is because they can be accessed either way that indexed files are so popular. Batch processing of indexed files may use either direct or sequential access, depending on the activity and volatility of the file. However, online processing normally requires direct access to records. Activity and volatility are measured somewhat differently when processing is online. Instead of measuring the amount of change in a processing run, as we do with batch processing, we look at the amount of change per unit of time (for example, amount of change per day).

We will examine three methods of indexing that are used today: the *indexed sequential-access method* (*ISAM*), the *virtual-storage access method* (*VSAM*), and the *full index*. The differences between these techniques have little or no impact on the writing of programs, but a knowledge of the differences helps in understanding how the use of a particular indexing method affects processing.

ISAM Files

ISAM is one of the oldest indexing methods in use today. The space used on disk by an ISAM file is divided into three main areas: the prime data area, the index, and the overflow area, as shown in Figure 9-3. The *prime data area* is used for the records themselves at the time the file is created. These must be *fixed-length records* (that is, records that all require the same amount of storage), and they are stored in sequence by a key field.

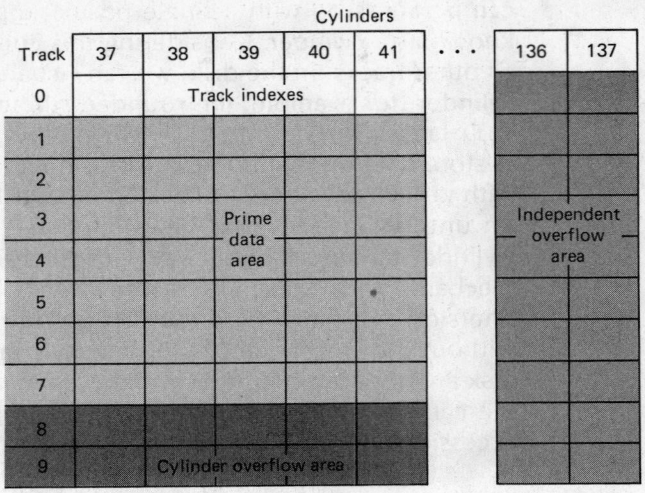

FIGURE 9-3 Layout of ISAM file.

An ISAM file may have three indexes, though only two are commonly used. At the lowest level is the *track index*. This is found in track 0 of each cylinder. The contents of this index will be examined more fully when creating an ISAM file and adding records to the file are discussed. For the time being, it is enough to know that the track index for a cylinder contains the highest key in each track of the prime data area in the cylinder. That is, there is an entry in the track index for every prime data area track in the cylinder. Because the records are in sequence, so is the index.

The next-higher-level index is the *cylinder index*, which contains the highest key in each cylinder of the prime data area. Very large ISAM files also have a *master index*, which contains the highest key in each track of the cylinder index.

When a specific record is to be retrieved directly from an ISAM file, the highest-level index is searched first, using the key of the record wanted as a search argument. If there is a master index for the file, the search looks for the first key in the master index that is greater than or equal to the key of the record being sought. This search yields the address of the track in the cylinder index that must be searched. If there is no master index, the entire cylinder index is searched.

The search of the cylinder index reveals in which cylinder of the file the record should be found. The track index in that cylinder is then searched to identify which track of that cylinder should contain the record. Finally, that track is searched until the record is found or until it is determined that no record with that key exists in the file. The cylinder and master indexes are not located in the same cylinders as the prime data area. The movement of the accessing mechanism between the prime data area and the higher-level indexes, and the time required to search the various indexes make ISAM a relatively slow method for directly accessing records. In some cases, the master or cylinder index may be stored in main memory. This reduces—or even eliminates—the amount of access-arm movement required to search the indexes, thereby increasing the speed with which records may be retrieved.

Overflow areas allow for the addition of records to the file. All available space on the tracks in the prime data area is used at the time the file is created. Any attempt to insert a record in its proper place in the file causes overflow; a record—either the one being added or another one—must be placed in an overflow area. There is a *cylinder overflow area* in each cylinder that provides space for overflow when a record is added to a track in the cylinder. There is an *independent overflow area* on another part of the disk in which records can be placed if a cylinder overflow area is filled. Overflow areas will be examined in more detail in the discussion of adding records to an ISAM file.

Creating an ISAM File   Since the records in an ISAM file are stored in the prime data area in sequence, the records from which the ISAM file is created must be in sequence on the key field. The *input/output control system (IOCS)* of the computer will terminate processing if there is a sequence error or if an attempt is made to write two records with the same key field value. The program to create an ISAM file is thus very simple: it consists of a loop to read and write records. IOCS handles all the work of setting up the indexes and overflow areas.

The track index that is created actually contains two entries for each track: a normal entry and an overflow entry. When the file is created, the normal entry contains the highest key on the track and the address of the track; the overflow entry contains the same highest key and a chaining field that is initially set to indicate that no overflow has occurred. How these entries change when a record is added to the file is discussed below.

Updating an ISAM File   To access directly a record to be updated, the programmer must supply IOCS with the key of the record needed and then issue a read command. IOCS searches the indexes, and—if it can find it—moves the record into memory. IOCS also sets a special switch to indicate if it is able to find the record in the file. The program must check this switch before proceeding.

The structure chart for such a program is shown in Figure 9-4, the program flowchart in Figure 9-5, and the pseudocode in Figure 9-6. (These figures are applicable to all indexed files, not just ISAM files.) After a transaction has been read, the key of the transaction record is moved to the record key field used by IOCS. When the read command is executed, IOCS retrieves from this field the key that it uses as a search argument in

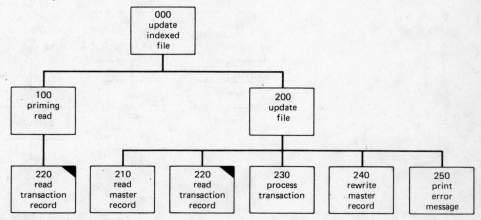

FIGURE 9-4   Updating indexed file.

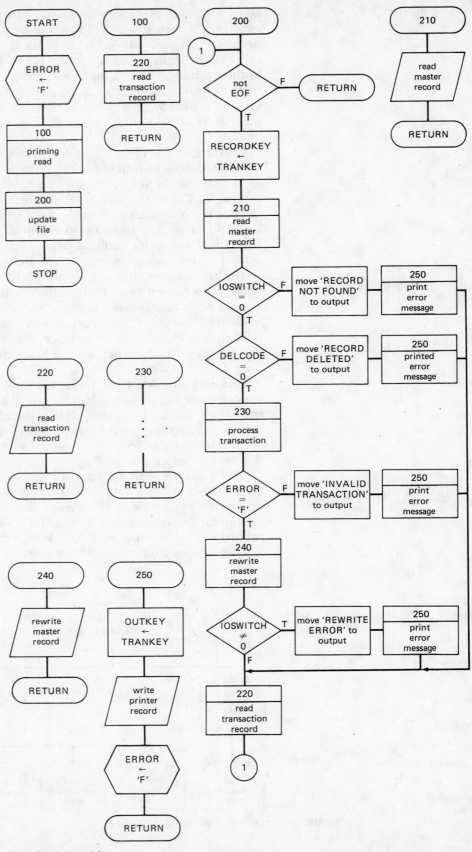

FIGURE 9-5 Updating indexed file.

```
000-update-indexed-file
set error to 'F'
call 100-priming-read
call 200-update-file
stop


100-priming-read
call 220-read-transaction-record
return


200-update-file
DO WHILE not EOF(transaction file)
    move transaction key to record key field
    call 210-read-master-record
    IF I/O switch = 0 THEN
        IF deletion code = 0 THEN
            call 230-process-transaction
            IF error = 'F' THEN
                call 240-rewrite-master-record
                IF I/O switch ≠ 0 THEN
                    move 'REWRITE ERROR' to printer output
                        area
                    call 250-print-error-message
                ELSE
                    (null)
                END IF
            ELSE
                move 'INVALID TRANSACTION' to printer
                    output area
                call 250-print-error-message
            END IF
        ELSE
            move 'RECORD DELETED' to printer output area
            call 250-print-error-message
        END IF
    ELSE
        move 'RECORD NOT FOUND' to printer output area
        call 250-print-error-message
    END IF
    call 220-read-transaction-record
END DO
return


210-read-master-record
read master record
return


220-read-transaction-record
read transaction record
return


230-process-transaction
  •••
  PSEUDOCODE FOR UPDATE PROCESSING GOES HERE
  •••
return


240-rewrite-master-record__
rewrite master record
return


250-print-error-message
move transaction key field to printer output area
write printer record
set error to 'F'
return
```

FIGURE 9-6   Updating indexed file.

searching the indexes and the prime data area. IOCS uses a special I/O switch to indicate the result of its search. If the record is found, IOCS sets the I/O switch to zero; if a record with the desired key is not found, the I/O switch is set to one. The switch is tested after the read operation, and if no record is found, an error message is printed and the next transaction is read. If a record is found, a deletion code field in the record is checked to see if the record is marked for deletion. In this example, a record is assumed to be active if the deletion code contains a zero. Clearly, a record marked for deletion should not be updated. The deletion of records in an ISAM file is discussed below.

If an active record is found, the transaction can be processed. An error switch is used to flag an invalid transaction (for example, one that contains an erroneous record code). A record is updated and written back to the master file only if there is no error. After attempting to rewrite the record, the I/O switch is checked again to be sure that the operation has been successful.

If the activity rate for a file is low, directly accessing an ISAM file to update it will take less time than updating the file sequentially. The time required to search the indexes and the prime data area is less than the time required to read a lot of unneeded records.

If the activity rate for an ISAM file is relatively high, which is true for certain applications, it may be more efficient to batch and sort the transactions and then update the file sequentially. Because of the higher activity rate, more of the records read will be updated. The time spent reading records that are not updated will be less than the time required to search the indexes if the file were accessed directly. The logic for processing an ISAM file sequentially is the same as for a sequential disk file.

Adding Records to an ISAM File Figure 9-7 shows the structure chart, Figure 9-8 the program flowchart, and Figure 9-9 the pseudocode for adding a record to an ISAM file. The processing may be batch or online; if batch is used, access may be direct or sequential. Unless the file is highly volatile, direct access is normally used.

The key of the record to be added is moved to the record key field, and the command to write an additional record is given. IOCS will set the I/O

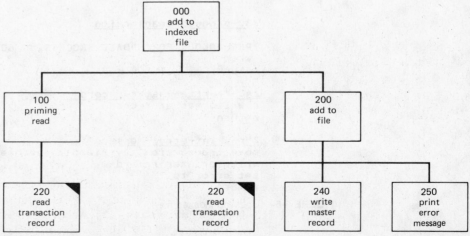

FIGURE 9-7   Adding records to indexed file.

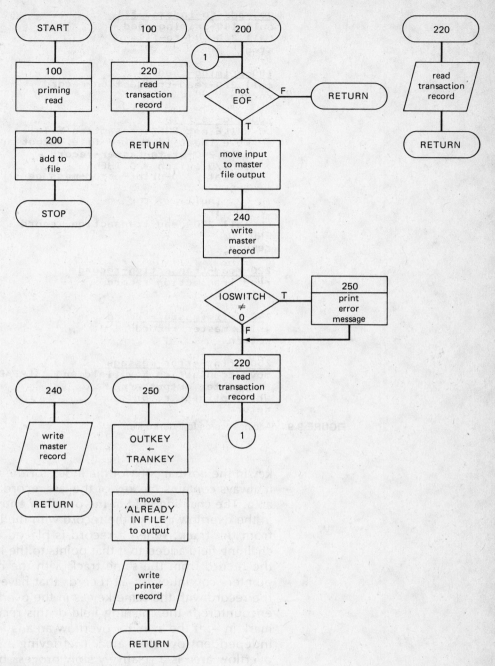

FIGURE 9-8 Adding records to indexed file.

switch to zero unless a record with that key already exists in the file; in that case the I/O switch is set to one.

The record being added will be inserted in its proper sequential position on the disk. The new record belongs on the first track with an overflow entry key in the track index that is greater than the key of the new record. Space is found for the new record by putting it or another record into the overflow area. IOCS takes care of all this, and it also makes adjustments to the track index entry for the track to which the new record belongs. The

```
000-add-to-indexed-file
call 100-priming-read
call 200-add-to-file
stop

100-priming-read
call 220-read-transaction-record
return

200-add-to-file
DO WHILE not EOF(transaction file)
   move input to master file output area
   call 240-write-master-record
   IF I/O switch ≠ 0 THEN
      call 250-print-error-message
   ELSE
      (null)
   END IF
   call 220-read-transaction-record
END DO
return

220-read-transaction-record
read transaction record
return

240-write-master-record
write master record
return

250-print-error-message
move transaction key field and 'ALREADY IN FILE' to
   printer output area
write printer record
return
```

FIGURE 9-9   Adding records to indexed file.

key in the normal entry of the index for the track may have to be changed; it always contains the key of the last record on the track in the prime data area. The chaining field in the overflow entry will now contain the address in the overflow area of the record with the lowest key that has overflowed from the track. When a record is placed in the overflow area, it has a chaining field added to it that points to the location in the overflow area of the record from the same track with the next-higher key. This chain of pointers continues for all records that have overflowed from a track until the record with the same key as in the overflow entry of the track index is encountered; the chaining field of this record has a special end-of-chain mark in it. If the cylinder overflow area is filled, a record is written in the independent overflow area. (Retrieving a record from the independent overflow area is a relatively slow process because this area is in another cylinder of the disk, and the access arm must first move to that cylinder.) The chaining makes it possible to locate a record in the overflow area when accessing the file directly and to process the file sequentially without missing any records.

As the above discussion indicates, adding a record to an ISAM file may involve a lot of work for IOCS: records may have to be shifted to make room for the new record; chaining fields in the overflow area may need to be changed; and track index entries have to be adjusted.

Deleting Records from an ISAM File   Records are deleted from an ISAM file in two stages. The first stage places in a special delete field in the record a code to indicate that the record is deleted. The structure chart for a program to do this is shown in Figure 9-10. It is similar to the updating structure chart of Figure 9-4, except it does not have an updating module. All we need to do in this program is to update the deletion code field. The module-200 logic for doing this is shown in Figures 9-11 and 9-12. In this case, we are replacing the zero in the deletion code field with a nine, which serves as a deletion flag. Programs that access the file must check this field to ensure that deleted records are not used.

Deletions, like additions, may be batched or done online. Direct access is normally used, but if a large percentage of the records is to be deleted, the transactions may be batched and processed sequentially.

Stage two of the deletion process requires *file reorganization.* An ISAM file is reorganized by reading it sequentially and creating a new version of the file in another location on the disk. Two things are accomplished by reorganizing the file: First, any records marked for deletion are not written to the new file; second, all overflow is eliminated because all records are written in the prime data area of the new file space. A highly volatile ISAM file uses disk space inefficiently because records that have been deleted are retained in the file until it is reorganized. Processing a highly volatile ISAM file may also be inefficient because large numbers of additions may result in long searching times to locate records in the overflow areas. This is particularly true if the independent overflow area must be used, for time is required to move the access arm to the overflow cylinders. ISAM files are reorganized regularly as a means of reducing accessing time and of using disk space as efficiently as possible. Even files with few deletions are reorganized if the number of additions has resulted in excessive overflow. The frequency of reorganization will be determined by the volatility of the file. Highly volatile files must be reorganized more frequently than less volatile files.

VSAM Files

Although VSAM provides two methods of accessing files that do not use indexes, these methods are not widely used. Therefore, any reference to a VSAM file here is to a *key-sequence data set,* that is, a data set (or file) in

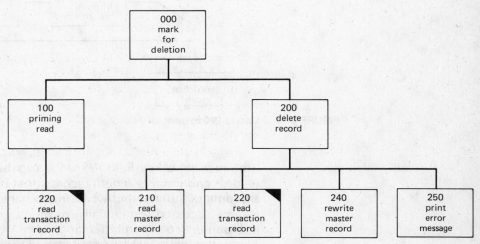

FIGURE 9-10   Marking records for deletion.

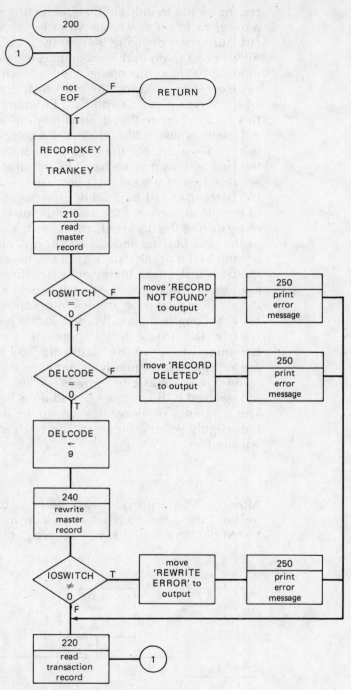

FIGURE 9-11   Module 200 to mark for deletion.

sequence on a key field. VSAM is capable of handling both fixed-length records and *variable-length records* (that is, records which require differing amounts of storage and which may change in length over time), and they may be accessed sequentially, or directly via indexes. To make VSAM files independent of any particular type of disk, tracks and cylinders are not part of the logical scheme for locating records. Instead, records are located

```
200-mark-for-deletion
DO WHILE not EOF(transaction file)
    move transaction key to record key field
    call 210-read-master-record
    IF I/O switch = 0 THEN
        IF deletion code = 0 THEN
            move 9 to deletion code field
            call 240-rewrite-master-record
            IF I/O switch ≠ 0 THEN
                move 'REWRITE ERROR' to printer output area
                call 250-print-error-message
            ELSE
                (null)
            END IF
        ELSE
            move 'RECORD DELETED' to printer output area
            call 250-print-error-message
        END IF
    ELSE
        move 'RECORD NOT FOUND' to printer output area
        call 250-print-error-message
    END IF
    call 220-read-transaction-record
END DO
return
```

FIGURE 9-12   Module 200 to mark for deletion.

by their displacement from the start of the file. The space for the file is broken down into control intervals and control areas. The *control interval* is the unit of storage that is transferred on a read or write operation. A control interval may contain one or more records, or—for very large records—more than one control interval may be required for a record. Several control intervals are collected into a *control area*.

The lowest-level index in a VSAM file is called the *sequence set*. In the sequence set there is an index record for each control area; it contains the highest key in each control interval within the control area and the starting location of each control interval. There are as many entries in a sequence-set record as there are control intervals in a control area. All higher-level index records are part of the *index set*. Index-set records at the level just above the sequence set contain the highest key in each control area and the location of the start of the sequence set for the control area. If more than one index-set record is required at this second level, there will be a third level which contains the highest key in each second-level index-set record, along with the location of the start of that record. The highest level in the index set always consists of a single record.

IOCS accesses a record directly by starting at the highest-level index-set record and working down to the sequence set and finally to the record itself. Accessing time can be reduced if all or part of the index set is loaded into main memory. Although the records are stored sequentially when the file is created, the addition of records may destroy this arrangement. Therefore, if the records are to be accessed sequentially, they cannot simply be read in the order in which they are stored on disk. Instead, the sequence set is used to access the records in the proper order.

No overflow area is required for a VSAM file.

Creating a VSAM File   The input to the program that creates a VSAM file must be in sequence on the key field. Records are written to the disk in sequential order, but unlike ISAM, VSAM does not fill the available space with records. *Free space* is normally—but not necessarily—set aside at the end of each control interval; this space is not used when the file is created, but is available for the addition of records when needed. Entire control intervals can also be reserved as free space. Because this free space is used when records are added to the file, VSAM avoids the processing inefficiencies encountered with ISAM files, where the addition of a record results in overflow.

Updating a VSAM File   As was indicated earlier, the structure chart and pseudocode for updating an ISAM file are applicable to VSAM files as well. The earlier discussion of updating an ISAM file can be applied to VSAM files.

One point worth noting is that the indexing method used with VSAM files generally results in faster access to records than is possible with ISAM files. As a result, direct processing can be used efficiently with VSAM files having higher activity rates.

Adding Records to a VSAM File   VSAM additions may be batched or made online. The faster access speeds of VSAM cause the volatility rate at which it is no longer efficient to make direct additions to be higher for VSAM files than for ISAM files.

While the logic of Figures 9-8 and 9-9 applies equally well to VSAM files, what happens when a record is added differs considerably. If free space is allocated in each control interval at the time the file is created, a record can be inserted in its proper place in sequence by shifting other records within the control interval to make room for it. If there is no room left in a control interval to add a record, VSAM does a control-interval split. Some of the records in the full control interval are moved to one of the free control intervals. The index set and the sequence set are altered to reflect this split. Adjustments to the sequence set allow for the sequential processing of the file even though records are no longer physically in sequence on the disk itself.

One of the sources of inefficiency with ISAM files is the involved procedure for locating records in the overflow area, a problem that can be mitigated to some extend by reorganizing the file periodically. With a VSAM file, processing is just as efficient after a control-interval split as before.

What happens when there is no free control interval in a control area to permit a control interval to be split? VSAM provides for a control-*area* split, with no reduction in processing efficiency.

Deleting Records from a VSAM File   VSAM has the capability of physically removing a record from a file and adding its space back into the available free space within the control interval. This space thus becomes available for records that must be added. A record is not marked for deletion; instead, a special delete command is issued.

For a highly volatile file, VSAM is more efficient than ISAM both in storage utilization and in processing. It is possible, however, that additions and deletions will be made at different places in the file, with the result that space is being freed by deletions in some control intervals, while other control intervals must be split. For this reason, even a VSAM file may occasionally be reorganized—not because the processing itself is inefficient but because the available disk storage is not being used efficiently.

If deleted records must be retained in the file, a deletion code can be inserted in the records. Once they are no longer needed, these records can be removed by processing the file sequentially and removing records marked for deletion.

Deletions can be batched or made online, depending on the volatility rate.

Fully Indexed Files

A fully indexed file is conceptually quite different from an ISAM or VSAM file, and yet the programming for using it is logically the same. A full index contains an index entry for every record in the file. The entry contains the record key and the address on the disk of the record. The index is ordered by record key. Because the key of every record in the file appears in the index, the records do not need to be stored in sequence and they may be fixed or variable in length. The index itself is kept in sequence to facilitate searching for a specific record key. A fully indexed file needs no overflow area, nor does it need to reserve free space to add records.

Creating a Fully Indexed File   The input to the create program may be in any order. The records are written to the disk in the order read, leaving as little unused space as possible on each track. As each record is stored on the disk, an entry is made in the index to record both the key and the location of the record. When all records have been stored, the index is sorted so that it can be searched efficiently. Any attempt to create more than one record with the same key is detected when the index is sorted.

Updating a Fully Indexed File   A fully indexed file can be updated from batch or online, and it can be accessed both directly and sequentially. As with other indexed files, to access a record directly the programmer must supply the system with the key of the record desired and issue a read command. The system will search the index for the key. If it finds the key in the index, it will go to the location indicated in the index to retrieve the record. Depending on whether the index search was successful or not, the I/O switch field will contain a zero or a one. Note that only the index needs to be searched to determine that a record with a given key is not in the file.

With large files, much time can be spent by IOCS in searching the index, so an efficient searching algorithm is essential. This is an obvious place to use a binary search, but other algorithms are also appropriate. For example, a *spaced sequential search* may be used. In this search, every nth entry in the index is examined. When an index key is found that is greater than the search key, a sequential search of the preceding $n - 1$ index entries is made. To speed up the searching process, every nth entry in the index may be loaded into the computer's memory. This reduces the delay caused by the access-arm movement that occurs if the entire index must be searched on the disk.

If the programmer wishes to access the file sequentially for an application with a high activity rate, the system will read the index entries sequentially, extract the location of each record in turn from the index, and go to that location for the record. This is a more time-consuming method of sequential processing than that used in ISAM and VSAM.

Adding Records to a Fully Indexed File   Records can be added to a fully indexed file simply by extending the file (another example of a piggyback file). The records to be added can be in any order. They are not inserted in any sequence, and they do not even need to be written in disk locations that are adjacent to the original file. For each record added, the record's key and location—wherever it is—are placed in the index. When all records have been added, the index is again sorted. Thus, the process of adding records to a fully indexed file is much simpler than adding records to ISAM and VSAM files. Additions create no overflow problem. Even though what the system does when records are added to a fully indexed file is quite different from what is done for ISAM and VSAM files, the logic of Figures 9-8 and 9-9 still works for the programmer.

Deleting Records from a Fully Indexed File   The procedure for deleting records is essentially the same as for an ISAM file. Records are simply marked for deletion and subsequently removed in a reorganization of the file. For a highly volatile file, it may be more efficient to batch the deletion transactions and process them sequentially against the sequential index. In reorganizing the file, accessing the file serially (in the order in which it is stored) will be faster than accessing it sequentially.

RANDOM FILES

Another type of file that can be accessed directly is the random file. The organization is random in the sense that if we look at the keys of adjacent records in the file, there is no obvious reason for the records to be where they are. While the reason may not be obvious, the location of each record is determined by its key. These files are sometimes inappropriately referred to as "direct" files. However, "direct" refers to the way a file is accessed and "random" to the way the records in a file are organized, and since records in an indexed file can also be accessed directly, we will use the more accurate term "random."

Determining the Location of Records

The location or address at which a record is stored in a random file is determined by manipulations performed on the record key. The manipulations are expressed as a *hashing* algorithm. The algorithm yields an address that is either a *relative track number* (the number of a track in the file relative to the beginning track of the file) or both a relative track number and the position of the record on the track. Since all programs needing to access a random file must use the same hashing algorithm, this algorithm will normally be written as an external subroutine. The details of the algorithm will not appear in any of the documentation for a program that uses it.

A more detailed discussion of hashing belongs in a systems design course. For our purposes it is enough to know that the design of a good algorithm is a very difficult task. A "good" algorithm is one which assigns addresses in such a way that the records are spread evenly over the storage available for the file. The poorer the algorithm, the more likely it is that the same address will be generated for more than one key. If the address consists of just a relative track number, this is not immediately a problem, for a track can usually accommodate a number of records. However, at some point the track may have no room for more records, and then overflow occurs.

If the address is both a track number and a record position, an overflow problem exists as soon as two record keys yield the same address. There are a variety of ways of dealing with the overflow associated with random files, but that topic is also more appropriate for a systems design course.

Overflow in an ISAM file occurs when records are added to a file; with a random file, it can even occur when a file is created. We will assume that the system handles all problems associated with overflow. It should be noted, however, that overflow in random files does result in slower access times. That is why it is so important to devise a hashing algorithm that assigns addresses in a way that minimizes overflow.

Unlike indexed files, random files cannot be processed sequentially without first sorting the file. Why then bother with a random file if good hashing algorithms are so difficult to design and the file must be sorted before it can be processed sequentially? A random file has one distinct advantage over indexed files: speed of access. Searching indexes to determine the location of a record generally requires the relatively slow mechanical movement of the access mechanism from cylinder to cylinder. Determining the address of a record in a random file can be done completely within the CPU, with no mechanical movements at all. Thus random files are used in those situations in which speed of access is the overriding consideration. This is true, for example, of *online real-time* systems (for example, a reservation system) where the output generated affects the transaction.

Random File Processing

Random file processing—at least from the programming standpoint—is very similar to indexed file processing.

Creating a Random File   A random file is created by reading a record, calling the external subroutine to apply the hashing algorithm to the record key, and then writing the record at the indicated address. The hashing subroutine must be supplied with the record key, and it will return the address on disk where the record is to be written. The call of the external subroutine looks like this:

call hashing-algorithm (record key, address)

The absence of a module number identifies "hashing-algorithm" as an external subroutine. The input to the create program may be in any order, but to reduce the impact of overflow, the records should be in order by probability that they will be used. In that way, if any overflow problems are encountered, they will be with records that are less likely to be accessed.

Updating and Maintaining a Random File   The logic for updating, adding records, and marking records for deletion is almost the same as for indexed files. There is one change: instead of moving the transaction key to a record key field before performing an I/O operation, we call the external hashing algorithm to get the record's address. How the system actually retrieves a record will, of course, be quite different from the methods used with indexed files. If the address is just a relative track number, the system has to search the track to find the desired record. If the address also includes the position of the record on the track, the system can go directly to that position.

The quality of the hashing algorithm, the volatility of the file, and the amount of space allocated for the file determine how long it takes before overflow becomes a problem. Records can always be added as long as there is room in the file. Records to be deleted are marked for deletion, but the space is not made immediately available for another record.

When overflow makes access times unacceptable, the file must be reorganized. In reorganizing a random file, the file can be read serially; the algorithm is modified to store the records in a new area on the disk. Records marked for deletion will simply be ignored. If the probabilities of particular records being used have changed significantly since the file was last created, the file can first be rearranged so that the records most likely to be accessed will be assigned storage locations on the disk first.

SELECTING A FILE ORGANIZATION

We have investigated three ways to organize data in a file: sequential, indexed, and random. We have also examined three versions of indexed files: ISAM files, VSAM files, and fully indexed files. Each of these methods of organizing data in a file has characteristics which make it advantageous in certain situations and less attractive in others.

Sequential organization is most suitable for files that have high activity and volatility rates, and it should be avoided for files with low activity and volatility rates. (If a file with a low activity rate is to be organized sequentially, disk is the preferred medium because only updated records need to be written.) What do we do with files that have high activity and low volatility, or low activity and high volatility, or low activity and low volatility?

These situations seem to be designed for indexed files. On closer examinations, however, it is apparent that not all types of indexed files are equally suitable under a given set of circumstances. For example, ISAM files are less suitable for the low activity–high volatility situation than either VSAM or fully indexed files. High volatility quickly causes processing inefficiencies with ISAM files because of the problems with overflow. Frequent reorganization is necessary to overcome this problem.

For the high activity–low volatility file, the fully indexed file is least suitable. The high activity rate would seem to indicate that the file should be updated sequentially, but the fully indexed file is not well suited for sequential processing. VSAM files can be processed sequentially quite efficiently, and—since the volatility rate is low—so can ISAM files.

For low activity–low volatility files, any of the indexing methods is suitable. In the final analysis, of course, the programmer must work with the indexing methods available on the computer system being used. If only one method is available, this whole discussion is academic, but on those systems which offer a choice, an awareness of the advantages and disadvantages of the available indexing methods can lead to a more informed decision.

And where do random files find their niche? Because of the difficulty in developing a good hashing algorithm, and the overflow problems encountered with a poor algorithm, the use of random files is largely limited to online applications in which speed of access is the primary concern. High volatility may aggravate the overflow problems, and so an investment in the development of a good algorithm can usually be justified.

It should be recognized that the advantage in access speed enjoyed by random files is not nearly as great as it once was. Disk drives are faster than they used to be and index searching has improved, and so for most applications an indexed approach yields a satisfactory access time.

SUMMARY

Disk files do not have to be processed sequentially. In this chapter we examined alternative ways of organizing disk files so that a user can go directly to a desired record. We considered three types of indexed files—ISAM, VSAM, and fully indexed—as well as random files. Even though there are considerable differences in how these different types of files are actually stored on disk and how records are accessed, from the programming standpoint they are actually quite similar.

We concluded this chapter with a brief discussion of the factors that enter into a decision about which of the methods for organizing a data file is most appropriate in a given situation.

KEY TERMS

control area	indexed sequential-access method
control interval	(ISAM)
cylinder	input/output control system (IOCS)
cylinder index	master index
cylinder overflow area	online real-time
direct access	prime data area
direct-access storage device (DASD)	random file
file reorganization	relative track number
fixed-length record	sequence set
free space	spaced sequential search
full index	track
hashing	track index
independent overflow area	variable-length record
index set	virtual-storage access method
indexed file	(VSAM)

EXERCISES

1 The situation in Exercise 3 of Chapter 8 is changed so that random transactions will be processed against a random file. The master record now includes a delete field that will contain a code of nine if the record is deleted, zero if it is not deleted. Prepare the structure chart, program flowchart, and pseudocode for this new situation.

2 The situation in Exercise 4 of Chapter 8 is changed so that random transactions will be processed against an indexed file. The master record now includes a delete field that will contain a code of nine if the record is deleted, zero if it is not deleted. Since the transactions are not batched by customer, the customer number and name are to be printed whenever a balance exceeds the credit limit. Prepare the structure chart, program flowchart, and pseudocode for this new situation.

NUMERIC CONSIDERATIONS

OBJECTIVES

Upon completing the appendix the student should be able to:

1 Determine the field size needed for results of arithmetic operations.
2 Round results.
3 Represent numbers using scientific notation.
4 Explain the purpose of output editing.
5 Define and use the key terms at the end of the appendix.

INTRODUCTION

In this text we have sidestepped some problems that arise in the manipulation of numbers. It seems somewhat ironic that the user of a computer, a machine that was originally developed to process large quantities of numeric data, should have to exercise so much care with numbers. Among the concerns that arise in working with numbers are the following:

- Dealing with decimal fractions
- Rounding answers
- Determining how much storage to reserve for the results of calculations
- Handling negative results
- Avoiding division by zero

Decimal fractions can be particularly troublesome; they are included in the discussions that follow of rounding and determining the size of results. As was noted in our examination of tables in Chapter 7, decimal points do not appear in numeric fields in the computer's memory. Higher-level languages keep track of the location of decimal points and align them before performing addition or subtraction; these tasks are left to the programmer when an assembler language is used.

ROUNDING

If someone works 37.5 hours at a pay rate of $8.33 per hour, the employee's gross pay is computed as 37.5 × $8.33 = $312.375. Since we cannot pay a half cent, the result is rounded to $312.38. *Rounding* is a process for adjusting a number so that the portion retained will be as close in value as possible to the original number. In general, any time that decimal positions are to be dropped from a result, the result should first be rounded. The technique for doing this can be described very simply:

Add five to the decimal position following the last one that is to be retained in the result; then drop all decimal positions to the right of the one that is to be retained.

To round an answer to the nearest whole integer, we add five to the tenths position and then drop all decimal positions. If the integer appearing in the tenths position is less than five, the units position will not change; if it is five or more, the units position will be increased by one, as shown in Table A-1. COBOL and RPG make it very easy for the programmer to round a result. All the programmer has to do is specify that the result is to be rounded, what the size of the result is to be, and how many decimal positions are to be retained. Some languages may (depending on the compiler) automatically round any result before it is printed, whereas others may require the programmer to do the rounding, using the technique described above.

If a result may be negative, special care must be taken. For example, if −12.3456 is to be rounded to the nearest hundreth, what is the result? It should be −12.35, but if we add five to the thousandths position, we will get −12.3406, which becomes −12.34 when we *truncate* (drop) the two low-order positions. To get the correct answer, we must round by subtracting:

$$
\begin{array}{r} -12.3456 \\ +5 \\ \hline -12.3406 \end{array}
\qquad
\begin{array}{r} -12.3456 \\ -5 \\ \hline -12.3506 \end{array}
$$

Before rounding a result that can be negative, its sign must be checked. If the result is negative, round by subtracting; otherwise, round by adding.

DETERMINING THE SIZE OF A RESULT

Most programming languages require the programmer to know how large a result is so that enough space can be allocated for it in storage or in an output record. The different arithmetic operations present us with a variety of problems in determining the size of results.

Addition

Before numbers can be added, the decimal points must be aligned. (As was noted earlier, this is done automatically in high-level languages.) There will be as many decimal positions in the sum as there are in the number with the most decimal positions. The size of the integer portion (the part preceding the decimal point) is not as easy to determine. It depends on how many numbers are being added and how large their integer portions are.

Known Quantity and Size of Numbers   If two integers are added, the size of the result can be no more than one digit larger than the size of the larger integer. For example, the sum of a six-digit integer and a five-digit in-

TABLE A-1   EXAMPLES OF ROUNDING

230.06	*to*	230.46		230.56	*to*	230.96
+ 5		+ 5		+ 5		+ 5
230.56		230.96		231.06		231.46
or		or		or		or
230		230		231		231

teger will be no larger than seven digits. If we add the largest such integers, we get

$$
\begin{array}{r}
999999 \\
+\ \ 99999 \\
\hline
1099998
\end{array}
$$

No result larger than this seven-digit number can be obtained by adding a six-digit integer and a five-digit integer. Similarly, if we add the smallest such negative integers, we get

$$
\begin{array}{r}
-999999 \\
+\ \ -99999 \\
\hline
-1099998
\end{array}
$$

This is the smallest possible result. The sum of any other six-digit and five-digit integers will lie between these two sums.

If we add 3 six-digit integers, the result will also be no larger than seven digits. In fact, we have to add more than 10 six-digit integers before we can possibly get an eight-digit result (if we sum 999999 ten times, we will get only 9999990), and more than 100 six-digit integers before we can get a nine-digit result. In general:

If we are adding integers of size S, the result will contain no more than S + 1 digits if 10 or fewer numbers are added, S + 2 if 11 to 100 numbers are added, S + 3 if 101 to 1000 are added, and so on.

Unknown Quantity of Numbers What do we do when the quantity of numbers is not known at the time the program is written? Sometimes, examination of comparable totals developed by some other procedure will tell us how large the result field should be. For example, if a manual system is being converted to the computer, we can use the size of the manually developed totals as a guide. If the total has never exceeded eight digits in the past, then eight may be the size we want. If, however, the current total is a large eight-digit number, or if we anticipate an increase in the number of amounts being accumulated in the future, we might decide to use a size of nine. (Adding one more position allows for a total field that is at least 10 times larger than the current one.)

We usually have some idea of how large a result field should be, but if we do not, we can simply choose a very large field size. If we underestimate the size of the total, however, high-order digits will be truncated and our answer will be wrong. COBOL provides an easy way for the programmer to determine if the result has become too large, so that a warning message may be printed. With some languages, the computer may halt processing when this type of error occurs. In other cases, there may be no indication that truncation has occurred; the only way to determine that there is a problem is to review the output.

Unknown Size of Numbers In business data processing, we usually know how large individual numbers will be. This is not always the case in mathematical problems. FORTRAN, BASIC, and Pascal deal with this problem by using a *scientific notation*, in which data can be expressed as a number multiplied by 10 to some power. For example, 123.45678 can be expressed as 1.2345678×10^2, and 0.0000123 can be expressed as 1.23×10^{-5}. The first significant digit (an integer between 1 and 9) precedes the decimal point; the rest of the number appears in the fractional part. The exponent of 10 is determined by the number of places the decimal point is shifted in going from the original representation to the scientific notation. Count the number of places shifted left or right; this number goes into the exponent as a positive number if the shift is to the left and as a negative number if the shift is to the right. Scientific programming languages represent the number 10 raised to a power by means of the letter "E" followed by the exponent. Thus 1.2345678×10^2 and 1.23×10^{-5} appear in this form as 1.2345678E+2 and 1.23E−5, respectively. Table A-2 shows further examples of this scientific notation and the corresponding programming-language representation.

Subtraction

The problems encountered with subtraction are very similar to those found with addition. Subtraction sometimes leads to another unexpected problem. This is illustrated by Exercise 1 of Chapter 1. In this exercise an employee's net pay is calculated by subtracting from the gross pay the amounts for income tax, union dues, and other deductions. If an employee is absent from work for a major part of a week and has large "other deductions" (for example, a payment to the credit union for a car loan), we may get the result shown in Table A-3. How do we pay an employee −$3.50? There are situations, and this is one of them, in which a negative result, even though it is correct, is unacceptable. The programmer must watch for such possibilities and include appropriate checks and processing procedures in the program to deal with them.

Multiplication

The rule for determining the field size of the result of a multiplication is very simple:

If S1 and S2 are the sizes of two fields, the size of the product of the two fields will be no greater than S1 + S2.

TABLE A-2   SCIENTIFIC NOTATION

Decimal number	Scientific notation	Programming representation
−6.827	-6.827×10^0	−6.827E+0
295,000	2.95×10^5	2.95E+5
−0.000365	-3.65×10^{-4}	−3.65E−4
0.00763	7.63×10^{-3}	7.63E−3

TABLE A-3   TROUBLESOME CALCULATION OF NET PAY

Gross pay	48.00
Less:	
Income tax	12.00
Union dues	1.00
Other deductions	38.50
Net pay	−3.50

This rule is quite easy to demonstrate:

9999	−9999	9999	−9999
× 999	× 999	× −999	× −999
9989001	−9989001	−9989001	9989001

The largest product of a four-digit number and a three-digit number is no larger than a seven-digit number.

Determining the number of decimal positions in the result is also quite simple:

> The number of decimal positions in the product of two fields with D1 and D2 decimal positions is D1 + D2.

Rounding should be applied if fewer decimal positions are to be retained.

The largest integer portion for the product is of size (S1 + S2) − (D1 + D2).

Division

Division presents a different set of problems in determining the size of the integer portion of the result.

If we try to draw an analogy for division from our rule for determining the field size of a product, we will be misled. The size of the integer portion is *not* the difference in the lengths of the integer portions of the two fields. Let us refresh our memory about the terms used to describe the numbers involved in division:

$$\frac{Dividend}{Divisor} = quotient$$

The largest possible integer portion of a quotient is obtained by dividing by the smallest possible divisor.

> If the integer portion of a dividend is of length I, and the divisor has D decimal positions, the quotient may have as many as I + D positions in its integer portion.

Consider the following examples:

$$\frac{999.99}{0.1} = 9999.9 \qquad \frac{999.99}{0.01} = 99999 \qquad \frac{999.99}{0.0001} = 9999900$$

The number of decimal positions in the quotient depends on the values of the dividend and divisor and the number of digits the computer is capable of using to represent a number. (See the discussion below of precision.) The quotient may contain a repeating fraction (for example, 0.333...) or a nonrepeating fraction (for example, 0.25). Unwanted decimal positions may be dropped (after rounding, of course).

One other problem associated with division is illustrated by Table A-4. Since when does 1 + 1 = 1? There is nothing wrong with the algebra shown, but there obviously is *something* wrong. Substitute 1 for Y in each line until you find a line on which the equality no longer holds. The problem appears in the fifth line. What happened in going from the fourth to the fifth line? We divided by Y − 1. And what does Y − 1 equal?

TABLE A-4 ANOTHER PROBLEM WITH DIVISION

1 Given		$Y = 1$
2 Multiply by Y		$Y^2 = Y$
3 Subtract 1		$Y^2 - 1 = Y - 1$
4 Factor		$(Y + 1)(Y - 1) = 1(Y - 1)$
5 Divide by Y $-$ 1		$Y + 1 = 1$
6 Substitute 1 for Y		$1 + 1 = 1$

Just a reminder: Do not attempt to divide by zero. What will happen depends on the language and the compiler being used, but of one thing you can be assured: attempting to divide by zero can only lead to problems. If there ever is a chance that a divisor may be zero, it should be checked before the division is performed. If a zero divisor is detected, the division should not be attempted. The alternative action taken will depend on what a zero divisor implies in the given program.

OUTPUT EDITING

Decimal points are not part of numbers when they are in the computer's memory or stored on tape or disk. When we print a report that includes fields that contain decimal fractions (for example, dollars and cents), the insertion of the decimal point makes it easier for the reader to understand the report.

The insertion of decimal points is one example of *output editing*. We previously used the term "editing" to refer to checking steps that are performed on input data to ensure that the data is acceptable. Output editing is done to make the output easier to use.

Output editing also includes—among other things—the insertion of commas in numbers, the printing of dollar signs, and the suppression of leading zeros. Table A-5 shows how output editing can cause the contents of fields in storage to appear when they are printed. Note that in these examples the suppression of leading zeros stops at the decimal point. The dollar sign is "floated" to a position just to the left of the first significant digit or the decimal point, whichever comes first. Editing of this type is handled very easily by COBOL, RPG, and most versions of BASIC.

ACCURACY AND PRECISION

"Accuracy" and "precision" are two terms that are frequently used interchangeably with regard to numeric data. They refer, however, to different

TABLE A-5 EXAMPLES OF OUTPUT EDITING

Field	Output
300000	$3,000.00
030000	$300.00
003000	$30.00
000300	$3.00
000030	$0.30
000003	$0.03

characteristics of data. *Accuracy* refers to the extent to which a data value corresponds to the actual state of what is being measured. *Precision* refers to the number of digits used to represent a measurement. Greater precision may result in improved accuracy, but precision does not ensure accuracy. A particular piece of data may be both accurate and precise; it may also be accurate and imprecise, or precise and inaccurate.

Let us consider an example involving temperature readings. Suppose I am concerned about the outside temperature. I consult a new "weather station" I have just purchased; its digital readout of the temperature is 36.4789°F. I also check my old thermometer hanging up outside the window; it seems to register a temperature of 28 or 29°F. The discrepancy between the weather station and the thermometer is somewhat disconcerting to me, so I decide to check with the local office of the National Weather Service. I am told that the current temperature is 28.8°F (which is close enough for government work). What can I conclude about the thermometer and the weather station? The weather station is more precise because it provides a six-digit reading, whereas the thermometer—at best—enables me to read the temperature to the nearest degree. The thermometer, however, provides a more accurate reading of the temperature. I had better take my weather station back to the store.

KEY TERMS

accuracy	rounding
output editing	scientific notation
precision	truncation

EXERCISES

In Exercises 1, 2, and 3, the notation (A, B) is used to represent a number containing A digits, of which B follow the decimal point.

1 What is the largest result of the following? Express your answer in the form (A, B).
   a (4, 2) + (6, 3)
   b (3, 0) − (7, 2)
   c Sum of up to 50 (6, 2) numbers
   d Sum of up to 10,000 (5, 2) numbers
2 What is the largest product of the following? Express your answer in the form (A, B).
   a (4, 2) × (6, 3)
   b (3, 0) × (7, 2)
   c (5, 1) × (2, 2)
   d (5, 3) × (5, 2)
3 How large may the integer portion of the quotient of the following divisions be?
   a (4, 2) ÷ (6, 3)
   b (3, 0) ÷ (7, 2)
   c (5, 1) ÷ (2, 2)
   d (5, 3) ÷ (5, 2)
4 Express the following numbers in scientific notation and in the form used in programming languages.
   a −3648.2
   b 90.317
   c 0.00836
   d 0.000006

GLOSSARY

accuracy   The extent to which a data value corresponds to the actual state of what is being measured.

action entry   An indication of an action to be taken under a rule in a decision table.

action stub   The list of actions in a decision table.

activity rate   A measure of the relative number of records in a file that are altered in an updating run.

algorithm   A sequence of steps that describe a method for solving a problem.

AND   A Boolean operation, as in the statement A AND B, in which the statement is true only if both A and B are true.

argument table   A table that is searched.

array   *See* Table.

backing up   Providing a way to restore a master file in case the current version of the file can no longer be used.

batch processing   Processing in which data is accumulated over a period of time and then processed as a group, or batch.

binary   Refers to a numbering system that represents all values with a combination of ones (1s) and zeros (0s).

binary search   A technique for searching an ordered argument table that is efficient for large tables.

Boolean algebra   A form of algebra in which symbols have the values of either "true" or "false," and are subject to the operations AND, OR, and NOT (also known as Boolean logic).

branch   Transfer control to another part of a program.

bug   An error in a computer program.

call   Instruction that transfers control to a subroutine.

coding   Writing instructions for a computer to perform a particular task.

character   A letter of the alphabet, a digit, or a special character ($, %, +, etc.).

compound condition   More than one condition combined by means of the Boolean operators AND and/or OR.

computer program   A group of instructions for a computer that causes it to perform a task.

condition   A situation which may be true or false, used to control a loop or to select from among two alternatives for processing.

condition entry   An indication of the status of a relevant condition for a rule in a decision table.

condition stub   The list of conditions in a decision table.

constant   A value that does not change.

contradiction   A situation in a decision table in which the same combinations of conditions lead to different actions.

control area   In a VSAM file, a collection of control intervals.

control break   A change in the value in a control field between consecutive records in a file.

control field   A field in input records that is used to sequence the file and that is checked to determine when a subtotal is to be printed.

control interval   In a VSAM file, the unit of storage that is transferred on a read or write operation.

counter   A device for recording the number of times something occurs.

cylinder   The collection of tracks of the same number on a disk, that is, the tracks that can be read from or written to with a single positioning of the accessing mechanism.

cylinder index   In an ISAM file, the index that contains the keys of highest record in each cylinder of the file.

cylinder overflow area   In an ISAM file, the tracks set aside in a cylinder to provide for records that overflow from the cylinder's prime data area when additions are made to the file.

DASD   Direct-access storage device; the most common example of a DASD is magnetic disk.

debugging   Removing the errors from a program.

decision table   A tool for planning and documenting processing that involves complex combinations of conditions.

desk checking   A reviewing process in which a representative sample of data is manually processed through an algorithm, flowchart, pseudocode, or coded program to locate logic errors.

detail line   A printed line that contains information about a single entity (person, thing, etc.).

detail-printed   Refers to a report which contains detail lines.

direct access   The ability to go directly to a record without having to first read all preceding records.

direct-access storage device   *See* DASD.

direct table addressing   A technique for accessing a function table (without searching an argument table) by deriving the position in the function table directly from the search argument.

discrete table   An argument table in which each entry represents a particular value that will be compared with a search argument in an attempt to find an exact match.

documenting   Preparing a written record of all activities associated with the programming process.

DO WHILE   The representation of the loop structure in pseudocode.

dummy record   A record placed at the end of a file to signal that there is no more data to be processed.

EOF   End-of-file condition when reading a file.

error routine   Instructions that are executed when an error is encountered during processing.

execute   Cause a program or group of instructions to perform its intended task.

execution-time error   An error, detected during the execution of a program, that is of such a severe nature (e.g., trying to divide by zero) that execution cannot be continued.

external subroutine   A set of instructions for performing a particular task that can be used by any program because the instructions reside in a library that is external to the using program.

false control break   A control break—encountered when processing the first record in an ordered file—that does not actually reflect a change in the value in a control field.

field   A collection of characters used to represent a unit of information about an entity; a subdivision of a record. Also referred to as an *item*.

file   A collection of related records.

file reorganization   Creating a new version of a direct-access file to eliminate inefficiency in storage utilization and/or processing as a result of the addition and/or deletion of records.

fixed-length record   A record that will never change in size.

free space   In a VSAM file, space set aside for the addition of records.

full index   An index in order by record key that contains the key and location of every record in a file.

function table   A table that contains values that are to be retrieved for use in processing.

GOTOless programming   Programming without the use of branch instructions.

grandfather-father-son A technique for backing up master files stored on magnetic tape.

group indication The printing in a report of only those control field values that have changed since they were last printed.

group-printed Refers to a report in which a line of data summarizes information from more than one record; a report without detail lines.

hashing Deriving the location for a record in a random file from the record key.

heading line Line printed at the top of the pages of a report.

hierarchy chart Another name for structure chart; a tool for top-down program planning.

high-level language A language in which one source program instruction may be translated into one or more object program instructions.

HIPO (hierarchical input-process-output) chart A technique for planning and documenting structured programs that utilizes a hierarchy (structure) chart, a description of the input and output for each module, and a description in pseudocode of the processing steps for each module.

IF-THEN-ELSE The representation of the selection structure in pseudocode.

increment Increase the value of a counter.

independent overflow area In an ISAM file, one or more cylinders that are used for records that have overflowed from the prime data area when there is no longer any room left in the appropriate cylinder overflow area.

index Used in conjunction with a table name to specify a particular element of a table; a part of an indexed file.

index set In a VSAM file, the index that contains the highest key in each control area; also includes any higher-level indexes that may be required.

indexed file A file from which records may be retrieved directly by means of one or more indexes; can be accessed sequentially as well.

indexed sequential-access method *See* ISAM.

initialize Define an initial value for a field, e.g., set a counter or total field to zero.

input Data that is to be read and processed by a program; the operation of reading such data.

input editing Processing that checks the validity of data.

input/output control system *See* IOCS.

intermediate control field A control field, other than the major or minor control field, present only when there are three or more control fields.

internal subroutine A set of instructions for performing a particular task that is written as a part of the using program.

I/O Input/output.

IOCS A part of the operating system of a computer that handles the reading and writing of records.

ISAM (indexed sequential-access method) A means of organizing records on a direct-access storage device that provides for both direct and sequential access.

item *See* field.

key field The field or fields that are used to identify a record; used in sorting a sequential file and in retrieving records from a direct file.

listing Output on a printer.

logic error An error that occurs as a result of faulty reasoning; cannot be detected by a translation program, but will produce incorrect results.

loop A group of instructions that is executed repeatedly until a condition is encountered that causes control to be transferred to the instruction following the loop.

loop structure One of the three fundamental programming structures; provides for the repetition of certain instructions as long as a condition is true.

maintaining Processing, with the purpose of keeping a master file current, that changes the number of records in a file, e.g., adding or deleting records.

major control field The most significant field in the ordering of a file; the one that changes least frequently.

master file A relatively permanent file that contains information used regularly; a file that must be updated and maintained.

master index   In an ISAM file, the highest-level index; an optional index that contains the highest key in each track of the cylinder index.

memory   A portion of the computer in which data, instructions, and the results of processing can be stored.

minor control field   The least significant field in the ordering of a file; the one that changes most frequently.

modular programming   An early stage in the development of structured programming. A program is broken down into pieces, or modules which can be coded and tested separately.

module   A piece of a program that performs a single, limited function.

multidimensional table   A table that can be visualized as containing more than a single column. A two-dimensional table contains rows and columns; a three-dimensional table is a stack of two-dimensional tables.

multilevel control break   Refers to processing that produces more than one level of subtotal, i.e., subtotals for groupings of records on more than one field.

Nassi-Shneiderman flowchart   A compact and easily understood technique for planning and documenting structured programs; includes no provision for branching.

nested   Included within another, as a loop structure within another loop structure (nested loop), or a selection structure within another selection structure (nested IF).

NOT   A Boolean operation, as in NOT A, that changes the value of a statement from true to false or from false to true.

null ELSE   A situation in which no action is taken if the condition for an IF-THEN-ELSE is false.

object program   The machine-language (binary) program produced by the translation program from the source program.

one-dimensional table   A table that can be visualized as containing a single column of values.

online real-time   A system, such as a reservation system, in which the output from processing a transaction is received immediately and affects the activity taking place.

OR   A Boolean operation, as in A OR B, in which the statement is true if either A or B (or both) is true.

output   The results of processing by the computer; the process of producing such results.

output editing   Operations performed on output to be printed to make it easier for a human being to read and understand, such as inserting commas and decimal points, suppressing leading zeros, and including dollar signs.

paired table   Argument and function table used together. When the proper entry in the argument table is found, the corresponding element of the function table is retrieved.

parameter   Value used in a program where the value is subject to change and is read in at the time the program is executed.

piggyback file   A file to which records are added by placing them after the records already in the file.

precision   The number of digits used to represent a measurement.

prime data area   In an ISAM file, the area in which records are placed when the file is created.

priming read   Reading the first record in a file prior to entering a loop that is executed until EOF is detected.

program flowchart   A representation using standard outlines of the processing steps to be used to solve a problem.

program switch   A field in memory, having the value of true or false, that is used to record a condition.

programming process   The procedure followed in developing a program: defining the problem, preparing an algorithm, preparing a flowchart (or pseudocode, Nassi-Shneiderman flowchart, etc.), coding, debugging and testing, and documenting.

pseudocode   A way to represent instructions that uses ordinary English; a planning tool for structured programming.

random file   A file in which records appear to be in no particular order because the location of a record is determined by manipulations performed on the key of the record (hashing).

record   A component of a file containing information about an entity; a collection of fields.

redundancy   A situation in which more than one rule of a decision table may be applied for a given combination of conditions.

referencing   Retrieving information from a file without altering its contents.

relative track number   A way of identifying the location of a track for a file on disk by determining how far it is from the first track used for the file.

restricted-value test   A test applied to an input field to determine if its value is acceptable, e.g., equal to one or several values, or within a range of values.

return   The instruction within a subroutine that returns control to the calling program.

rounding   Adjusting a number prior to printing it so that the digits printed will be as close as possible to the original value of the number.

rule   A part of a decision table that indicates what actions are to be taken under a given combination of conditions.

run   *See* execute.

scientific notation   A way of expressing a number by writing it with one nonzero digit preceding the decimal point and the remainder of the digits in the fractional part, multiplied by 10 raised to the appropriate power.

search argument   The value that is compared with argument table entries.

segmented table   An argument table in which the argument entry is the upper (for an ascending table) or lower (for a descending table) limit of a range of values.

selection structure   One of the three fundamental programming structures; provides the ability to choose between two alternative courses of action on the basis of whether a condition is true or false.

sentinel value   A specific value placed in a field in a dummy record to signal the end of the file.

sequence checking   A method for verifying that a file is in order by comparing key fields of consecutive records.

sequence set   In a VSAM file, the lowest-level index. Consists of a record for each control area containing the highest key in each control interval in the control area; allows for the sequential processing of the file.

sequence structure   One of the three fundamental programming structures; provides for the execution of instructions in the order in which they are encountered.

sequential access   A special case of serial access in which the records in the file are in order on one or more fields.

sequential search   A method for searching an argument table that examines the entries in the order in which they appear in the table, starting with the first entry.

serial access   Processing records in a file by starting with the first record and taking each succeeding record in turn.

simple condition   A single condition that by itself controls a loop or selects one of two alternatives for processing.

single table   An argument table with no corresponding function table (used in editing data) or a function table with no corresponding argument table (used in direct table addressing).

source program   Instructions for the computer written in a form that is relatively easy for the programmer to work with; must be converted to machine language by a translation program before it can be run on a computer.

spaced sequential search   A searching method in which table or index entries at fixed intervals are examined until either the desired entry is found or it can be determined that the desired entry has been passed over; in the latter case the entries between the last two entries examined are then searched serially.

structure chart A tool to use in the top-down planning of a structured program that shows the modules that comprise the program, and also shows the modules called by each module.

structured programming A collection of techniques for the planning and writing of programs that increases programmer productivity, e.g., top-down programming and the use of loop, selection, and sequence structures.

stub That portion of a decision table that lists all the conditions to be examined and the various possible actions to be taken.

subroutine A set of instructions for performing a particular task that can be called when needed.

subscript *See* index.

syntax error A violation of the rules of a programming language.

table A collection of items of the same type and size.

table file A file in which the data that makes up a table is stored.

table lookup *See* table search.

table search The examination of an argument table to find an entry that is equal to the search argument (in the case of a discrete table), greater than or equal to the search argument (in the case of a segmented table in ascending order), or less than or equal to the search argument (in the case of a segmented table in descending order).

testing Running a program with sample data to identify logic errors.

top-down programming A technique for planning a structured program in which the entire program is first broken down into three modules: (1) the processing that takes place before any data is processed, (2) the processing of the data, and (3) the processing that takes place after all data records have been read. These modules in turn are successively subdivided until each module performs a single, limited function.

total line A line that summarizes data obtained from one or more input records.

track One of a series of concentric rings on the surface of a magnetic disk on which data is recorded.

track index In an ISAM file, the lowest-level index. Located on track 0 of each cylinder for the file, the track index contains the highest key on each prime data track in the cylinder as well as pointers to records that have overflowed from those tracks.

transaction file A relatively temporary file that contains information that is used to update or maintain a master file.

translation program A program that converts a source program into a machine-language object program; it also provides a listing of the source program and diagnostic messages.

truncation The dropping of digits from either end of a number.

truth table A tool for analyzing all possible combinations of values of a Boolean expression.

updating Changing the contents of records in a master file to keep it current without changing the number of records in the file.

user The people who will use the output produced by the computer.

variable A field whose contents can change.

variable-length record A record which may change in size over time because of a change in the number of fields in the record, a change in the size of fields, or both.

virtual-storage access method *See* VSAM.

visual table of contents *See* VTOC.

volatility rate A measure of the relative amount of change in the number of records in a master file.

VSAM (virtual-storage access method) A means of organizing records on a direct-access storage device that provides for both direct and sequential access.

VTOC (visual table of contents) Another name for a structure chart; a tool for the top-down planning of a structured program.

INDEX

INDEX

Access:
    direct, 185
    sequential, 156
    serial, 156
Accuracy, 209
Action entry, 79
Action stub, 79
Activity rate, 182
Algorithm, 6
    desk-checking, 8
AND, 53
Argument, search, 130
Argument table, 130
Array, 128

Backing up, 157
Batch processing, 62
Binary, 13
Binary search, 139
Boolean algebra, 53
Branch, 7
Bugs, 16

Call, 27
Character, 2
Coding, 13
Compound condition, 60
Computer program, 1, 13
Condition, 36
    compound, 60
    simple, 60

Condition entry, 79
Condition stub, 79
Constant, 63
Contradiction, 80
Control area, 197
Control break, 87
    false, 89
    multilevel, 107
Control field, 87
    intermediate, 108
    major, 108
    minor, 108
Control interval, 197
Counter, 7
Cylinder, 187
Cylinder index, 188
Cylinder overflow area, 189

DASD (direct-access storage device),
    185
Debugging, 16
Decision table, 77
Desk-checking, algorithm, 8
Detail line, 17
Detail-printed report, 110
Direct access, 185
Direct-access storage device
    (DASD), 185
Direct table addressing, 130
Discrete table, 130
DO WHILE, 41
Documenting, 2

Dummy module, 33
Dummy record, 65

Editing:
  input, 62
  output, 209
Entry:
  action, 79
  condition, 79
EOF, 12
Error:
  execution-time, 8
  logic, 12
  syntax, 14
Error routine, 64
Execute, 7
Execution-time error, 8
External subroutine, 28

False control break, 89
Field, 2
  control, 87, 108
  key, 156
File, 2
  indexed, 187
  maintaining, 156
  master, 155
  piggyback, 179
  random, 200
  referencing, 156
  table, 135
  transaction, 155
  updating, 156
File reorganization, 195
Fixed-length record, 187
Flowchart:
  Nassi-Shneiderman, 93
  program, 8
Free space, 198
Full index, 187, 199
Function table, 130

GOTOless programming, 35
Grandfather-father-son method, 172
Group indication, 110
Group-printed report, 110

Hashing, 200
Heading line, 88

Hierarchical input-process-output
    (HIPO) chart, 123
Hierarchy chart, 30
High-level language, 13
HIPO (hierarchical input-process-
    output) chart, 123

I/O (input or output), 35
IF-THEN-ELSE, 42
Increment, 7
Independent overflow area, 189
Index, 134
  cylinder, 188
  full, 187, 199
  master, 188
  track, 188
Index set, 197
Indexed file, 187
Indexed sequential-access method
    (ISAM), 187
Initialize, 8
Input, 2
Input or output (I/O), 35
Input editing, 62
Input/output control system (IOCS),
    189
Intermediate control field, 108
Internal subroutine, 27
IOCS (input/output control system),
    189
ISAM (indexed sequential-access
    method), 187
Item, 2

Key field, 156

Listing, 16
Logic error, 12
Lookup, table, 136
Loop, 19
Loop structure, 36

Maintaining, file, 156
Major control field, 108
Master file, 155
Master index, 188
Memory, 6
Minor control field, 108
Modular programming, 26

Module, 26
   dummy, 33
Multidimensional table, 147
Multilevel control break, 107

Nassi-Shneiderman flowchart, 93
Nested instruction, 42
NOT, 53
Null ELSE, 42

Object program, 13
One-dimensional table, 147
Online real-time system, 201
OR, 53
Output, 2
Output editing, 209
Overflow area:
   cylinder, 189
   independent, 189

Paired table, 128
Parameter, 63
Piggyback file, 179
Precision, 209
Prime data area, 187
Priming read, 36
Program, 1
   object, 13
   source, 13
   translation, 13
Program flowchart, 8
Program switch, 71
Programming:
   GOTOless, 35
   modular, 26
   structured, 26
   top-down, 30
Programming process, 1
Pseudocode, 41

Random file, 200
Record, 2
   dummy, 65
   fixed-length, 187
   variable-length, 196
Redundancy, 79
Referencing, file, 156
Relative track number, 200
Reorganization, file, 195

Restricted-value test, 63
Return, 27
Rounding, 204
Rule, 79
Run, 16

Scientific notation, 206
Search:
   binary, 139
   sequential, 136
   spaced sequential, 199
   table, 130
Search argument, 130
Segmented table, 130
Selection structure, 38
Sentinel value, 65
Sequence checking, 63
Sequence set, 197
Sequence structure, 35
Sequential access, 156
Sequential search, 136
Serial access, 156
Simple condition, 60
Single table, 128
Source program, 13
Spaced sequential search, 199
Structure:
   loop, 36
   selection, 38
   sequence, 35
Structure chart, 30
Structured programming, 26
Stub, 78
   action, 79
   condition, 79
Subroutine, 26
   external, 28
   internal, 27
Subscript, 134
Switch, program, 71
Syntax error, 14

Table, 128
   argument, 130
   decision, 77
   discrete, 130
   function, 130
   multidimensional, 147
   one-dimensional, 147
   paired, 128
   segmented, 130

Table (*Cont.*):
  single, 128
  truth, 56
Table file, 135
Table lookup, 136
Table search, 130
Testing, 16
Top-down programming, 30
Total line, 18
Track, 185
Track index, 188
Transaction file, 155
Translation program, 13
Truncate, 205
Truth table, 56

Updating, file, 156
User, 32

Variable, 53
Variable-length record, 196
Virtual-storage access method
  (VSAM), 187, 195
Visual table of contents (VTOC),
  30
Volatility rate, 182
VSAM (virtual-storage access
  method), 187, 195
VTOC (visual table of contents),
  30